MINDFUL L2 TEACHER EDUCATION

Taking a Vygotskian sociocultural stance, this book demonstrates the meaningful role that L2 teacher educators and L2 teacher education play in the professional development of L2 teachers through systematic, intentional, goal-directed, theorized L2 teacher education pedagogy. The message is resoundingly clear: Teacher education matters! It empirically documents the ways in which engagement in the practices of L2 teacher education shape how teachers come to think about and enact their teaching within the sociocultural contexts of their learning-to-teach experiences. Providing an insider's look at L2 teacher education pedagogy, it offers a close-up look at teacher educators who are skilled at moving L2 teachers toward more theoretically and pedagogically sound instructional practices and greater levels of professional expertise.

First, the theoretical foundation and educational rationale for exploring what happens inside the practices of L2 teacher education are established. These theoretical concepts are then used to conduct *microgenetic analyses* of the moment-to-moment, asynchronous, and at-a-distance dialogic interactions that take place in five distinct but sometimes overlapping practices that the authors have designed, repeatedly implemented, and subsequently collected data on in their own L2 teacher education programs. *Responsive mediation* is positioned as the nexus of *Mindful L2 Teacher Education* and proposed as a psychological tool for teacher educators to both examine and inform the ways in which they design, enact, and assess the consequences of their own L2 teacher education pedagogy.

Karen E. Johnson is Kirby Professor in Language Learning and Applied Linguistics, The Pennsylvania State University, USA.

Paula R. Golombek is Clinical Associate Professor, Linguistics, University of Florida, USA.

ESL & Applied Linguistics Professional Series

Visit **www.routledge.com/education** for additional information on titles in the ESL & Applied Linguistics Professional Series

MINDFUL L2 TEACHER EDUCATION

A Sociocultural Perspective on Cultivating Teachers' Professional Development

Karen E. Johnson
Paula R. Golombek

Routledge
Taylor & Francis Group

NEW YORK AND LONDON

First published 2016
by Routledge
711 Third Avenue, New York, NY 10017

and by Routledge
2 Park Square, Milton Park, Abingdon, Oxon, OX14 4RN

Routledge is an imprint of the Taylor & Francis Group, an informa business

© 2016 Taylor & Francis

The right of Karen E. Johnson and Paula R. Golombek to be identified as authors of this work has been asserted by them in accordance with sections 77 and 78 of the Copyright, Designs and Patents Act 1988.

Library of Congress Cataloging in Publication Data
Johnson, Karen E., author. | Golombek, Paula R., author.
Title: Mindful L2 teacher education : a sociocultural perspective on cultivating teachers' professional development / by Karen E. Johnson and Paula R. Golombek.
Description: New York, NY : Routledge, 2016. | Series: ESL & applied linguistics professional series | Includes bibliographical references and index.
Identifiers: LCCN 2015035488 | ISBN 9781138189782 (hardback) | ISBN 9781138189799 (pbk.) | ISBN 9781315641447 (ebook)
Subjects: LCSH: Language teachers—Training of. | English teachers—Training of. | Language and languages—Study and teaching. | English language—Study and teaching—Foreign speakers.
Classification: LCC P53.85 .J65 2016 | DDC 418.0071—dc23
LC record available at http://lccn.loc.gov/2015035488

ISBN: 978-1-138-18978-2 (hbk)
ISBN: 978-1-138-18979-9 (pbk)
ISBN: 978-1-315-64144-7 (ebk)

Typeset in Bembo
by diacriTech, Chennai

To Glenn, Elizabeth, and Lillian
To Michael, Alex, and Anya

CONTENTS

PREFACE

The 'training' of teachers is a topic about which many people—from politicians to parents—have strong emotional opinions, opinions that are rarely grounded in a theoretical understanding of how humans learn, and subsequently how teachers should teach. Indeed, uttering the word 'theory' when discussing teacher education often sparks negative reactions as being abstract drivel. The current public rhetoric surrounding the education of teachers has contributed to a de-skilling of teachers and a de-professionalization of the field of teacher education—similarly affecting second language (L2) teachers and L2 teacher education. The goal of this book, while in some sense a response to this rhetoric, is to demonstrate the meaningful role that L2 teacher educators and L2 teacher education play in the professional development of L2 teachers through systematic, intentional, goal-directed, theorized L2 teacher education pedagogy. We resoundingly say, "Teacher education matters!"

Over the past 25 years, we have consistently sought to understand what we do, why we do it, and the consequences of what we do through Vygotskian sociocultural theory. Our Vygotskian sociocultural stance has not only framed our thinking and activity as teacher educators, but also our analyses as researchers of L2 teacher cognition and professional development. And it is this interaction between our thinking and doing as teacher educators and as researchers of L2 teacher learning that inspired the writing of this book. By looking closely at the teachers with whom we work as they learn to teach and our activity in mediating their learning, we have, true to our Vygotskian sociocultural stance, explicitly externalized our own L2 teacher education pedagogy. And as a consequence, we have become increasingly mindful of our role in cultivating teachers' professional development.

In this book, we empirically document the ways in which engagement in the practices of L2 teacher education shapes how L2 teachers come to think about and enact their teaching within the sociocultural contexts of their learning-to-teach experiences. Because we view teacher educators as having greater responsibility within teaching/learning interactions, our obvious audience for this book is L2 teacher educators. Yet we also know from experience that graduate students preparing to enter academia as well as experienced classroom teachers often find themselves thrust into teacher educator positions with little or no preparation. Thus, this book will provide both seasoned and newly minted teacher educators with an insider's look at L2 teacher education pedagogy. But in describing our pedagogy, this book will also hold appeal for L2 teachers and researchers who wish to examine the thinking and doing of their own pedagogy as well as the pedagogy of others.

An overview of the book

In Parts I and II we establish the theoretical foundation and educational rationale for exploring what happens inside the practices of L2 teacher education. In Part I, we lay the theoretical foundation for our own pedagogy, what we have come to conceptualize as *Mindful L2 Teacher Education*. In Chapter 1, we provide an overview of Vygotskian sociocultural theory and how it informs how we conceptualize L2 teacher learning and L2 teacher education pedagogy. Since we characterize the nexus of *Mindful L2 Teacher Education* through the concept of *responsive mediation*, we originally sought to fit this key concept into our title, but through pointed queries from our editors realized how the word 'mediation' can have no meaning for some (what is that?) or a specific meaning for others (like in a legal matter?). To rectify this, in Chapter 2, we articulate the central role of mediation in teacher conceptual development, trace the ways that mediation has been conceptualized within a Vygotskian sociocultural perspective, and discuss what such conceptualizations offer L2 teacher education pedagogy. We then argue for the central role of *responsive mediation* in enabling L2 teachers to internalize new psychological tools that support the development of L2 teacher/teaching expertise.

In Part II, we draw on Vygotsky and Vygotskian-inspired theoretical concepts that we use throughout the remainder of the book to conceptually articulate and operationally define the concept of *responsive mediation*. In Chapter 3 we define Vygotsky's *obuchenie* (teaching/learning) and *perezhivanie* (emotional experience) in order to establish a conceptual articulation of the qualities that necessitate teacher educator mediation to be responsive to the dialogic interactions they have with teachers. We also draw on McNeil's (2000) construct of *growth points* as a moment or series of moments when teachers' cognitive/emotional dissonance comes into being and argue that *responsive mediation* directed at the *growth point* creates the potential for productive teacher learning and development.

In Chapter 4 we define Mercer's (2000) *interthinking*, or how humans use language to carry out joint intellectual activity and to make joint sense of experience, and the *intermental development zone*, or how teacher educators and teachers stay attuned to each other's changing states of knowledge and understanding over the course of an educational activity. These two Vygotskian-inspired concepts are central to how we frame and trace the emergence of *responsive mediation* in the practices highlighted in Part III of the book. We also outline our rationale for taking up sociocultural discourse analysis (Mercer, 2004) as a methodological tool for conducting *microgenetic analyses* (Vygotsky, 1981) of the quality and character of teacher/teacher educator dialogic interactions and their educational significance for the development of L2 teacher/teaching expertise.

In Part III, Chapters 5–9, we then use these theoretical concepts to conduct *microgenetic analyses* of the moment-to-moment, asynchronous, and at-a-distance dialogic interactions that take place in five distinct but sometimes overlapping practices that we have designed, repeatedly implemented, and subsequently collected data on in our own L2 teacher education programs. For each practice, we outline our educational goals and pedagogical procedures. We then situate each practice in the unique institutional and sociocultural context in which it occurred as well as provide sociohistorical information about the teachers who participated in these practices. For each practice we highlight the linguistic, rhetorical, and pragmatic characteristics of teacher educator/teacher dialogic interaction, describe the quality and character of the *responsive mediation* that emerges, and explore the consequences of *responsive mediation* on the ways in which teachers begin to think about and/or attempt to enact their instructional practices. Yet, we offer our analyses of the *responsive mediation* that emerges inside these practices as illustrative. We do not wish to promote or promulgate 'best practices' in L2 teacher education. Instead, we seek to provide readers with an insider's view of what *responsive mediation* looks like as it unfolds and make visible what is required of teacher educators to create conditions that support productive L2 teachers' professional development.

In Part IV, we position *responsive mediation* as the nexus of *Mindful L2 Teacher Education*. In Chapter 10 we propose *responsive mediation* as a psychological tool for teacher educators to both examine and inform the ways in which they design, enact, and assess the consequences of their own L2 teacher education pedagogy. We offer *Mindful L2 Teacher Education* as theoretical learning that is intentional, deliberate, and goal-directed by teacher educators who are skilled at moving L2 teachers toward more theoretically and pedagogically sound instructional practices and greater levels of professional expertise.

References

McNeill, D. (Ed.) (2000). *Language and gesture*. Cambridge: Cambridge University Press.

Mercer, N. (2000). *Words & minds: How we use language to think together*. London: Routledge.

Mercer, N. (2004). Sociocultural discourse analysis: Analyzing classroom talk as a social mode of thinking. *Journal of Applied Linguistics, 1*(2), 137–168.

Vygotsky, L. S. (1981). The genesis of higher mental functions. In J. V. Wertsch (Ed.), *The concept of activity in Soviet psychology* (pp. 144–188). Armonk, NY: Sharpe.

ACKNOWLEDGMENTS

This book has truly been a labor of love, involving personal and professional introspection, theorizing, and insights about what we have thought, felt, and done over our years as teacher educators, and importantly as teacher educators in dialogue with each other. The process of writing this book has strengthened our commitment to L2 teachers and L2 teaching as professionals and a profession. An enormous debt of gratitude goes to the many L2 teachers from across the globe with whom we have worked over the years, especially those featured in this book. Their struggles, success, and growth have consistently motivated us to become more conscious of what we do, to experiment with Vygotsky's ideas concretely in practice, and to grow as teacher educators. We are grateful that they opened their 'inner' worlds and their classroom worlds to us. We would like to thank a special group of teachers with whom we worked at American University, as our interweaving of the theoretical and practical with them pushed our thinking in the later stages of writing this book. We would also like to thank our good friend and colleague James P. Lantolf and the Sociocultural Reading Group at The Pennsylvania State University for deepening our understanding of dialectical logic and the ideal/material dialectic. We are very grateful to Rebecca Zoshak for her meticulous copyediting and attention to clarity in the written word. Finally, we would like to thank the reviewers commissioned by Routledge for their supportive feedback on an earlier draft of this book and acquisitions editor Naomi Silverman and series editor Eli Hinkel for their professionalism and recognition of the book's potential contribution to the ESL and Applied Linguistics Professional Series.

NOTES ON TRANSCRIPTIONS

T:	teacher
TE:	teacher educator
S:	student (not identified)
S1, S2, etc.:	identified student
Ss:	several students at once or the whole class
CM:	classmate, CM1, classmate 1
[	[do you understand? overlap between teacher/student, student/ student
=	turn continues, or one turn follows another without any pause
(.)	a dot indicates a just noticeable pause
(2.0)	a number indicates a timed pause, e.g., 2 seconds
?	rising intonation—question or other
___	emphatic speech, usually on a <u>word</u>
wo (h) rd	(h) to indicate the word is expressed with laughter
wor-	a dash indicates a word that has been cut off
wo:rd	colons indicate elongation of a sound
(word)	a guess at unclear or unintelligible talk
( )	talk occurs but unintelligible
((laughter))	indicates paralinguistic sounds like laughter, crying, etc
((*italics*))	notes on gestures, actions, eye gaze, etc.

(adapted from van Lier 1988; Johnson 1995)

Johnson, K. E. (1995). *Communication in second language classrooms*. New York: Cambridge University Press.

van Lier, L. (1988). *The classroom and the language learner*. London: Longman.

PART I

Laying the Foundation for Mindful L2 Teacher Education

1

A SOCIOCULTURAL PERSPECTIVE ON L2 TEACHER EDUCATION

Introduction

This book is about what happens inside the practices of L2 teacher education. By practices, we mean the activities in which teachers and teacher educators engage within L2 teacher education programs. Our interest in these practices is not so much with the practices themselves, but what we, as teacher educators, are attempting to accomplish through these practices, how we go about accomplishing our goals through the quality and character of our interactions with teachers, and most importantly, what our teachers are learning as they engage in these practices. We are deeply committed to seeing the ways in which engagement in the practices of L2 teacher education influence how teachers come to think about and interact with their students and the ways in which teachers come to understand both the scope and impact of their teaching. We believe that it is inside the practices of L2 teacher education, both the 'moment-to-moment' interactions (oral and written) between teacher educators and teachers as well as the assignments and activities that teacher educators ask teachers to engage in, perhaps face-to-face but many times 'at-a-distance,' where teacher educators can best see, support, and enhance the professional development of L2 teachers. By exploring these interactions as they unfold and within the sociocultural contexts in which they occur, we, as teacher educators, not only open ourselves up for closer scrutiny, but we also hold ourselves accountable to the teachers with whom we work and, of course, the L2 students they teach. Our goal in writing this book is to highlight the unique contributions that teacher educators and teacher education can make in cultivating L2 teachers' professional development. We firmly believe that learning to teach should not be a process of 'discovery learning' or 'learning by doing,' but rather learning that is intentional, deliberate, and goal-directed by expert teacher educators who are skilled at moving teachers toward more theoretically and pedagogically sound instructional practices and greater levels of professional expertise.[1]

A sociocultural perspective on teacher learning

It will come as no surprise to readers of our previously published work[2] that our epistemological stance on teacher learning is grounded in Vygotskian sociocultural theory (Vygotsky, 1978, 1981, 1986). Representing a coherent *theory of mind*, we take seriously Vygotsky's conceptualization of the development of human cognition as inherently social; that is, it emerges out of participation in external forms of social interaction that become internalized psychological tools for thinking (*internalization*). We acknowledge Vygotsky's claim that this transformation, from external (*interpsychological*) to internal (*intrapsychological*), is not direct, but mediated. In fact, we see the dialogic interactions that unfold in the practices of L2 teacher education as the very external forms of social interaction and activities that we hope, as teacher educators, will become internalized psychological tools for teacher thinking, enabling our teachers to construct and enact theoretically and pedagogically sound instructional practices for their L2 students. Moreover, our Vygotskian sociocultural stance is a transformative model of the human mind, since Vygotsky argued that individuals transform what is appropriated for their own purposes and in/for particular contexts of use. It does not represent an apprenticeship or reproduction model of the human mind. Rather, we recognize individuals as actors in and on the social situations in which they are embedded, being both shaped by and shaping the social situations of cognitive development. Thus, psychological processes are at the same time both socially derived—embedded within the historical practices of a culture—and individually unique. For L2 teachers, this means that they are shaped in and through their experiences as learners, the cultural practices of teacher education, and the particulars of their teaching context, all embedded within larger sociocultural histories yet appropriated in individual ways.

With that said, we know from our more than two decades of working with L2 teachers that the Vygotskian notion of *internalization*, that is, from external (*interpsychological*) to internal (*intrapsychological*), does not happen independently or automatically. In fact, decades of public lament has chided the lack of lasting impact that teacher education programs have on moving teachers beyond teaching the way they were taught when they were students or implementing what they learn in their teacher education programs in the classrooms and schools where they eventually work (Ball & Forzani, 2010; Cochran-Smith, Feiman-Nemser, & McIntyre 2008; Edwards & D'Arcy, 2004; Kennedy, 2008). We recognize that developing L2 teacher/teaching expertise takes prolonged and sustained participation in the social practices of both becoming and being a L2 teacher. Yet, in line with our Vygotskian sociocultural stance, we see teacher education programs (school learning) as the ideal venue for the systematic learning of L2 teaching through intentional, well-organized instruction. Vygotsky proposed that learning in the everyday world emerges out of common, concrete activities and immediate social interactions resulting in *everyday concepts*, a kind of unconscious, empirical knowledge that may actually be incorrect or misinformed. School learning, involving what Vygotsky called *academic (scientific) concepts*,[3] a more systematic and generalized knowledge, enables learners to think in ways that transcend their *everyday* experiences. Obvious parallels can be made between Lortie's (1975) *apprenticeship of observation* as learning about teaching in the everyday world of being a student and school learning as instantiated in the content and processes of L2 teacher education programs. In essence, teacher education is designed to expose teachers to relevant *academic concepts* that once internalized will enable them to overcome their everyday notions, possible misconceptions, of what it means to be a teacher, how to teach, and how to support student learning. Interestingly, Vygotsky did not privilege *academic concepts* over *everyday concepts* since he argued that neither is sufficient for a child to become fully self-regulated. In fact, in his critique of formal schooling he claimed that the "direct teaching of concepts is impossible and fruitless. A teacher who tries to do this usually accomplishes nothing but *empty verbalism*, a parrot like repetition of words by the child, simulating a knowledge of the corresponding concepts but actually covering up a vacuum" (Vygotsky, 1986, p. 150). Instead, he argued that the goal of concept development is for *academic concepts* and *everyday concepts* to become united into *true concepts*; an academic concept "gradually comes down to concrete phenomena" and an everyday concept "goes from the phenomenon upward toward generalizations" (p. 148). The internalization of *true concepts* through formal schooling has several significant outcomes for teachers. Initially, *true concepts* help to transform teachers' tacit knowledge and beliefs acquired through their schooling histories, enabling them to rethink what they thought they knew about teachers, teaching, and student learning. When teachers begin to use *true concepts* as tools for thinking (psychological tools), they begin to see classroom life and the activities of teaching/learning through new theoretical lenses. Likewise, when teachers *think in concepts* (Karpov, 2003), they are able to reason about and enact their teaching effectively and appropriately in various instructional situations, for different pedagogical purposes, and are able to articulate theoretically sound reasons for doing so.

Although not drawing on Vygotskian sociocultural theory, a similar argument has been made in general educational research by Kennedy (1999) who characterizes 'expertise' in teaching as emerging out of the ways in which teachers make sense of 'expert' knowledge, or knowledge that is propositional, written down, codified in textbooks, and publicly accepted as a principled way of understanding phenomena within a particular discourse community (*academic concepts*), and their own 'craft' or 'experiential' knowledge that emerges through their own lived experiences as learners (*everyday concepts*). As teachers begin to link this 'expert' knowledge to their own 'experiential' knowledge, they tend to reframe the way they describe and interpret their lived experience. These new understandings enable them to reorganize their experiential knowledge and this reorganization creates a new lens through which they interpret their understandings of themselves and their classroom practices. Thus, 'expertise' has a great deal of experiential knowledge in it, but it is organized around and transformed through 'expert' knowledge. From this perspective, teacher learning is clearly not the straightforward internalization of 'expert' knowledge from the outside in. Instead, teachers populate 'expert' knowledge with their own intentions, in their own voices, and create instruction that is meaningful for their own objectives (A.F. Ball, 2000). This, others have argued, positions teachers not as passive recipients of theory but as active users and producers of theory in their own right, for their own means, and as appropriate for their own instructional contexts (Cochran-Smith & Lytle, 1993).

Teacher education, whether for beginning or experienced teachers, may be the only occasion when the learning of teaching is the result of the kind of systematic, intentional, well-organized instruction that embodies the range of psychological tools that will enable teachers to enact theoretically and pedagogically sound instructional practices and thus develop greater levels of teacher/teaching expertise. We contend that the quality and character of the mediation that emerges in the practices of L2 teacher education plays a pivotal role in enabling teachers to come to understand their *everyday concepts* concerning teaching/learning through relevant *academic concepts* concerning language, language learning, and language teaching, thereby enriching the *academic* through the *everyday*, and building the capacity to think in and act through *true concepts* as they develop L2 teacher/teaching expertise.

We also recognize that the extent to which engagement in the practices of L2 teacher education will become internalized psychological tools for teacher thinking depends, in large part, on the agency and motives of our teachers and the affordances and constraints embedded within our and their professional worlds (Feryok, 2012). Therefore, in order to understand what happens inside the practices of L2 teacher education more fully, we need to look at the social/professional worlds from which teachers and teacher educators have come and now operate in. To do so, we draw on Freeman and Johnson's (1998) notions of *schools* and *schooling* to tease out the social influences of both settings and processes in the learning and doing of L2 teaching. Accordingly, we recognize *schools* as the physical and sociocultural settings in which learning-to-teach, teaching, and learning take place. *Schooling*, on the other hand, represents the sociocultural and historical processes that take place in schools over time. Combined, *schools* and *schooling* create and sustain certain meanings and values, representing the sociocultural terrain in which the work of teaching is thought about, carried out, and evaluated. Similar to Freeman and Johnson's original argument, the dialogic interactions that emerge in the practices of L2 teacher education cannot be understood apart from the sociocultural environments in which they take place and the processes of establishing and navigating the social values in which these practices are embedded (see also Edwards, 2010). It is against this backdrop that we explore what happens inside the practices in L2 teacher education.

Our view of second language teacher education

We recognize that the particular parameters of any L2 teacher education practice will no doubt reflect a particular view of what second language education is supposed to be about, including the dispositions, or habits of mind, for what constitutes good L2 teaching. Thus, by design, these parameters impart this view on learners of L2 teaching through direct social interactions (teacher–teacher educator interaction) and cultural artifacts (theory and research, i.e., *academic concepts* instantiated in books, articles, curricular materials, assessments), and through the internalization of ways of talking about language, teaching, learning, and students that represent this particular view. In fact, our Vygotskian sociocultural stance requires that we take stock of our own theoretical orientation to L2 education and the professional development of L2 teachers. Vygotsky was quite clear that formal education must engage with what matters in society, and that education itself implies transmitting something that is worthwhile, socially valued, and culturally significant. Indeed, we feel it is imperative to articulate what we believe to be informed habits of mind, productive instructional concepts and practices that support student language learning, and the particular view of L2 teaching that we expect our teachers to internalize and enact in the L2 classroom.

As teacher educators, our particular practices are imbued with values that position second language education as, in essence, providing language learners with a repertoire of semiotic resources for *how to be* and *how to mean* in the L2 world (Byrnes, 2012; Kramsch, 2014). Through theoretical learning in L2 teacher education, we likewise are providing a repertoire for *how to be* and *how to mean* in the L2 teaching world. Therefore, our theoretical orientation toward language, language teaching, and the learning of language teaching positions social interaction and meaning as central. We believe teachers, as well as the L2 learners they teach, develop through the mediation of others, as Vygotsky's often quoted phrase suggests, "through others, we become ourselves" (1931/1997, p. 105). Moreover, we view L2 teacher/teaching expertise as the development of what Johnson (1999) calls *reasoning teaching*, defined as

> the complex ways in which teachers conceptualize, construct explanations for, and respond to the social interactions and shared meanings that exist within and among teachers, students, parents, and administrators, both inside and outside the classroom. Simply put, reasoning teaching reflects the complex ways in which teachers figure out how to teach a particular topic, with a particular group of students, at a particular time, in a particular classroom, within a particular school. (p. 1)

By fostering *reasoning teaching* through our particular practices, we hope to address the time, experience, and interactional constraints inherent in any instructional context. *Reasoning teaching*, as a form of *teacherly thinking* (Golombek, 2011), is very much in line with Edwards' (2010) notion of promoting "resourceful teaching for resourceful learning" (p. 72), an educational stance that involves much more than the delivery of curriculum or the acquisition of skills, including the building of teacher agency by strengthening teachers' knowledge of and ability to manipulate a repertoire of linguistic, cultural, pedagogical, and interactional resources that enable them to support productive student learning. And we believe that the development of L2 teacher/teaching expertise is best accomplished through high quality mediational activities with expert teacher educators engaged in the practices of L2 teacher education.

Before we move on, what we mean by 'teachers' in this book needs some elaboration. We recognize that our own BA and MA TESOL programs typically cater to pre-service teachers since the majority who enroll are often newcomers to L2 teaching and the university settings in which our academic departments are situated. However, we note that a significant number of our teachers have extensive L2 teaching experience, draw on multilingual resources, and have had an array of international and intercultural experiences. Many of our teachers are teaching part-time while enrolled in our teacher education programs. So, for us, the traditional pre-service/in-service distinction becomes somewhat blurred. We, thus, use the word 'teachers' in most cases to represent the varied sociocultural histories and instructional experiences our teachers may have.

In sum, to understand the learning and development of L2 teachers/teaching as it takes place in formal teacher education, it is imperative to examine the interactions that unfold inside the practices of L2 teacher education. Empirically documenting the dialogic interactions that emerge inside the practices of L2 teacher education, tracing L2 teacher development as it is unfolding, and detailing the consequences of these interactions on the ways in which L2 teachers begin to think about and attempt to enact their instructional practices with L2 students is the ultimate goal of this book.

The development of knowledge of and for second language teaching

All professions have an accepted conception of what it is that people need to know and be able to do to carry out the work of a particular profession. However, it is also the case that a so-called *professional knowledge base* is not a static or neutral entity, but instead grounded in certain values, assumptions, and interpretations that are shared by members of a particular professional community. Johnson (2009b) has argued that the knowledge base of L2 teacher education informs three broad areas: (1) the content of L2 teacher education programs, *what L2 teachers need to know*; (2) the pedagogies that are taught in L2 teacher education programs, *how*

L2 teachers should teach; and (3) the institutional forms of delivery through which both the content and pedagogies are learned, *how L2 teachers learn to teach* (p. 21). It is this third area, *the institutional forms of delivery through which both the content and pedagogies are learned*, that constitute what we are calling the practices of L2 teacher education and the focus of this book. As we stated at the outset, we believe that it is inside these practices, the moment-to-moment dialogic interactions as well as the assignments and activities that teacher educators ask teachers to engage in at a distance, where teacher educators are best able to cultivate teachers' professional development. Likewise, the choices teacher educators make about the particular practices they enact in their L2 teacher education programs are neither static nor neutral but emerge from and are situated in the social, political, economic, and cultural histories that are located in the contexts where teacher educators and teachers live, learn, and teach. Therefore, the development of knowledge of and for language teaching is embedded in and emerges out of "located L2 teacher education," which entails constructing locally appropriate responses (i.e., practices) that support the preparation and professionalism of L2 teachers within the settings and circumstances in which they live and work (Johnson, 2006, p. 245).

Attempts to document knowledge of and for teaching in general education began in the mid-80s, most notably when Shulman (1987) and his colleagues at Stanford University embarked on a research project to define the knowledge base of teaching. They were interested in documenting not only the disciplinary foundations of what teachers need to know about the subject matter that they are expected to teach, but also the knowledge that teachers rely on to make that subject matter accessible, relevant, and useful to students. Coined *pedagogical content knowledge*, because it combines knowledge of content, pedagogy, curriculum, learners, and educational context, Shulman emphasized *pedagogical content knowledge* as being "of special interest because it identifies the distinctive bodies of knowledge for teaching" (p. 8). Accordingly, *pedagogical content knowledge* is neither fixed nor stable, but instead emergent, dynamic, and contingent on teachers' knowledge of particular students, in particular contexts, who are learning particular content, for particular purposes. As a result, the development of *pedagogical content knowledge* emerges out of engagement in the activities of teaching since its very nature constitutes and is constitutive of the interconnectedness of content, context, students, and pedagogical purpose.

Given its dynamic nature, *pedagogical content knowledge* develops as teachers engage in the actual activities of teaching. And this creates a conundrum for teacher education programs because it requires that learners of teaching perform as self-regulated teachers before they have the necessary competence to do so, or before they have the appropriate pedagogical content knowledge to do so. Yet, we see the developmental value of *performance preceding competence* (Cazden, 1981; Miller, 2011), in a sense, placing teachers ahead of themselves, as it is precisely through engaging in the activities of teaching and the dialogic interactions (spoken and written) related to those activities that teachers will develop deeper understandings of their actions and become consciously aware of the subject matter content and pedagogical resources that form the basis of their instructional decisions and activities. With that said, we also recognize that conscious awareness is not enough. While teachers may be consciously aware of the difficulties that learners might encounter while completing an instructional task, they may be unable to enact the most beneficial instructional strategies at critical points in time so as to assist learners in accomplishing that task. Conscious awareness is essential if teachers are to develop voluntary control, or self-regulation, over their instructional decisions and practices. Enabling teachers to become consciously aware of the *academic concepts* and pedagogical resources that form the basis of their instructional decisions and activities is an essential, albeit insufficient, element of the development of teacher/teaching expertise.

While most L2 teacher education programs do require a supervised practicum and/or internship experiences, these often come near the end of the program, remain disconnected from academic coursework, and are apprenticeship-like, in that they invoke a 'discovery learning' conceptualization of teacher learning. If, as the current research on teacher cognition suggests (see Kubanyiova & Feryok, 2015), participation in particular sociocultural practices and contexts shape what and how teachers learn to teach, then L2 teacher education programs must create multiple and varied opportunities for teachers to engage in theoretically and pedagogically sound instructional practices within the sociocultural contexts in which they are currently teaching or will eventually teach. More importantly, these opportunities, by design, must create spaces for teacher educators to offer expert mediation that supports teachers as they are engaged in the processes of being and becoming teachers. While traditional practicum activities tend to include teaching a class, self-observation, observing other teachers, the use of teaching journals, or discussions in seminars (Gebhard, 2009), new technologies that support computer-mediated communication (discussion boards, Moodle, blogs) have helped to open up these activities by exposing teachers' thoughts, feelings, and concerns as they are participating in the processes of learning to teach while simultaneously fostering greater teacher/teacher educator dialogue around the activities of planning, teaching, and reflecting on teaching (see Johnson & Golombek, 2013; Yoshida, 2011). Additionally, various forms of inquiry-based professional development (i.e., teacher study groups, peer coaching, lesson study) (see Johnson, 2009a), particularly those that allow for self-directed, collaborative, inquiry-based learning that is directly relevant to teachers' classrooms, have helped to create structural arrangements where teachers and teacher educators can engage in sustained collaborative dialogue that make explicit the dynamic nature of the *pedagogical content knowledge* that teachers come to rely on as they make the content of their instruction accessible, relevant, and useful to students.

In addition, we believe that teacher educators must frame their interactions with teachers in such a way as to enable them to gain an expert's understanding of the subject matter content being taught and the instructional resources to teach it for their own purposes and within/for particular contexts of use. This requires that teacher educators assist teachers in developing a deep conceptual understanding of the subject matter content they are expected to teach as well as conscious knowledge of the *academic concepts* that represent the scientific foundation of that content. For example, most L2 teachers know, from their everyday experience, that the present progressive tense in English is marked for regular verbs with the suffix –ing. Yet, few may be consciously aware of the complex relationship between tense (*location of time*), aspect (*flow of time*), and mood (*degree of necessity, obligation, probability, ability*) that work in concert to trigger language users to make certain choices about how to denote actions in time and space or "the construal of a situation based on the viewer's perspective" (Langacker, 2001, p. 16). In most L2 teacher education programs, teachers do have opportunities to learn the *academic concepts* that represent the systematic generalized knowledge that has emerged from theory and research of their subject matter content (i.e., knowledge about language, second language acquisition, multi-literacies, etc.); however, more often than not these *academic concepts* are not linked to the day-to-day activities of teaching/learning in L2 classrooms. General educational research has made a distinction between the accepted disciplinary knowledge of a particular field and the *pedagogical content knowledge* (Shulman, 1987) that teachers use to make the content of their instruction relevant and accessible to students (D.L. Ball, 2000). We see, from our Vygotskian sociocultural stance, this disciplinary knowledge and *pedagogical content knowledge* as being in a dialectical relationship, with each shaping and transforming the other (i.e., *true concepts*) through mediated engagement in the activities of L2 teaching.

A persistent challenge for language teacher education is to create learning/teaching opportunities that foster the development of L2 teacher *pedagogical content knowledge*. What makes this challenge so persistent is that, as the original definition suggests, because it is emergent, dynamic, and contingent on teachers' knowledge of particular students, in particular contexts, who are learning particular content, for particular purposes, it cannot be acquired in one context and then simply applied to another. At the same time, we recognize that teacher educator *pedagogical content knowledge* is also partial and dynamic, and thus what we know about particular content or the particular pedagogical resources we suggest will most certainly shape how we mediate teacher learning and development. This is precisely why some have described the activities of teaching as 'unnatural work' (Ball & Forzani, 2010) as it requires teachers to unpack something that they presumably know so well, and may have fully internalized, yet now must make accessible to and learnable by others. We argue that the same can be said for teacher educators. Exploring our practices as teacher educators, as we do in this book, is one way to unpack our expertise.

The development of knowledge of and for second language teaching involves a complicated, dialectic, socioculturally situated process of becoming and being an L2 teacher within various communities of practice (Lave & Wenger, 1991).

Yet, from our Vygotskian sociocultural stance, knowledge of and for second language teaching is not, and cannot be, separated from the individuals who both internalize and enact it in the settings in which they live, learn, and work. Thus, we next turn to the development of L2 teacher identity, another critical dimension in cultivating teachers' professional development.

The development of L2 teacher identity

Research on language teacher cognition within the last decade has argued that teacher identity is a fundamental component of what teachers know and do in the language classroom (Duff & Uchida, 1997; Kanno & Stuart, 2011; Morgan, 2004; Varghese et al., 2005). For beginning and experienced teachers alike, there is an "inextricable relationship between teacher identity and classroom practice" (Kanno & Stuart, 2011, p. 250). Though Vygotsky never used the term 'identity' in his work (Cross & Gearon, 2007; Penuel & Wertsch 1995), others have theorized about the social origin and formation of identity by highlighting how cultural tools (re)shape action in goal-oriented activity (Penuel & Wertsch, 1995), so that identity is "a being in continuous becoming" (Roth, 2003, p. 8) through activity. Our work as teacher educators and our Vygotskian sociocultural stance align well with Cross (2006) and Cross and Gearon's (2007) construct of *identity-in-activity* as a way to unify identity as concrete practice and discursively constructed practice. More specifically, they posit that language teacher identity involves a dialectic between the microgenetic activity that a teacher realizes as a *subject* within an *activity system* (Engeström, 1987; Leont'ev, 1978), with its associated rules, community members, tools, and objects, and the larger social, cultural, historic domain from which that activity emerged and is shaped. The construct of *identity-in-activity* can thus be used to analyze the development of teacher identity because it can be applied initially to characterize a teacher's identities in different *activity systems*, or instructional contexts, and the larger discourses shaping those identities in different contexts. If there is a sense that tensions exist, it can then be used to identify possible *contradictions* between identity and activity within and between *activity systems*. Identity, along with motive, is thus a byproduct of emotion, suggesting that emotion and motive are central to understanding the formation of identity (Roth, 2007).

Teachers trying to develop particular identities often face contradictions because the various *activity systems* in which they participate have different values, norms, and expectations for what constitutes 'good' language teachers and 'good' language teaching. What is imparted in teacher education programs, or in literature advocating particular approaches to or goals in language teaching, may be at odds with the larger sociocultural, institutional, and historical discourses shaping a particular teaching context. In his work, Cross (2006) detailed the contradictions between *activity systems* by showing how an in-service Japanese as a foreign language teacher's *identity-in-activity* did not feature widespread use of the Japanese language to develop students' communicative competence in the target language, what Cross suggests is advocated as 'good practice' in L2 teaching. Rather, the teacher's activity focused on using English to establish classroom order and using Japanese as a means to enhance English literacy skills, what he characterizes as the socioculturally constructed activity of being a 'good Japanese language teacher' in this particular context. Thus, as the *subject* of different *activity systems*, teachers experience *contradictions* between identities, and between identities and activity within and between those *activity systems* because those systems have different objects or goals, communities, norms of behavior, and histories.

Yet, teachers will no doubt experience contradictions differently even within the same *activity system*, because of their varied social historical circumstances, and the affordances and constraints these provide (Dang, 2013). Mediating teachers as they encounter such *contradictions* in their identities across *activity systems* should thus be part of the process of unifying their emotion, cognition, and activity of teaching within the practices of L2 teacher education. Developing teacher identity means not only introducing new identities to teachers, but also enabling them to develop activities that align with that identity in a 'located' teaching setting.

One way that teacher educators have attempted to mediate teacher identities, to encourage them to envision and possibly adopt more empowering teacher identities, is through reading and reflecting on research and theories that challenge the dominant discourses of idealized English language teachers. A line of such research has sought to transform the identities of nonnative speaking English teachers explicitly by challenging the *native speaker myth* (Phillipson, 1992) through various mediational activities such as exploring theories of bilingualism and multicompetence (Cook, 1992) in courses of MA TESOL programs or teacher supervision courses in PhD programs. By exploring these theories and more empowering identities, and re-storying their own identities through reflective activities, typically reflective journals, teachers are able to reimagine themselves as multicompetent and multilingual teachers of English, viewing themselves more positively as part of an imagined community of multicompetent speakers of English (Golombek & Jordan, 2005; Pavlenko, 2003; Reis, 2011a, 2011b). A fundamental weakness of these studies is that although they describe teachers' adoption of idealized conceptions of an alternative teacher identity, they do not show the teachers transforming the material activity of their teaching to align with their incipient identities. Moreover, as Kanno and Stuart (2011) demonstrated, formation of teacher identity is a sustained process of *learning-in-practice* (Lave 1996), through which developing basic instructional skills, content expertise, and an understanding of what is important to teachers in their own teaching is particularly constructive in identity building. This raises a practical and ethical concern for teacher educators as to how to maximize opportunities for teachers to design instructional activities for specific teaching contexts that are congruent with both identities appropriate for those contexts, and teachers' conceptions of teaching and learning, in order to enhance the development of located teacher identities that form part of 'located' teacher education (Johnson, 2006). A common and long-standing mechanism for uncovering disempowering teacher identities as well as reimagining more empowering ones is engagement in narrative activity, to which we turn next as we complete this overview of our Vygotskian sociocultural stance on L2 teacher education.

The transformative power of narrative activity

While narrative has long been viewed as the quintessential way through which teachers' knowledge is structured and rationalized as a productive vehicle for teacher inquiry and knowledge building (Cochran-Smith & Lytle, 2009; Elbaz, 1983), from our Vygotskian sociocultural stance, we have argued that the transformative power of narrative activity lies in its ability to ignite cognitive processes that can foster L2 teacher professional development (Johnson & Golombek, 2011b). We thus positioned narrative activity as a mediational tool arguing that:

> The act of narrating, as a cultural activity, influences how one comes to understand what one is narrating about. The telling or retelling (either oral or written) of an experience entails a complex combination of description, explanation, analysis, interpretation, and construal of one's private reality as it is brought into the public sphere. (p. 490)

In order to tease apart the complex means by which narrative activity functions as a mediational tool, we proposed three interrelated and often overlapping functions: narrative as externalization, narrative as verbalization, and narrative as systematic examination.

When narrative activity functions as externalization, it allows teachers to express their understandings and feelings by giving voice to their past, present, and even imagined future experiences. Narrative as externalization fosters introspection, explanation, and sense-making, while simultaneously opening up teachers' thoughts and feelings to social influence. In this sense, narrative as externalization has value not only for teachers themselves but also for teacher educators. When narrative activity functions as externalization, it concretizes, in teachers' own words, how, when, and why new understandings emerge, understandings that can enable teachers to gain increasing control over their thinking, feelings, and actions. Once externalized, these same understandings offer teacher educators insights into teachers' ways of 'seeing and being' in the world. Such insights offer teacher educators an orienting basis for action from which they can work to support and enhance the professional development of L2 teachers.

When narrative activity functions as verbalization, it assists teachers as they attempt to internalize the *academic concepts* that they are exposed to in their teacher education programs. Narrative as verbalization allows teachers to deliberately and systematically use *academic concepts* to reexamine, rename, and reorient their everyday experiences, engaging in what Vygotsky (1986) described as *ascending from the abstract to the concrete*. If internalized, *academic concepts* "have the potential to function as psychological tools, which enable teachers to have greater awareness and control over their cognitive processes, and in turn, enable them to engage in more informed ways of teaching in varied instructional contexts and circumstances" (Johnson & Golombek, 2011b, p. 493). For narrative activity to function as verbalization, the *academic concepts* that teachers are exposed to in teacher education programs must be situated within the settings and circumstances of teachers' professional worlds and realized through the concrete goal-directed activities of actual teaching. When narrative activity functions as verbalization, it becomes a powerful mediational tool that supports teachers' *thinking in concepts* (Karpov, 2003) as they make sense of their teaching experiences and begin to regulate both their thinking and teaching practices.

Narrative as systematic examination represents the procedures or parameters for how teachers engage in narrative activity. Drawing again from our Vygotskian sociocultural stance, human cognition is understood as originating in and fundamentally shaped by engagement in social activity, and consequently, cognition cannot be removed from activity. Put quite simply, *what is learned* is fundamentally shaped by *how it is learned*. Therefore, different forms of narrative activity will entail different types of systematic examination, ultimately having different consequences for learning and development. As an example, the parameters associated with writing a learning-to-teach history might focus the teacher's attention more on the (re)construction of self as a teacher, whereas the parameters of an action research project might focus the teacher's attention more on the particulars of classroom activity. Ultimately, the consequences of engagement in narrative activity will be shaped by the parameters that frame its systematic examination.

From our Vygotskian sociocultural stance, we find transformative power in teachers engaging in narrative activity. Taken together, when narrative activity functions as externalization, it enables teachers to make their tacit thoughts, feelings, and hopes explicit and create cohesion out of their lived experiences. When narrative activity functions as verbalization, it enables teachers to use theoretical constructs to inform and increasingly regulate their thinking and teaching activities. The parameters of any narrative activity will determine the focus of its systematic examination, enabling teachers to recognize the intentions and reasoning behind their thinking and teaching activities, and perhaps alter the ways in which they think about and engage in the activities of teaching. For teacher educators, recognizing the transformative power of narrative activity is critical to the design, enactment, and assessment of the consequences of what happens inside the practices of L2 teacher education.

In this book we seek to highlight the unique contributions that teacher educators and teacher education make to L2 teacher professional development. Specifically, we focus on how teacher learning and development are assisted by the dialogic interactions that emerge inside the practices of L2 teacher education. The ultimate goal of this book is to empirically document these dialogic interactions and their consequences for teacher development because it is inside these practices and the *responsive mediation* that emerges as they unfold that we find the key to enabling teacher educators to understand, support, and enhance L2 teacher professional development.

Notes

1 This argument is an expanded version of Johnson, K.E. (2015). Reclaiming the relevance of L2 teacher education. *The Modern Language Journal 99*(3), 515–528.
2 Johnson, 2006, 2007, 2009, 2015; Johnson & Golombek, 2003, 2011a, 2011b; Golombek & Johnson, 2004; Golombek & Doran, 2014; Golombek, 2015.
3 We recognize *scientific* and *academic concepts* as interchangeable but have given preference to *academic concepts* as this is how Vygotsky (1935/1994) referenced them in his later writings about formal (schooling) education.

References

Ball, A. F. (2000). Teachers' developing philosophies on literacy and their use in urban schools: A Vygotskian perspective on internal activity and teacher change. In C.D. Lee & P. Smagorinsky (Eds.), *Vygotskian perspectives on literacy research: Constructing meaning through collaborative inquiry* (pp. 226–255). New York: Cambridge University Press.

Ball, D. L. (2000). Bridging practices: Intertwining content and pedagogy in teaching and learning to teach. *Journal of Teacher Education, 51*(6), 25–27.

Ball, D. L., & Forzani, F. M. (2010). The work of teaching and the challenge for teacher education. *Journal of Teacher Education, 60*, 497–511.

Byrnes, H. (2012). Of frameworks and the goals of collegiate foreign language education: Critical reflections. *Applied Linguistics Review, 3*, 1–24.

Cazden, C. (1981). Performance before competence: Assistance to child discourse in the zone of proximal development. *Quarterly Newsletter of the Laboratory of Comparative Human Cognition, 3*, 5–8.

Cochran-Smith, M., & Lytle, S. (1993). *Inside/outside: Teacher research and knowledge.* New York: Teachers College Press.

Cochran-Smith, M., & Lytle, S. L. (2009). *Inquiry as stance: Practitioner research for the next generation.* New York: Teachers College Press.

Cochran-Smith, M., Feiman-Nemser, S., & McIntyre D. J. (Eds.) (2008). *Handbook of research on teacher education: Enduring questions in changing contexts* (3rd Edition). New York: Routledge.

Cook, V. J. (1992). Evidence for multicompetence. *Language Learning, 42*, 557–591.

Cross, R. (2006, November). Identity and language teacher education: The potential for sociocultural perspectives in researching language teacher identity. In *Languages, Teaching, and Education at the Australian Association for Research in Education Annual Conference: Engaging Pedagogies* (pp. 27–30).

Cross, R., & Gearon, M. (2007). The confluence of doing, thinking and knowing: Classroom practice as the crucible of foreign language teacher identity. In A. Berry, A. Clemans, & A. Kostogriz (Eds.), *Dimensions of professional learning: Identities, professionalism and practice* (pp. 53–67). Rotterdam, Netherlands: Sense Publishers.

Dang, T. K. A. (2013). Identity in activity: Examining teacher professional identity formation in the paired-placement of student teachers. *Teaching and Teacher Education, 30,* 47–59.

Duff, P. A., & Uchida, Y. (1997). The negotiation of teachers' sociocultural identities and practices in postsecondary EFL classrooms. *TESOL Quarterly, 31,* 451–486.

Edwards, A. (2010). How can Vygotsky and his legacy help us to understand and develop teacher education? In V. Ellis, A. Edwards, & P. Smagorinsky (Eds.), *Cultural-historical perspectives in teacher education and development* (pp. 61–77). London: Routledge.

Edwards, A., & D'Arcy, C. (2004). Relational agency and disposition in sociocultural accounts of learning to teach. *Educational Review, 56*(2), 147–155.

Elbaz, F. (1983). *Teacher thinking: A study of practical knowledge.* London: Crown Helm.

Engeström, Y. (1987). Learning by expanding: An activity-theoretical approach to developmental research. Retrieved April 11, 2003 from http://lchc.ucsd.edu/MCA/Paper/Engestrom/expanding/toc.htm.

Feryok, A. (2012). Activity theory and language teacher agency. *The Modern Language Journal, 96,* 95–107.

Freeman, D., & Johnson, K. E. (1998). Reconceptualizing the knowledge-base of language teacher education. *TESOL Quarterly, 32*(3), 397–417.

Gebhard, J. G. (2009). The practicum. In J. C. Richards & A. Burns (Eds.), *The Cambridge guide to language teacher education* (pp. 250–258). Cambridge: Cambridge University Press.

Golombek, P. R. (2011). Dynamic assessment in teacher education: Using dialogic video protocols to intervene in teacher thinking and activity. In K. E. Johnson & P. R. Golombek (Eds.), *Research on second language teacher education: A sociocultural perspective on professional development* (pp. 121–135). New York: Routledge.

Golombek, P. R. (2015). Redrawing the boundaries of language teacher cognition: Language teacher educators' emotion, cognition, and activity. *The Modern Language Journal, 99*(3), 470–484.

Golombek, P. R., & Doran, M. (2014). Unifying cognition, emotion, and activity in language teacher professional development. *Teaching and Teacher Education, 39,* 102–111.

Golombek, P. R., & Johnson, K. E. (2004). Narrative inquiry as a mediational space: Examining emotional and cognitive dissonance in second language teachers' development. *Teachers and Teaching: Theory and Practice, 10*(2), 307–327.

Golombek, P. R., & Jordan, S. R. (2005). Becoming "black lambs" not "parrots": A poststructuralist orientation to intelligibility and identity. *TESOL Quarterly, 39*, 513–533.

Johnson, K. E. (1999). *Understanding language teaching: Reasoning in action.* Boston: Heinle, Cengage Learning.

Johnson, K. E. (2006). The sociocultural turn and its challenges for L2 teacher education. *TESOL Quarterly, 40*(1), 235–257.

Johnson, K. E. (2007). Tracing teacher and student learning in teacher-authored narratives. *Teacher Development, 11*(2), 1–14.

Johnson, K. E. (2009a). *Second language teacher education: A sociocultural perspective.* New York: Routledge.

Johnson, K. E. (2009b) Trends in second language teacher education. In J. C. Richards & A. Burns (Eds.), *The Cambridge guide to language teacher education* (pp. 20–29). Cambridge: Cambridge University Press.

Johnson, K. E. (2015). Reclaiming the relevance of L2 teacher education. *The Modern Language Journal, 99*(3), 515–528.

Johnson, K. E., & Golombek, P. R. (Eds.) (2011a). *Research on second language teacher education: A sociocultural perspective on professional development.* New York: Routledge.

Johnson, K. E., & Golombek, P. R. (2011b). The transformative power of narrative in second language teacher education. *TESOL Quarterly, 45*(3), 486–509.

Johnson, K. E., & Golombek, P. R. (2013). A tale of two mediations: Tracing the dialectics of cognition, emotion, and activity in teachers' practicum blogs. In G. Barkhuizen (Ed.), *Narrative research in applied linguistics* (pp. 85–104). Cambridge: Cambridge University Press.

Kanno, Y., & Stuart, C. (2011). Learning to become a second language teacher: Identities-in-practice. *The Modern Language Journal, 95*, 236–252.

Karpov, Y. V. (2003). Vygotsky's doctrine of scientific concepts: Its role for contemporary education. In A. Kozulin, B. Gindis, V. S. Ageyev, & S. M. Miller (Eds.), *Vygotsky's educational theory in cultural context* (pp. 65–82). Cambridge: Cambridge University Press.

Kennedy, M. M. (1999). Ed schools and the problem of knowledge. In J. Rath & A. McAninch (Eds.), *What counts as knowledge in teacher education?* (pp. 29–45). Stamford, CT: Ablex Publishing Corporation.

Kennedy, M. (2008). The place of teacher education in teachers' education. In M. Cochran-Smith, S. Feiman-Nemser, & D. J. McIntyre, (Eds.), *Handbook of research on teacher education: Enduring questions in changing contexts* (pp. 1199–1203). New York: Routledge.

Kramsch, C. (2014). Teaching foreign languages in an era of globalization: Introduction. *The Modern Language Journal, 98*, 296–311.

Kubanyiova, M., & Feryok, A. (2015). Language teacher cognition in Applied Linguistics research: Revisiting the territory, redrawing the boundaries, reclaiming the relevance. *The Modern Language Journal, 99*(3), 435–449.

Langacker, R. W. (2001). Cognitive linguistics, language pedagogy, and the English present tense. In M. Pütz, S. Niemeier, & R. Dirven (Eds.), *Applied cognitive linguistics: Theory and language acquisition* (pp. 3–39). Berlin: Walter de Gruyter.

Lave, J. (1996). Teaching as learning in practice. *Mind, Culture, and Activity, 3,* 149–164.

Lave, J., & Wenger, E. (1991). *Situated learning: Legitimate peripheral participation.* New York: Cambridge University Press.

Leont'ev, A. N. (1978). *Activity, consciousness, and personality.* Englewood Cliffs, NJ: Prentice Hall.

Lortie, D. (1975). *Schoolteacher: A sociological study.* Chicago: University of Chicago.

Miller, R. (2011). *Vygotsky in perspective.* Cambridge: Cambridge University Press.

Morgan, B. (2004). Teacher identity as pedagogy: Towards a field-internal conceptualisation in bilingual and second language education. *International Journal of Bilingual Education and Bilingualism, 7,* 172–188.

Pavlenko, A. (2003). "I never knew I was a bilingual": Reimagining teacher identities in TESOL. *Journal of Language, Identity, and Education, 2,* 251–268.

Penuel, W. R., & Wertsch, J. V. (1995). Vygotsky and identity formation: A sociocultural approach. *Educational Psychologist, 30,* 83–92.

Phillipson, R. (1992). *Linguistic imperialism.* Oxford: Oxford University Press.

Reis, D. S. (2011a). "I'm not alone": Empowering non-native English-speaking teachers to challenge the native speaker myth. In K. E. Johnson & P. R. Golombek (Eds.), *Research on second language teacher education: A sociocultural perspective on professional development* (pp. 31–49). New York: Routledge.

Reis, D. S. (2011b). Non-native English-speaking teachers (NNESTs) and professional legitimacy: A sociocultural theoretical perspective on identity transformation. *International Journal of the Sociology of Language, 208,* 139–160.

Roth, W. M. (2003). Review essay: Culture and identity. *Forum Qualitative Sozialforschung/Forum: Qualitative Social Research, 4*(1), 1–34.

Roth, W. M. (2007). Emotion at work: A contribution to third-generation cultural-historical activity theory. *Mind, Culture, and Activity, 14,* 40–63.

Shulman, L. S. (1987). Knowledge and teaching: Foundations of the new reform. *Harvard Educational Review, 57*(1), 1–22.

Varghese, M., Morgan, B., Johnston, B., & Johnson, K. A. (2005). Theorizing language teacher identity: Three perspectives and beyond. *Journal of Language, Identity, and Education, 4,* 21–44.

Vygotsky, L. S. (1978). M. Cole, V. John-Steiner, S. Scribner, & E. Souberman (Eds.) *Mind in society.* Cambridge, MA: Harvard University Press.

Vygotsky, L. S. (1981). The genesis of higher mental functions. In J. V. Wertsch (Ed.), *The concept of activity in Soviet psychology* (pp. 144–188). Armonk, NY: Sharpe.

Vygotsky, L. S. (1986). *Thought and language* (A. Kozulin, Trans.). Cambridge, MA: MIT Press.

Vygotsky, L. S. (1931/1997). The development of thinking and formation of concepts in the adolescent. In R. W. Rieber (Ed.), The *collected works of L. S. Vygotsky. Vol. 5: Child psychology* (pp. 29–81). New York: Plenum Press.

Vygotsky, L. S. (1935/1994). The development of academic concepts in school aged children. In R. van der Veer & J. Valsiner, (Eds.) (1994), *The Vygotsky reader* (pp. 355–370). Oxford: Blackwell.

Yoshida, T. (2011). Moodle as a mediational space: Japanese EFL teachers' emerging conceptions of curriculum. In K. E. Johnson & P. R. Golombek (Eds.), *Research on second language teacher education: A sociocultural perspective on professional development* (pp. 136–152). New York: Routledge.

2

MEDIATION IN L2 TEACHER PROFESSIONAL DEVELOPMENT

The word 'mediation' in our daily lives has different connotations for different people in different contexts. Some may automatically comprehend it in the sense of a third-party arbiter brought in to reconcile differences, whether it be a professional brought in to settle a legal dispute or a caregiver brought in to settle a squabble between siblings. Our use of mediation is not as an *everyday concept* but rather as an *academic concept*, which we detail in this chapter as the foundation for our concept of *responsive mediation*. From our Vygotskian sociocultural stance, mediation is key in the development of higher mental processes of all humans. In this chapter, we articulate the pivotal and complicated role of mediation in the development of higher mental processes, especially in terms of L2 teacher development. Beginning with Vygotsky, we trace how mediation is conceptualized within a sociocultural theoretical perspective. We then follow with how various Vygotskian scholars have interpreted mediation and extended it for psychological and educational applications. We offer *responsive mediation* as playing a crucial role in exploiting the potential of what Vygotsky called symbolic tools—social interaction, artifacts, and concepts—to enable teachers to appropriate them as *psychological tools* in learning-to-teach and ultimately in directing their teaching activity.

Mediation: The central concept in Vygotsky's theory of the mind

To start, Vygotsky argued that the relationship between the world and humans is indirect, that is, *mediated*. This relationship is typically represented in Vygotsky's (1978) triadic model connecting sign, tool, and mediated activity (adapted from p. 54) (Figure 2.1).

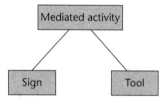

FIGURE 2.1

Humans do not act directly with or on the world, but use culturally and historically molded physical tools that expand their physical abilities and thus enable them to change the conditions in which they live. In short, physical tools are externally oriented to shape the material world. For example, using a mortar and pestle in certain cultures and time periods enabled cooks to transform ingredients and thus transform cuisine in the process, while food processors in other cultures and time periods have shortened the time needed to transform ingredients. Whether using a mortar and pestle or a food processor, something will be gained, perhaps time, while something may be lost, perhaps texture or taste. Humans also have the unique capacity to use *psychological tools*, such as literacy, to mediate their thinking and activities that likewise expand their mental processes, transforming themselves and their activity in the process. *Psychological tools*, or *signs*, have also been historically and culturally shaped, passed on, and adapted by successive generations in response to individual and community needs, but they are internally oriented to shape cognitive development. As such, *psychological tools* represent unique cultural manifestations of artifacts and activities, concepts and social relations, or *mediational means*.

Within Vygotskian sociocultural theory, how we learn to use these *psychological tools* to develop our higher mental processes—to transform ourselves—is explained through the role of *mediation*. Children learn to use these tools in and through sustained social interaction with adults, first on the social plane (external or *interpsychological*) and later on the mental plane (internal or *intrapsychological*) plane as the child begins to self-regulate. Adults use verbal tools initially in joint activity, which has a clear purpose (*goal-directed activities*), as a way to regulate, or mediate, the child's behavior. Children appropriate these tools and begin to use them in the form of *egocentric* (private) speech to organize, or plan, direct, and evaluate, their own behavior. For example, children may initially tell themselves 'hot' when near a stove, as their caregivers have done, to deter any impulse to touch it. Children likewise regulate others' behavior (social speech), for example when a child tells a caregiver to 'get the ball.' As children master verbal tools, these tools gradually become internalized, transforming into *inner speech* through which children regulate their own mental functioning and activity. This ongoing process of transformation from the external to the internal, resulting in new forms of cognition, is what Vygotsky expressed as *internalization*.

Teacher educators need to engage teachers in appropriate practices of L2 teacher education, and in the context of engaging in these practices, expose them to the psychological tools needed for successful performance of these activities, with the goal of developing L2 teacher/teaching expertise. Psychological tools grounded in the sociocultural histories of language teaching/teacher education mediate teachers' mental processes. Teachers are not born with these psychological tools, nor do they need to discover or reinvent these tools themselves. Instead, psychological tools should be presented explicitly to teachers through theoretical learning. This is precisely what L2 teacher education programs are supposed to do. Teacher educators who work in these programs have already internalized the psychological tools they use to enact theoretically and pedagogically sound instructional practices. To make these psychological tools available to novice teachers, teacher educators first need to externalize them. That is, they need to present them to teachers as external signs through moment-to-moment and at-a-distance dialogic interactions.

The child and adult (or teacher and teacher educator) will inevitably have different *motives* as they engage in joint activity. Thought does not exist in itself but is "engendered by motivation, i.e., by our desires and needs, our interests and emotions" (Vygotsky, 1986, p. 252). Although learners engage in activity with their own motives, part of what more expert others do is promote the development of new motives through mediation. The new motive "always ripens under the umbrella of the person's current motive, that is, within his or her current activity" (Karpov, 2014, p. 28). For example, a teacher's motive in writing a reflection journal may be to meet a requirement of a course. Alongside that teacher's motive, the teacher educator may mediate that activity through written comments and questions intended to encourage a new motive—journal writing as self-inquiry to promote the development of teacher/teaching expertise. Thus, within the joint activity of L2 teacher education, teacher educators must have a clear sense of their own motives, try to elicit what teachers' motives are, and work to promote new motives in teacher activity when necessary. The process of doing this is demanding for teacher educators, so we hope the case studies of teachers engaged in learning-to-teach that follow (Chapters 5–9) provide some insights.

Mediational means: Artifacts and activities, concepts and social relations

Mediational means have widespread, value-laden social and ideological implications. Researchers have shown how literacy, as a psychological tool, is multifaceted, with different practices that embody different values and goals for different social groups (Brice Heath, 1983; Scribner & Cole, 1981). The literacy of formal schooling, established and valued as normative by certain groups, confers power to those groups while disempowering other groups enacting different literacy practices (Brice Heath, 1983; Scollon, 2001). Additionally, although these tools facilitate certain actions, they simultaneously restrict them (Scollon, 2001), exemplified by the mortar and pestle and food processor comparison. A more relevant example for L2 teacher education would be that while using a lesson plan provides affordances for a beginning teacher in terms of sequencing a considerable amount of information and activity within a lesson, it may constrain the teacher's classroom teaching, so that finishing the lesson as planned becomes the goal itself. Though Vygotsky discussed these mediational means, within the domain of child cognitive development, they are implicated in all human cognitive development, and for our purposes, the development of L2 teacher/teaching expertise.

Cultural artifacts and activities, as mediational means, appear to be simple concepts but are in fact multifaceted. Language has been singled out as the most powerful cultural artifact that transforms, or mediates, mental functioning, allowing humans to perform increasingly complex activities. Artifacts can be symbolic, such as language, as well as concrete, such as the physical object of a videotape of a teacher teaching. Artifacts have an ideal-material quality in human activity "that are not only incorporated into the activity, but are constitutive of it" (Lantolf & Thorne, 2006, p. 62). For example, a lesson plan is ideal in a teacher's conceptualization of it in the mind and representation on paper, but then becomes material both as a physical copy of it written out and then enacted in the classroom. For a teacher, the physicality and sociality of a lesson plan interact, but its sociality, or how it is used to organize the activities of instruction, shapes how the lesson plays out in the actual class. Humans are unique in that they can create a mental plan, symbolically through speaking or writing, of their physical activity before they engage in that activity (Ilyenkov, 1977). The phrase 'lesson plan' is ideal and material as well in that we have a conceptual understanding of its meaning, but it has a material sense in how it is represented in terms of the alphabetic or phonetic system of English.

Concepts, both *everyday* and *academic*, as detailed in Chapter 1, also mediate the ongoing process of *internalization*. As we know, Vygotsky envisioned that learning involved a dialectic between *everyday concepts*, subconscious, empirical knowledge that may actually be incorrect or misinformed, and *academic concepts*, more systematic and generalized knowledge that is the purview of school learning. For Vygotsky, it is only through explicit and systematic instruction that learners will transcend their *everyday* experiences and reach a deeper understanding of and control over the object of study (*true concepts*). Conceptual development emerges over time, depending on the affordances and constraints of the learning environment and learner agency. According to Lantolf and Thorne (2006), "human agency appears once we integrate cultural artifacts and concepts into our mental and material activity" (p. 63). In L2 teacher education, teacher educators mediate teacher's cognition through *academic concepts* so they become psychological tools that teachers use to enact their agency and regulate their mental and material activity of teaching in locally appropriate, theoretically and pedagogically sound instructional practices for their students and contexts.

Social relations, or human mediation, are also important in terms of how the adult's involvement with the child in joint activity promotes *internalization*. From the time children are born, they participate in different culturally specified activities and relations that are part of their historical legacy and are involved in dialogic interactions with caregivers who use language to regulate the child.

Though language is important in human mediation, "the construction of meaning is regulated (or mediated) by social relationships" (Moll, 2014, p. 33). The social in relations is not only the dialogic interactions between child and adult, but the longstanding historical and sociocultural inheritance that shapes the interaction. In L2 teacher education, we view the social relations between the teacher educator and teacher as functioning as a powerful and demanding form of mediation. The specific forms of human mediation used will no doubt differ depending on the goal-directed activities in which teachers and teacher educators are engaged, as well as the institutional settings in which that mediation is embedded.

The zone of proximal development: An arena of learner potentiality

The transformation of mental processes from the external to the internal through the introduction of verbal tools into activity emphasizes "qualitative rather than quantitative increments" (Wertsch, 2007, p. 179), and is intimately tied to the child's relationship to the environment. Environment does not mean a description of the features in the context in which the child is situated but that the child's mental–personal is always in relation to the material–social. Vygotsky sought to explain the basis of qualitative change through the notion of the *social situation of development*: "The social situation of development represents the initial moment for all dynamic changes that occur in development during the given period" (Vygotsky, 1988, p. 198). Within such a critical period, a contradiction emerges between what the child can actually do, the child's emotional–affective needs, and emerging mental formations. Vygotsky proposed that children go through varied stages in their development characterized by dialectical interaction of stable and critical periods initiated by a contradiction. The unity of the contradiction indicates that the mental–personal has been transformed, as has the material–social, so that the child has a new relation to the environment. As teacher educators, we believe L2 teacher education programs represent a similar sort of critical period in teachers' professional development. Just as Vygotsky proposed critical periods as times of qualitative transformation in children's development (i.e., the introduction of literacy through formal schooling), thus causing a restructuring of social relations (i.e., being asked reading comprehension questions by the teacher), L2 teacher education programs are often a period of tremendous emotional/cognitive dissonance. Students are repositioned as teachers, *everyday concepts* about teachers and teaching (i.e., the apprenticeship of observation) are reconceptualized through *academic concepts* (i.e., theoretical learning), new identities, meanings, and ways of being emerge, and teachers form new *perezhivanie* about their experiences. It is a time during which human mediation, as we illustrate in Chapters 5–9, is absolutely critical in cultivating teachers' professional development.

Given Vygotsky's notions of the social situation of development, critical periods, and the development of higher mental processes as mediated, beginning as joint activity in which the tool is externalized for a child by a caregiver, it follows that the child's independent use of a psychological tool will naturally lag behind the use of the tool with assistance. Vygotsky's innovation is that he conceptually framed this distance between a learner's level of independent performance and the level of assisted performance as the *zone of proximal development* (ZPD):

> The zone of proximal development of the child is the distance between his[1] actual development, determined with the help of independently solved tasks, and the level of the potential development of the child, determined with the help of tasks solved by the child under the guidance of adults and in cooperation with his more intelligent partners. (1933/1935, p. 42)

The ZPD offers an alternative conception of instruction and cognitive development than the underlying conventional schooling practices where instruction follows development. In other words, a child is assumed to be at a certain level of development and then instruction focuses on content considered appropriate for that level. For Vygotsky (1986) however, correctly organized instruction "marches ahead of development and leads it," focusing on "ripening" mental processes (p. 188). This is possible through Vygotsky's conception of the ZPD as a metaphoric space of potentiality. In order to understand the causes, characteristics, and forces surrounding a child's social situation of development, Chaiklin (1993) suggests that Vygotsky intended the ZPD as a diagnostic tool. The ZPD thus has direct implications for assessing what learners need instructionally at any given point in time, and consequently, for how a more expert-other can mediate responsively. Rather than instruction focusing on a learner's independent activity or what has already been internalized, a learner's ZPD emerges in and through the activity of assisted performance. Expert-others, such as teachers, observe that assisted performance and then work with learners at the boundaries of their potential, or their ZPD—that is, the level at which they begin to perform only with considerable help from expert-others. Mediation aimed at the upper threshold of a learner's abilities means that learner frustration is always a possibility, so expert-others should stay attuned to learner affect during ZPD activity as well (Mahn & John-Steiner 2002).

Vygotsky (1987) did discuss ways that more expert-others could observe and mediate learner activity, such as "demonstration, leading questions, and by introducing elements of the task's solution" (p. 209). More specifically, he describes the expert's role as showing how a problem could be solved and then seeing if the student could solve the problem through imitation, by beginning to solve the problem and seeing if the student could finish it, by enabling the student to solve the problem through interaction with a more capable other, or by explaining the principle underlying the problem (Vygotsky, 1988, p. 202). Yet, he and many who have taken up sociocultural theory argue that educational applications should not simply focus on identifying exemplary mediation patterns but on ensuring that in whatever interactive activity the child and expert-other are engaged, the focus of attention should be on whether the child is able to take part in the activity in ways that could not be done on his/her own and that the interactive activity results in a specific psychological function becoming appropriated by the child (Kozulin, 2003; Mahn, 2003; Wertsch & Stone, 1985). This issue is core to our argument as well; it is not the practices of L2 teacher educators themselves, but what happens inside those practices that enable teachers to engage in activities that are beyond their current capabilities and have significant consequences for how they begin to think about and enact their teaching.

Furthermore, the ZPD is always rooted in cultural and historical values; that is, people/society have a vision of the end goals of a ZPD, of where development should go (Newman & Holtzman, 1993). The same holds for us as teacher educators involved in L2 teacher education programs. We have a vision of our end goals, of where our teachers' development should go, although this, of course, will be shaped by the fact that 'located L2 teacher education' (Johnson, 2006) is about constructing locally appropriate responses that meet the needs of teachers and teacher educators in the settings and circumstances where they live, learn, and work.

In addition to the collaboration that occurs in the joint activity during the ZPD, Vygotsky (1987) viewed imitation as a major component of developmental activity directed at maturing mental functions. As he noted, it is during collaboration that the child can "move from what he has to what he does not have through imitation" (p. 210). Imitation is not simply verbatim copying of what someone does. Rather, imitation is potentially transformative activity in which a child, having some understanding of the goals and means of the activity, intentionally and creatively tries to reproduce adult performance (Vygotsky, 1988). In sum, children imitate what they are in the process of learning, and imitation "is the chief means by which early childhood human beings are related to as other than and in advance of who they are" (Newman & Holzman, 1993, p. 151).

Play, as Vygotsky (1933/1966) defined it, is also a rich source of higher mental development and creates a zone of proximal development:

> In play the child is always behaving beyond his age, above his usual everyday behavior; in play he is, as it were, a head above himself. Play contains in a concentrated form, as in the focus of a magnifying glass, all developmental tendencies; it is as if the child tries to jump above his usual level. The relation of play to development should be compared to the relation between instruction and development. . . . Play is a source of development and creates the zone of proximal development. (p. 74)

Vygotsky posited that what children are doing through play, in essence, is working through their understandings of signs and cultural artifacts in ways that initially imitate interactions in which they have participated or observed, a kind of 'practice' in a 'safe zone.' For example, when a caregiver observes a child playing 'teacher,' the caregiver may marvel at the cleverness of the child as he or she uses grammatically complex and semantically appropriate expressions, for example 'if you misbehave like that, I'm going to have to put you in a timeout.' In fact, the child is imitating in his or her play activity what has been experienced in activity with the caregiver. For Vygotsky (1988), both play and imitation are not copying or acting, but complex and transformative processes, a chief means of being in advance of oneself, requiring an ability to understand the minds of others.

Teacher educators thus play a vital role in enacting mediation directed at each teacher's potentiality during ZPD activity. And it is the quality and character of the mediation that teacher educators provide that is instrumental in understanding and supporting the development of teacher/teaching expertise. Also critical to this process are the *structured mediational spaces*, or 'safe zones,' where teachers are allowed to 'play' at being and becoming teachers, where they can, with assistance, function ahead of themselves as they write about, talk about, and enact teaching activity, advancing their understanding of what it takes to think, talk, and act like an L2 teacher.

A major challenge for teacher educators is to recognize both the lower and upper thresholds of this metaphoric space for each teacher, identifying what a teacher can do in joint activity interacting with peers, and more importantly with expert-others, while accomplishing a task that is beyond his/her abilities. This enables teacher educators to gauge teachers' potential for development and their capabilities as they are emerging, so that teacher educators relate to teachers in advance of themselves. Subsequently, another challenge for teacher educators is to provide activities in advance of a teacher's independent functioning but accompanied by supportive interactions. If all goes as planned, teachers will imitate the use of these tools, that is, use them in the same way that teacher educators used them, but this imitation marks only the beginning. Teacher educators need to orchestrate and monitor teachers' use of these externalized psychological tools until teachers gain increasing control over them. As teachers begin to internalize these external psychological tools, teacher educators can be less and less involved in assisting teachers. Ultimately, teachers move beyond imitation and can independently use these psychological tools to address the challenges they face and/or the instructional problems at hand.

Vygotskian-informed scholars' interpretations of mediation

Van der Veer and Valsiner (1991) argue that Vygotsky's intellectual work was motivated by a "quest for synthesis" (p. 391), but that quest was thwarted by historical and personal circumstances during his lifetime. The political climate of the Soviet Union that became increasingly perilous during Vygotsky's life constrained what he could share and how he could share his ideas in writing. Vygotsky's poor health as a result of suffering from tuberculosis and his early death at 37 meant that his productive work time was relatively short. The incompleteness of his work, as well as its originality, has inspired a profusion of research based on his ideas. In particular, mediation and how it shapes how we come to control our mental worlds has been widely discussed by a range of scholars working within sociocultural theory (Cole, 1996; Daniels, 2002; Karpov & Haywood, 1998; Kozulin, 2003; Lantolf & Thorne, 2006; Lantolf & Poehner, 2014; van der Veer & Valsiner, 1991; Wertsch, 1985, 2007). Several interpretations of mediation are relevant when considering how teacher educators can intentionally integrate theoretical learning in the cultural practices of teaching and teacher education.

Explicit and implicit mediation

According to Wertsch (2007), Vygotsky expressed two perspectives on mediation in his writing—explicit mediation and implicit mediation. Wertsch argues that the different disciplinary perspectives influencing Vygotsky over the course of his life influenced his conception of and the very language used to explain mediation: explicit mediation is attributed to the discipline of Psychology, and implicit mediation, to poetics/semiotics.

Explicit mediation, what we would associate with formal schooling, has a two-fold nature according to Wertsch (2007). It is explicit in that someone, a teacher for example, intentionally and openly introduces a sign (i.e., meanings) into ongoing activity, and that sign is likewise ongoing and visible (see Chapter 3 for a detailed discussion of Vygotsky's maxim 'sign meaning develops'). This type of mediation is evident in Vygotsky's (1978, 1987) *functional method of dual stimulation*, in which an artificial stimulus, or sign, is overtly inserted into ongoing activity to study the development of higher mental processes as the object of the activity, as well as to facilitate the organization of it. We can think of this kind of mediation as that which we typically enact in L2 teacher education when we try to engage teachers in appropriate joint practices, and in the process of engaging in these practices, expose them to the psychological tools needed for successful performance of these activities. For example, Johnson & Dellagnelo (2013) exposed a team of teachers to a set of pedagogical tools designed specifically to foster greater student participation and engagement in L2 instruction. The explicit insertion of these tools into how they talked about and enacted their teaching activities assisted the teachers in becoming more fluent users of these tools in their L2 instruction.

Implicit mediation, however, is not "artificially and intentionally introduced into ongoing action" (Wertsch, 2007, p. 189) because, as it typically involves signs (i.e., meanings), it is often part of the communication that is connected to the activity. Wertsch notes that examples of implicit mediation include social and inner speech, which mediate psychological processes. As part of communication, they are less obvious and not purposefully deployed to organize goal-directed activity. Implicit mediation can most certainly be found in teacher/teacher educator dialogic interactions. For example, the way a teacher educator frames how language learners might engage in an instructional activity can mediate how teachers come to understand and enact that activity. As we illustrate in Chapter 7, the teacher educator's repeated reference to 'multiple right answers' not only shaped how the teachers came to understand the theoretical concept they were preparing to teach (parallelism), but also how they eventually taught it.

Wertsch (1985) also developed the concept of strategic mediation, which represents cognitive assistance that moves from implicit to explicit, is responsive to immediate need, and is concerned more with cognitive transformation than behavioral performance. Simply telling a teacher to 'ask for examples' might enable her to get through the interactive lecture part of a lesson, but it may not transform the way she thinks about her teaching or how she structures and enacts teaching activity in future lessons. Thus, strategic mediation, for Wertsch, must be minimally intrusive, allowing learners to exert and exhibit as much control over the task as possible. Likewise, assistance must be regulated, for example too much assistance decreases learner agency, while too little increases frustration. Essential to strategic mediation during the ZPD is the notion of *intersubjectivity* (Wertsch, 1985), defined as "when interlocutors share some aspect of their situation definition" (p. 159). In other words, a learner needs to understand the objects and events in a learning situation from the expert's point of view in order for their interactions on the external plane to move to the internal.

Metacognitive and cognitive mediation

Karpov and Haywood (1998) also argue that Vygotsky expressed two perspectives on mediation in his writing—metacognitive mediation and cognitive mediation. Metacognitive mediation refers to the process through which children develop the semiotic tools to control, or self-regulate, their thinking. This refers to Vygotsky's idea that we described in the earlier section of this chapter—higher mental processes are mediated by psychological tools, such as language, signs, and symbols that adults teach to children through joint activity.

Cognitive mediation is connected to formal schooling as it refers to the process through which humans develop the psychological tools "necessary for solving subject-domain problems" (Karpov & Haywood, 1998, p. 28). As we wrote in Chapter 1, learners, such as learners of teaching, enter school, or L2 teacher education, with *everyday concepts*, but can overcome them through the introduction of *academic concepts* in systematic formal instruction. As learners master *academic concepts*, they can use them to mediate themselves in relevant problem solving activity. Karpov and Haywood reiterate Vygotsky's assertion that *empty verbalism*, simple parroting of the concept, marks the beginning of the development of *academic concepts*, but note that Vygotsky did not explain how to link these concepts with instructional procedures. However, many of Vygotsky's followers did just that (see Davydov, 2004; Gal'perin, 1989, 1992; Karpov & Bransford, 1995).

Mediation as co-regulation during ZPD activity

Vygotsky's belief in formal educational activity as the leading activity of development has inspired many Vygotskian scholars to characterize mediation as co-regulation during ZPD activity. Co-regulation, according to Fogel (1991), involves mutual cooperation between mediator and learner so that it is not simply the mediator who is shaping the nature and direction of their joint activity but also involves how learners respond to, and in some ways regulate, the mediator's activities. Co-regulation is very much in line with our conceptualization of *responsive mediation* as being emergent, dynamic, and contingent on the interactions between teachers and teacher educators. In this sense, teachers' professional development is provoked when they are attempting to accomplish something that they cannot yet accomplish on their own, but they are in fact quite active, in both explicit (i.e., asking for help) and implicit (i.e., expression of negative emotions) ways, in shaping the quality and character of the mediation that emerges during interactions with teacher educators.

In the field of second language acquisition (SLA), Aljaafreh and Lantolf (1994) were the first Vygotskian scholars to conduct an in-depth study of how mediation might function as co-regulation during ZPD activity. In their study of an ESL writing tutor's meditational moves, they argued that mediation should be attuned to learner development, and therefore, must be graduated, negotiated, and contingent on moment-to-moment changes in learner need. Likewise, mediation should be minimally intrusive, allowing the learner greater opportunities to self-regulate and only becoming more explicit when needed to move forward with the task at hand. Thus, such mediational moves, from implicit to explicit, are contingent on learner responsiveness and continuously negotiated during ZPD activity. In their most recent book, Lantolf and Poehner (2014) argue that viewing mediation as co-regulation during ZPD activity positions mediation "not as a treatment that can be administered to individuals to move them from one level of development to another but rather as interaction that must remain attuned to learner needs and changes in learner contributions over time" (p. 159). We concur, emphasizing the tremendous responsibility placed on mediators, or for us, teacher educators, "in determining how to approach tasks, set goals, select strategies, to optimally involve learners and reformulate plans and actions" (p. 159). This reinforces the import of *learner reciprocity* (van der Aalsvoort & Lidz, 2002) and agency in teacher/teacher educator interactions as teachers' transformation of mental processes is contingent upon teachers taking up for their own purposes what teacher educators offer through mediation.

Given our Vygotskian sociocultural stance, as well as Lantolf and Poehner's influential work on *dynamic assessment* (DA) in second language learning, we need to distinguish what we mean by *responsive mediation* in relation to *dynamic assessment*, terminology Vygotsky did not use himself. Lantolf and Poehner (2004) define DA as a procedure

> that integrates assessment and instruction into a seamless, unified activity for simultaneously assessing and promoting learner development through appropriate forms of mediation that are sensitive to the individual's (or in some cases a group's) current abilities. In essence, DA is a procedure for simultaneously assessing and promoting development that takes account of the individual's (or group's) zone of proximal development (ZPD). (p. 50)

DA is a kind of dialogic cooperation between mediator and learner, with the mediator continually assessing the learner's understanding in order to determine an appropriate mediational response. Because there is no prescribed script for the mediator to follow, the mediator responds intentionally and spontaneously to the emerging needs of the learner. As we mentioned above, Aljaafreh and Lantolf (1994) propose that the mediator's assistance in a DA interaction be graduated, moving from implicit to explicit, contingent on a learner's needs, and dialogic. The goal of DA is "to unify assessment and instruction into a single activity, the goal of which is learner development" (Lantolf & Thorne, 2006, p. 351). In other words, the mediation enables the learner to go beyond the here and now of the task, eventually creating internalized psychological tools that can be used in novel problem solving activities.

Our concept of *responsive mediation* shares much in common with DA. We believe, however, that the nature of teacher educator mediation of teachers, especially those engaged in the act of teaching, makes enacting Aljaafreh and Lantolf's (1994) proposal difficult, if not counterproductive, at times. The proposition that mediation moves ideally from implicit to explicit can be impractical given that more often than not, *responsive mediation* is not possible in the actual activity of teaching. Because we cannot mediate directly during the activity of teaching, mediation often takes place when teachers are preparing for teaching or while reflecting on a lesson after the fact. And sometimes such preparation and/or reflection may occur days or even weeks before or after the actual lesson is taught. The mediation that we provide may simply not be taken up as a result at times. Moreover, teacher educators have a limited amount of time to mediate teachers through the array of conceptual, practical, managerial, and interpersonal topics that need to be addressed in L2 teacher education programs. Often we have to mediate teachers in the throes of emotional/cognitive dissonance who still have to wake up the next day and teach a lesson. Without the luxury of time, we have to bolster teachers through other-regulation to enable them to fulfill their basic instructional and ethical responsibilities. Sometimes the most effectual thing we can do for a despairing teacher is to tell her what she could say to achieve a particular objective, or to tell him which kind of activity would help achieve an objective. This suggests, therefore, that the quality and character of *responsive mediation* in the practices of L2 teacher education will vary depending on the particular practice in which we are engaged and on our teachers' constellation of emotion, cognition, and activity.

Human and symbolic mediation

Kozulin (2003) argues that the agents of mediation in Vygotsky's writings represent two dimensions: human and symbolic. In human mediation, the focus is on how a child's involvement in joint activity with an expert-other is consequential for cognitive development; in other words, whether the child is capable of assuming greater responsibility for the activity in the future. In symbolic mediation, the focus is on how the introduction of symbolic signs, tools, and/or cultural artifacts might bring about change in a child's performance and ultimately his/her cognition. The distinction between the two, however, is somewhat blurred, as human mediation, or immediate interaction between individuals, typically entails the use of symbolic tools. Building on the example mentioned earlier, a lesson plan has both ideal and material qualities; it is the concrete instantiation of an idealized set of instructional goals and activities. Yet, when a teacher and teacher educator discuss, or co-construct a lesson plan, the teacher educator's vision of how that lesson plan should be enacted may differ considerably from the teacher's. Human mediation between the teacher and teacher educator will most likely entail bringing these two visions closer together, or in Vygotskian terms, establishing a sense of intersubjectivity. Critical to the relationship between human and symbolic mediation is Kozulin's (2003) claim that symbols may remain useless unless their meaning as cognitive tools is properly mediated. He explains this relationship:

> Symbolic tools have a rich educational potential, but they remain ineffective if there is no human mediator to facilitate their appropriation by the learner. By the same token, human mediation that does not involve sophisticated symbolic tools would not help the learner to master more complex forms of reasoning and problem solving. (p. 35)

Thus, a lesson plan might assist a teacher in enacting a lesson, but without human mediation with an expert-other, the mere use of the lesson plan risks denying the teacher the opportunity to master expert ways of thinking about and enacting teaching activity. In fact, it might also be the case that a lesson plan enacted without expert mediation could impede a teacher's development if getting through the lesson plan becomes the teacher's object, rather than being responsive to and supportive of meaningful student learning. Thus, we reiterate the pivotal role that human mediation plays in cultivating teachers' professional development.

Responsive mediation

Before we offer an initial definition of *responsive mediation*, we feel it is important to make one final comment about the unique nature of human mediation. As we mentioned in Chapter 1, a central tenet of Vygotskian sociocultural theory is that psychological functions appear twice, once in the actual interaction between people engaged in some sort of goal-directed activity and the other as an inner (internalized) tool for thinking that humans use to direct the material world. On the basis of this premise, Vygotskian scholars who are interested in delineating the quality and character of human mediation, most notably the mediator (i.e., caretakers, mediators, teachers), have deliberately attempted to classify types of human mediation that support cognitive development. For example, Palinscar and Brown's (1984) seminal work on reciprocal teaching included techniques such as questioning, summarizing, predicting, and clarifying strategies in supporting children's literacy development. Rogoff (1995), in her work with cultural communities, argued for three general forms of human mediation: apprenticeship, wherein community models are provided to a novice; guided participation, which occurs through joint activity by expert and novice; and appropriation, where the novice uses the tool without social mediation. However, we align with Kozulin (2003) in his argument that types, techniques, or scales for determining effective human mediation are too numerous and context-dependent to allow for a simple classification system. We wholeheartedly agree, and thus, in our work we intentionally refrain from classifying types of *responsive mediation*. Instead, our analyses of what happens inside the practices of L2 teacher education focus on what *responsive mediation* looks like as it unfolds, the intentions underlying it, how *responsive mediation* assists teachers as they attempt to accomplish tasks and develop dispositions that they do not yet have the capacity for, and the extent to which *responsive mediation* results in specific psychological functions becoming appropriated by teachers in their thinking and teaching activity.

This overview of the Vygotskian concept of mediation lays the theoretical foundation for an initial definition of *responsive mediation*. As we have argued thus far, the quality and character of mediation must be negotiated, cannot be predicted beforehand, and is dependent on the ability to recognize and target teachers' emergent needs as well as utilize their responses to mediation and/or requests for additional support. This does not mean, however, that teachers will automatically or willingly internalize the mediational support offered by teacher educators. Emotions, differing motives, and teacher constructed and/or imagined identities will shape these interactions and how teachers respond to the mediation they experience. The challenges for teacher educators are to recognize the upper limits of teachers' potential (ZPD) and be strategic in the sort of assistance given, while also recognizing and being responsive to teachers' responses. It is for these reasons that we intentionally use the term *responsive mediation* to emphasize the multidirectional nature of teacher educators' dialogic interactions with teachers and the fluidity with which *responsive mediation* evolves with twists and starts. Fundamental to our argument is when, where, and how *responsive mediation* emerges matters in L2 teacher education. In Chapters 3 and 4 we offer key Vygotsky and Vygotskian-inspired theoretical concepts that further articulate our definition of *responsive mediation* as the nexus of *Mindful L2 Teacher Education*.

Note

1. Throughout this book we have kept Vygotsky's original use of the pronoun 'he' but we intend for it to represent all genders.

References

Aljaafreh, A., & Lantolf, J. P. (1994). Negative feedback as regulation and second language learning in the zone of proximal development. *The Modern Language Journal*, 78, 465–483.

Brice Heath, S. (1983). *Ways with words: Language, life and working communities and classrooms*. Cambridge: Cambridge University Press.

Chaiklin, S. (1993). Understanding the social scientific practice of understanding practice. In S. Chaiklin & J. Lave (Eds.), *Understanding practice: Perspective on activity and context* (pp. 377–401). Cambridge: Cambridge University Press.

Cole, M. (1996). *Cultural psychology: A once and future discipline*. Cambridge, MA: The Bellknap Press of Harvard University Press.

Daniels, H. (2002). *Vygotsky and pedagogy*. London: Routledge.

Davydov, V. V. (2004). *Problems of developmental instruction: A theoretical and experimental psychological study*. Moscow: Akademiya.

Fogel, A. (1991). *Developing through relationships: Origins of communication, self, and culture*. Chicago: University of Chicago Press.

Gal'perin, P. Y. (1989). Mental actions as a basis for the formation of thoughts and images. *Soviet Psychology, 27*(3), 45–64.

Gal'perin P. Y. (1992). Stage-by-stage formation as a method of psychological investigation. *Journal of Russian and East European Psychology, 30*(4), 60–80.

Ilyenkov, E. (1977). *Dialectical logic. Essays on its history and theory*. Moscow: Progress Press.

Johnson, K. E. (2006). The sociocultural turn and its challenges for L2 teacher education. *TESOL Quarterly, 40*(1), 235–257.

Johnson, K. E., & Dellagnelo, A. (2013). How 'sign meaning develops': Strategic mediation in learning to teach. *Language Teaching Research, 17*(4), 409–432.

Karpov, Y. V. (2014). *Vygotsky for educators*. Cambridge: Cambridge University Press.

Karpov, Y. V., & Bransford, J. (1995). Vygotsky and the doctrine of empirical and theoretical learning. *Educational Psychologist, 30*(2), 61–66.

Karpov, Y. V., & Haywood, H. C. (1998). Two ways to elaborate Vygotsky's concept of mediation. *American Psychologist, 53*, 27–36.

Kozulin, A. (2003). Psychological tools and mediated learning. In A. Kozulin, B. Gindis, V. S. Ageyev, & S. M. Miller (Eds.), *Vygotsky's educational theory in cultural context* (pp. 15–38). Cambridge: Cambridge University Press.

Lantolf, J. P., & Poehner, M. E. (2004). Dynamic assessment of L2 development: Bringing the past into the future. *Journal of Applied Linguistics 1*, 49–74.

Lantolf, J. P., & Poehner, M. E. (2014). *Sociocultural theory and the pedagogical imperative in L2 education*. New York: Routledge.

Lantolf, J. P., & Thorne, S. (2006). *Sociocultural theory and the genesis of second language development*. Oxford: Oxford University Press.

Mahn, H. (2003). Periods in child development: Vygotsky's perspective. In A. Kozulin, B. Gindis, & S. M. Miller (Eds.), *Vygotsky's educational theory in cultural context* (pp. 119–137). Cambridge: Cambridge University Press.

Mahn, H., & John-Steiner, V. (2002). The gift of confidence: A Vygotskian view of emotions. In G. Wells & G. Claxton (Eds.), *Learning for life in the 21st century: Sociocultural perspectives on the future of education* (pp. 46–58). Cambridge, MA: Blackwell.

Moll, L. C. (2014). *L. S. Vygotsky and education*. London: Routledge.

Newman, F., & Holzman, L. (1993). *Lev Vygotsky: Revolutionary scientist*. London: Routledge.

Palinscar, A. S., & Brown, A. L. (1984). Reciprocal teaching of comprehension-fostering and comprehension-monitoring activities. *Cognition and Instruction*, *1*, 117–175.

Rogoff, B. (1995). Observing sociocultural activity on three planes. In J. Wertsch, P. Del Rio, & A. Alvarez (Eds.), *Sociocultural studies of mind* (pp. 139–164). New York: Cambridge University Press.

Scollon, R. (2001). *Mediated discourse: The nexus of practice*. London: Routledge.

Scribner, S., & Cole, M. (1981). *Psychology of literacy*. Cambridge, MA: Harvard University Press.

van der Aalsvoort, G. M., & Lidz, C. S. (2002). Reciprocity in Dynamic Assessment in classrooms: Taking contextual influences on individual learning into account. In G. M. van der Aalsvoort, W. C. M. Resing, & A. J. J. M. Ruijssenaars (Eds.), *Learning potential assessment and cognitive training* (pp. 111–144). Amsterdam: Elsevier.

van der Veer, R., & Valsiner, J. (1991). *Understanding Vygotsky*. Oxford: Blackwell.

Vygotsky, L. S. (1933/1935). Razvite zhitejskikh I nauchnykh ponjatij v skhol'nom vozraste. As cited in R. van der Veer & J. Valsiner (1991). *Understanding Vygotsky* (p. 328–348). Oxford: Blackwell.

Vygotsky, L. S. (1933/1966). Igra I ee rol' v psikhicheskom razvitii rebenka. *Voprosy Psikhologii*, 62–76. As cited in R. van der Veer & J. Valsiner (1991), *Understanding Vygotsky* (p. 328–348). Oxford: Blackwell.

Vygotsky, L. S. (1978). M. Cole, V. John-Steiner, S. Scribner & E. Souberman (Eds.), *Mind in society*. Cambridge, MA: Harvard University Press.

Vygotsky, L. S. (1986). *Thought and language* (A. Kozulin, Trans.). Cambridge, MA: MIT Press.

Vygotsky, L. S. (1987). Thinking and speech (N. Minick, Trans.). In R. W. Reiber (Ed.), *The collected works of L. S. Vygotsky, Vol. 3. Problems of the theory and history of Psychology* (pp. 37–285). New York: Plenum Press.

Vygotsky, L. S. (1988). The problem of age (M. Hall, Trans.). In R. W. Reiber (Ed.), *The collected works of L. S. Vygotsky, Vol. 5. Child psychology* (p. 215–231). New York: Plenum Press.

Wertsch, J. V. (1985). *Vygotsky and the social formation of mind*. Cambridge, MA: Harvard University Press.

Wertsch, J. V. (2007). Mediation. In H. Daniels, M. Cole, & J. V. Wertsch (Eds.), *The Cambridge companion to Vygotsky* (pp. 178–192). New York: Cambridge University Press.

Wertsch, J. V., & Stone, A. (1985). The concept of internalization in Vygotsky's account of the genesis of higher mental functions. In J. Wertsch (Ed.), *Culture, communication, and cognition: Vygotskian perspectives* (pp. 162–179). New York: Cambridge University Press.

PART II

Vygotsky and Vygotskian-Inspired Theoretical Concepts That Inform Responsive Mediation

3

OBUCHENIE, PEREZHIVANIE, AND GROWTH POINTS

In this chapter, we define Vygotsky and Vygotskian-inspired theoretical concepts that inform how we conceptually articulate and operationally define the concept of *responsive mediation*. We begin with an overview of Vygotsky's ideas on school teaching/learning or, in Russian, *obuchenie*, and build a rationale for why we use *obuchenie* as a lens through which to explore *responsive mediation* in the practices of L2 teacher education. To accomplish this, we turn to Vygotsky's views on emotion, in particular the notion of emotional experience or, in Russian, *perezhivanie*, a construct that enables us to better understand how teachers are experiencing and responding to the practices of L2 teacher education. We include Vygotsky's (1987) claim of the *affective and volitional tendency* as central to teacher cognition and explore the role of emotion in the learning-to-teach process, as well as how teacher educator and teacher emotions and motives shape their interactions. Finally, we invoke McNeill's (2000, 2005) construct of *growth points* as a moment or series of moments when teachers' cognitive/emotional dissonance comes into being and argue that *responsive mediation* directed at the *growth point* creates the potential for the development of L2 teacher/teaching expertise.

Obuchenie: The dialectical unity of school teaching/learning

In Vygotsky's (1935/1994) later writings he focused on the problem of teaching/learning in school and, in particular, the relationship between school teaching/learning (*obuchenie*) and cognitive development. He was highly critical of traditional approaches to formal schooling, claiming that

> a straightforward learning of concepts always proves impossible and educationally fruitless. Usually, any teacher setting out on this road achieves

nothing except a meaningless acquisition of words, mere verbalization in children, which is nothing more than simulation and imitation of corresponding concepts which, in reality, are concealing a vacuum. (p. 356)

Instead, he postulated that the development of *academic concepts* in the mind of the child is substantially different from the development of *everyday concepts*, which arise spontaneously through concrete experiences in the everyday world. For Vygotsky, *academic concepts* in children undergo a fundamental process of development, that is, "when a child assimilates a concept, he reworks it and in the course of this reworking, he imprints it with certain specific features of his own thoughts" (p. 361). Thus, while their developmental processes are different, *academic concepts* and *everyday concepts* are "tightly bound up with one another and . . . constantly influence one another" (p. 365). For school aged children, Vygotsky argued that the key to *internalization* (from the social to the psychological) is the extent to which the processes of school teaching/learning (*obuchenie*) interrelate *academic* and *everyday concepts* in goal-directed, practical activity that has relevance in the material world (see also Robbins, 2003).

We find Vygotsky's (1987) *obuchenie*, defined as "teaching/learning as collaborative interactions governed by a mutuality of purpose" (p. 212), to be a useful lens through which to explore the dialogic interactions that emerge in the practices of L2 teacher education. *Obuchenie* captures the actions and intentions of teaching *and* learning, rather than only a teacher who provides instruction to a child who learns (van der Veer & Valsiner, 1991). Importantly, *obuchenie* places greater focus on the instructional side of expert/novice interactions, suggesting that *obuchenie* leads rather than follows cognitive development (Cole, 2009). This distinction is important because Vygotsky argued against the prevailing notion of his time that a child's psychological functions must reach a certain level of maturity before instruction is beneficial. In fact, he argued that teaching/learning (*obuchenie*) and development are distinct processes but that *obuchenie* enables a series of developmental processes to undergo their own development. Therefore, *obuchenie* "is only effective when it points to the road for development" and while Vygotsky argued that it is the teacher "who creates conditions for certain cognitive processes to develop, it is the child who has to learn to transform an ability 'in itself' into an ability 'for himself'" (van der Veer & Valsiner, 1991, p. 331). *Obuchenie* is, therefore, not simply concerned with cognitive functions and/or capabilities that have already been fully formed, but also with those that are still developing and thus typically manifest in joint activity with others. It is here, Vygotsky argued, where instructional intervention will have its greatest significance.

Vygotsky's (1978) other major break with the field of Psychology at the time was the basic maxim that the relationship between the word (*sign form*) and thought (*sign meaning*) does not remain constant, but instead is unstable and undergoes fundamental change. His developmental or *genetic method* was designed to understand how this change happens by focusing almost exclusively on how the inclusion of new *tools* or *signs* leads to qualitative transformation in mental activity (Wertsch, 2007). And from this method, one can observe how the inclusion of particular sign forms, especially those of a symbolic nature (i.e., language) play a role in converting learning that emerges in social activity into psychological tools (*sign meanings*), or tools for thinking.

Much, if not all, of what teacher educators try to do is to intentionally insert new *tools* or *signs* into the activities that constitute teacher education with the goal of qualitative transformation in how novice teachers think as well as how they teach. Such *explicit mediation*, according to Werstch (2007) "involves the intentional introduction of signs into the ongoing flow of activity . . . designed and introduced by an external agent, such as a tutor, who can help reorganize an activity in some way" and it is throughout this process that "sign meaning develops" (pp. 185–186). Werstch goes on to claim that a sign form, or word,

> first appears in social and individual activity without the users' full understanding of its meaning or functional role. What then follows is a process of coming to understand the meaning and functional significance of the sign form that one has been using all along. (p. 186)

Thus, the sign form, or word, functions as a sort of *material sign vehicle* that allows novices to function at a level that is out ahead of their current mastery. According to Werstch (2007), "the general goal of instruction [*obuchenie*] is to assist students in becoming fluent users of a sign system" (p. 186). Werstch further stated:

> When encountering a new cultural tool, . . . the first stages of acquaintance typically involve social interaction and negotiation between experts and novices or among novices. It is precisely by means of participating in this social interaction that interpretations are first proposed and worked out and, therefore, become available to be taken over by individuals. (p. 187)

If we consider *obuchenie* as it unfolds in the practices of L2 teacher education, we would expect teacher educators to intentionally introduce new *sign forms* (e.g., genre) and in some cases entire *sign systems* (e.g., systemic functional linguistics) in order to reorganize how teachers think about and engage in the activities of L2 teaching. These new signs and/or sign systems typically represent the latest theory and research (*academic concepts*) on how language works, how languages are learned and used, as well as how languages can be taught in various instructional settings. The assumption, of course, is that the introduction of these new *sign forms*, through course readings, in-class discussions, and reflective activities, will enable teachers to work out the *sign meanings* and functional significance and eventually lead to changes not only in how teachers think about teaching but also in what they actually do in the classroom. However, this trajectory, from external to internal, does not happen automatically, nor does it occur in a straightforward manner. Instead it requires prolonged and sustained participation in concrete goal-directed activity (e.g., actual teaching), supported by *responsive mediation* offered by an expert (e.g., teacher educator, mentor teacher, and/or peer teacher) that leads the development of *sign meaning* (e.g., theoretical and pedagogical tools or signs) so that *sign meanings* become more like those of experts, with the ultimate goal of enabling teachers to use *sign meanings* and *sign systems* flexibly and fluently in the activities of L2 instruction.

Bringing Vygotsky's insights together, *obuchenie* entails high quality teacher–learner dialectics, in which learners interact with experts who offer pedagogically designed psychological tools (*sign forms* and/or *sign systems*) and semantic/pragmatic explanations of those tools (*sign meanings*) to promote a functional understanding of *academic concepts* in ways that facilitate the reorganization of the child's mental structures. If we overlay these insights on the practices of L2 teacher education, it is the teacher educator who must create the conditions for L2 teacher/teaching expertise to develop. Such conditions must be grounded in clearly articulated professional development goals, provide exposure to theoretically and pedagogically sound instructional practices (*sign forms* and/or *sign systems*), and make the reasoning behind those practices explicit (*sign meanings*). Enacting *obuchenie* therefore will entail context-specific, high-quality, teacher–teacher educator dialogic interactions that support *sign meaning development* as teachers engage in a broad range of activities associated with L2 teaching. In exploring what happens inside the practices of L2 teacher education, we are interested in both the teaching of teachers *and* the learning of teaching and, in particular, the interactional spaces, mediated through language, where *obuchenie* takes place.

Perezhivanie: The subjective significance of teachers' lived experiences

We acknowledge that carrying out *obuchenie*, as Vygotsky envisioned, requires a lot of teacher educators. First and foremost, it requires that we attend to what our teachers bring to our interactions: where they are coming from and how they understand what they are experiencing. And gaining access to such pre-understandings is no easy task. To do so, we invoke another Russian term, *perezhivanie*, used throughout Vygotsky's writings to capture the subjective significance of lived experiences that contribute to the development of one's personality, especially the emotional and visceral impact of lived experiences on the prism through which all future experiences are refracted (see van der Veer & Valsiner, 1994). Vygotsky stated that, "The emotional experience [*perezhivanie*] arising from any situation or from any aspect of his environment determines what kind of influence this situation or this environment will have on the child" (as cited in van der Veer & Valsiner, 1994, p. 339). Since individuals will most certainly experience the same event quite differently, one's *perezhivanie* is not the experience itself, but how that experience is interpreted and understood by the individual.

We know from the research on teacher cognition that teachers draw heavily on their lived experiences as learners in classrooms, yet their emotional experiences (*perezhivanie*) grounded in their schooling histories may be vastly different. For example, one teacher may express deep admiration and respect for a 'strict' teacher who held high expectations and presented material thoroughly and systematically through lecture while another might perceive that same 'strict' teacher as authoritarian and controlling and, thus, choose to establish closer social and personal relationships with and among students. For teacher educators, establishing a sense of a teacher's *perezhivanie*, both past (e.g., *apprenticeship of observation*) and present (e.g., how they are experiencing the practices of teacher education) is essential if we are to provide mediation that is responsive to how teachers are experiencing and responding to the practices of L2 teacher education.

Additionally, enacting *obuchenie* requires that we attend to what we, as teacher educators ourselves, bring to our interactions with teachers. Our mediation is shaped by the complex interplay of cognition and emotion, originating in and reshaped through our own *perezhivanie*. As teacher educators, our own emotions can influence the mediation we provide to teachers even though we may seemingly be engaging in consistent practices and feedback (Golombek, 2015). We should similarly identify the emotions we bring to particular relationships and how they affect what we mediate and how we articulate that in our interactions with particular teachers. Thus, enacting *obuchenie* requires teacher educators to stay attuned to our own subjectivities in the emergent, relational interactions we co-construct with teachers.

Affective and volitional tendency: The dialectic unity of cognition and emotion

Further complicating the process of enacting *obuchenie* is that in order to offer mediation that is responsive to teachers' maturing capabilities, teacher educators must be able to ascertain what those maturing capabilities are. This poses unique challenges for teacher educators as, more often than not, teachers' maturing capabilities are expressed as intensely emotional 'highs and lows' that emerge from being asked to perform as self-directed teachers before they have the necessary competence to do so. Once again, we know from our years of experience that teachers' expressions of emotion run the gamut: from the exhilaration of meaningful student engagement to anxiety and humiliation when lessons go awry. We also recognize that within most teacher education programs, expressions of emotion are at best recognized as normal and glossed over, or at worst seen as a serious character flaw. While teaching has long been considered an emotional practice (Denzin, 1984), with teachers' daily practices (lesson planning, managing instruction, interacting with students, colleagues, and parents, etc.) recognized as being permeated with emotional meanings and influences (Hargreaves, 1998, 2000), as teacher educators we often feel perplexed about how best to respond to teachers' expression of emotion. This quandary reminds us, however, that teacher education is fundamentally about people: people with rich histories, resilient beliefs, and multilayered identities that emerge from and are shaped by the social, cultural, political, and economic environment from which they have come and in which they learn and work (see also Cross, 2010).

Thus, learning to teach, regardless of the instructional context, is about trying on and taking up new identities. It is a deeply personal matter, and often emotionally charged in ways that are rarely officially recognized in teacher education programs. So it is from this stance that we ground our own professional development practices in the sociocultural dialectic unity of cognition, emotion, and activity and argue that the emotional dimensions of learning-to-teach, when tapped into as a resource rather than viewed as a distraction, are fundamental to being and becoming a teacher (Golombek & Doran, 2014; Johnson & Worden, 2014). Finally, given the emotionally charged nature of learning-to-teach, teachers also need to develop trust in the teacher educator, much like Karpov (2014) suggests a child must "accept a caregiver as a mediator who will create the kind of supportive environment necessary for development" (p. 38). Therefore, we recognize that teachers will experience some sort of cognitive/emotional struggle as they develop L2 teacher/teaching expertise. As we explore the dialogic interactions that emerge inside the practices of L2 teacher education, it is to this cognitive/emotional struggle that teacher educators must be attuned.

Cognitive/emotional dissonance as potential growth points

Numerous studies in L2 teacher education support Vygotsky's (1987) notion that cognitive/emotional dissonance acts as a catalyst that can, with the right mediation, create conditions that support the development of L2 teacher/teaching expertise (Childs, 2011; DiPardo & Potter, 2003; Golombek & Johnson, 2004; Johnson & Worden, 2014; Kubanyiova, 2012; Reis, 2011). However, the challenge for teacher educators is to stay attuned to instances of cognitive/emotional dissonance where *responsive mediation* may be most productive in terms of supporting teacher learning and development. Here we draw on elements of McNeill's (2000, 2005) theoretical construct of the *growth point* since it not only helps elucidate Vygotsky's (1987) dialectic unity of thought and language, but because we have also found it to be useful for marking critical junctures in teacher learning and development.

For Vygotsky (1987), speech is not a matter of putting pre-existing thoughts into words. Instead "thought is restructured as it is transformed into speech. It is not expressed but completed in the word" (p. 251). Thus, thoughts undergo continuous change during the process of speaking, which both shapes and is shaped by a speaker's history, social interactive context, and agency. Based on

Slobin's (1987) original notion of *thinking-for-speaking*, or how speakers organize their thinking during acts of speaking, McNeill's (2005) work on the *speech-gesture synchrony* defines the *growth point* as the "minimal unit of an imagery-language dialectic" that thus constitutes a particular starting point for a thought as it "comes into being" (p. 104). Moreover, because it combines the two semiotic opposites of imagery and linguistic form, the *growth point* "creates a benign instability that fuels thought and speech" and represents "a speaker's efforts to construct meaning" in a particular context and point in time (p. 104). For McNeill, the *growth point* in *thinking-for-speaking* represents what Vygotsky called the *psychological predicate*, providing a window into thinking as it arises in and is shaped by the activity of speaking (McNeill & Duncan, 2000).

While McNeill's *imagery-language dialectic* is manifested through gesture and speech, our work examines instances of the dialectic of cognition and emotion as it arises in the context of teachers learning-to-teach while engaged in the practices of L2 teacher education. Like McNeill, we see *growth points* as instantiations of a dialectic 'coming into being' in specific contexts that can, with *responsive mediation*, create conditions for teacher learning and development. In our work, we posit *growth points* in the learning of teaching as 'coming into being' when contradictions emerge between what a teacher envisions and the reality of what actually occurs while teaching, contradictions that can be inferred through a teacher's emotionally indexing language and behavior in such moments. Such contradictions create a sense of instability, or cognitive/emotional dissonance, that may be both mystifying and debilitating for teachers. In the face of such instability, teachers often turn inward, experience a crisis of confidence, and return to the sort of traditional monologic teaching that permeated their schooling histories. Moreover, teachers are typically unable to recognize what triggers moments of cognitive/emotional dissonance, and instead tend to blame their students or themselves.

In sum, we operationalize the *growth point* as a moment or series of moments when teachers' cognitive/emotional dissonance comes into being. And we argue that *responsive mediation* directed at the *growth point* creates the potential for productive teacher learning and development. Like McNeill, we see the *growth point* as emergent and contingent, and thus mediation directed at the *growth point* cannot be predicted beforehand. It is dependent on the teacher educator's ability to recognize and target teachers' emergent needs as well as utilize their responses to that mediation and/or requests for additional support. Critical as well is enabling teachers to become consciously awareness of the sources of their cognitive/emotional dissonance as this too can lead to productive teacher learning and development. The challenge for teacher educators is to be attuned to critical instances of teacher cognitive/emotional dissonance, recognize and capitalize on these as potential *growth points*, and create the conditions for *responsive mediation* to emerge in support of the development of L2 teacher/teaching expertise. With these concepts in mind, in Chapter 4 we introduce two additional

Vygotskian-inspired theoretical concepts that we believe function as powerful psychological tools for capturing *responsive mediation* as it emerges inside the practices of L2 teacher education.

References

Childs, S. S. (2011). "Seeing" L2 teacher learning: The power of context on conceptualizing teaching. In K. E. Johnson & P. R. Golombek (Eds.), *Research on second language teacher education: A sociocultural perspective on professional development* (pp. 67–85). New York: Routledge.

Cole, M. (2009). The perils of translation: A first step in reconsidering Vygotsky's theory of development in relation to formal education. *Mind, Culture, and Activity, 16*(4), 291–295.

Cross, R. (2010). Language teaching as sociocultural activity: Rethinking language teacher practice. *The Modern Language Journal, 94*, 434–452.

Denzin, N. (1984). *On understanding emotion.* San Francisco: Jossey-Bass.

DiPardo, A., & Potter, C. (2003). Beyond cognition: A Vygotskian perspective on emotionality and teachers' professional lives. In A. Kozulin, B. Gindis, & S. M. Miller (Eds.), *Vygotsky's educational theory in cultural context* (pp. 317–345). Cambridge: Cambridge University Press.

Golombek, P. R. (2015). Redrawing the boundaries of language teacher cognition: Language teacher educators' emotion, cognition, and activity. *The Modern Language Journal, 99*(3), 470–484.

Golombek, P. R., & Doran, M. (2014). Unifying cognition, emotion, and activity in language teacher professional development. *Teaching and Teacher Education, 39*, 102–111.

Golombek, P. R., & Johnson, K. E. (2004). Narrative inquiry as a mediational space: Examining emotional and cognitive dissonance in second language teachers' development. *Teachers and Teaching: Theory and Practice, 10*(2), 307–327.

Hargreaves, A. (1998). The emotional practice of teaching. *Teaching and Teacher Education, 14*(8), 835–854.

Hargreaves, A. (2000). Mixed emotions: Teachers' perceptions of their interactions with students. *Teaching and Teacher Education, 16*, 811–826.

Johnson, K. E., & Worden, D. (2014). Cognitive/emotional dissonance as *growth points* in learning to teach. *Language and Sociocultural Theory, 2*(1), 125–150.

Karpov, Y. V. (2014). *Vygotsky for educators.* Cambridge: Cambridge University Press.

Kubanyiova, M. (2012). *Teacher development in action: Understanding language teachers' conceptual change.* New York: Palgrave Macmillan.

McNeill, D. (2000). *Language and gesture.* Cambridge: Cambridge University Press.

McNeill, D. (Ed.) (2005). *Gesture and thought.* Chicago: University of Chicago Press.

McNeill, D., & Duncan, S. D. (2000). Growth points in thinking-for-speaking. In D. McNeill (Ed.), *Language and gesture* (pp. 141–161). Cambridge: Cambridge University Press.

Reis, D. S. (2011). "I'm not alone": Empowering non-native English-speaking teachers to challenge the native speaker myth. In K. E. Johnson & P. R. Golombek (Eds.), *Research on second language teacher education: A sociocultural perspective on professional development* (pp. 31–49). New York: Routledge.

Robbins, D. (2003). *Vygotsky's and A.A. Leontiev's semiotics and psycho-linguistics: Applications for education, second language acquisition, and theories of language.* New York: Praeger.

Slobin, D. (1987). Thinking for speaking. In L. Aske, N. Beery, L. Michaelis, & H. Filip (Eds.), *Papers from the 13th Annual Meeting of the Berkeley Linguistics Society.* Berkeley, CA: Berkeley Linguistics Society.

van der Veer, R., & Valsiner, J. (1991). *Understanding Vygotsky.* Oxford: Blackwell.

van der Veer, R., & Valsiner, J. (Eds.) (1994). *The Vygotsky reader.* Oxford: Blackwell.

Vygotsky, L. S. (1978). M. Cole, V. John-Steiner, S. Scribner, & E. Souberman (Eds.), *Mind in society.* Cambridge, MA: Harvard University Press.

Vygotsky, L. S. (1987). Thinking and speech (N. Minick, Trans.). In R. W. Reiber (Ed.), *The collected works of L. S. Vygotsky* (Vol. 3, pp. 37–285). New York: Plenum Press.

Vygotsky, L. S. (1935/1994). The development of academic concepts in school aged children. In R. van der Veer & J. Valsiner (Eds.) (1994). *The Vygotsky reader* (pp. 355–370). Oxford: Blackwell.

Wertsch, J. V. (2007). Mediation. In H. Daniels, M. Cole, & J. V. Wertsch (Eds.), *The Cambridge companion to Vygotsky* (pp. 178–192). New York: Cambridge University Press.

4

INTERTHINKING, THE INTERMENTAL DEVELOPMENT ZONE, AND SOCIOCULTURAL DISCOURSE ANALYSIS

In this chapter, we present two additional Vygotskian-inspired theoretical concepts that we believe function as powerful psychological tools for capturing *responsive mediation* as it emerges inside the practices of L2 teacher education. We draw heavily on the work of Mercer and his colleagues (Littleton & Mercer, 2013; Mercer, 2000; Mercer & Littleton, 2007; Mercer, Littleton, & Wegerif, 2004) who, from a Vygotskian sociocultural theoretical perspective, focus their analytic lens on the notion of *interthinking*, defined as how humans use language to carry out joint intellectual activity and to make joint sense of experience. Quite simply, *interthinking* allows humans to combine their intellectual resources, via language, to achieve more than they would be able to do on their own. Mercer's central argument, directed at large-scale public sector schooling, is that when children experience ways of using language collectively, such experiences support the development of using language for thinking individually. In their words, "thinking collectively provides a template for thinking alone" (Littleton & Mercer, 2013, p. 112). A central goal of Mercer's work is to empower teachers to encourage children to use talk to *interthink* effectively, as this not only helps develop children's capabilities to think and learn individually, it also increases their capacities to engage in reasoned arguments, to generate innovative ideas, and to consider alternative solutions to reoccurring problems: all important life skills that are essential to becoming a productive citizen in today's modern society.

Building on the notion of *interthinking*, Mercer also proposes the construct of an *intermental development zone* (IDZ), defined as how teachers and learners stay attuned to each other's changing states of knowledge and understanding over the course of an educational activity. The IDZ, like Vygotsky's ZPD, is not a thing or a place, but an activity where, in our case, teacher educators and teachers seek to stay attuned to each other's changing states of knowledge and understanding while engaged in the practices of L2 teacher education. And it is our contention that during an IDZ we can capture the quality and character of *responsive mediation* as it emerges, trace teachers' conceptual development as it unfolds, and acknowledge the key role that teacher educators play in supporting *obuchenie*, the processes of school teaching/learning. Finally, in line with Mercer's dual emphasis on the processes of education (i.e., what happens in formal schooling) as well as educational outcomes (i.e., what students learn), we take up sociocultural discourse analysis as a methodological tool for conducting microgenetic analyses of the quality and character of teacher/teacher educator dialogic interactions and their educational significance for the development of L2 teacher/teaching expertise.

Interthinking: Language as joint intellectual activity

Mercer's (2000) construct of *interthinking* is an attempt to explain how humans use language to carry out joint intellectual activity and to make joint sense of experience. *Interthinking*, or more simply *thinking together*, according to Mercer, is both an individual and social endeavor. Aligned with a Vygotskyian sociocultural perspective, language has two main functions: as a communicative or cultural tool and as a psychological tool. As a cultural tool, language is used for establishing interpersonal relationships and for sharing and jointly developing knowledge. It also functions as a symbolic tool that allows for collective cultural knowledge to carry over from generation to generation (i.e., cultural transmission). This cultural tool can in turn be employed as a psychological tool to shape individual thinking; that is, through language, collaborators can jointly organize, plan, and regulate their actions to solve problems. In this way, the individual (psychological realm) and society (culture) are connected by language, and this relationship constitutes a powerful dialectic that can be used to investigate and understand the dynamic and genetic (historical) nature of human interaction. Mercer goes on to argue that because language is often ambiguous, *thinking together* may generate misunderstandings since it relies on a mutually (often subconsciously) agreed upon context in which interaction takes place: specifically, a dialogical space in which there is shared common knowledge of the topics being discussed as well as socially acceptable conventions of interaction and behavior. These interactional conventions, or what Mercer calls *conversational ground rules*, are most often implicit yet they shape and organize the way we interact with one another based on the roles or positions we assume. For Mercer, effectively *thinking together* requires that we establish a collective understanding of the conversational ground rules that govern our interactions.

Likewise, Mercer (2000) also argues that any interaction has a historic and a dynamic aspect—historic in that it is located in particular institutional and cultural contexts, dynamic because the shared understanding is constantly being developed—always in a state of flux. How people construct the contextual foundations of their interactions is critical to understanding the unique qualities of human communication, a notion also foundational to Vygotskian sociocultural theory. Conversational ground rules are the conventions that language users employ to carry on particular kinds of conversations (oral/written), in particular social contexts, and are often implicitly understood rather than explicitly negotiated. Moreover, those who are in control of such conversations often act as if the people with whom they are dealing are familiar with the relevant ground rules and do not help novices by making the ground rules explicit or explaining why they are being followed.

In the practices of L2 teacher education, the conversational ground rules for teacher/teacher educator dialogic interactions cannot be taken for granted. Since teacher educators are institutionally positioned as experts, their status, from the perspective of teachers, is historically and dynamically constructed. When framed as supervisors or evaluators, teacher educators are expected to assess teachers' ideas/performance and in many institutional contexts around the world this is exactly what they do. They operate under normative conversational ground rules that allow them to do most of the talking/writing, evaluate teachers' ideas and/or teaching activities both positively and negatively, and offer substantive commentary about how teachers should be thinking or should be teaching.

Recognizing the expertise that teacher educators bring to the table, we are also cognizant, from our Vygotskian sociocultural stance, that in order to support the development of L2 teacher/teaching expertise, the conversational ground rules for teacher educator/teacher dialogic interactions need to be continually (re)negotiated. As we discussed in Chapter 3, a fundamental element of enacting *obuchenie* is to recognize teachers' pre-understandings as well as their *perezhivanie* and to offer mediation that is responsive to teachers' immediate needs, goals, emotions, and motives. To enact *obuchenie*, the conversational ground rules must shift and change depending on the particular practice teachers and teacher educators are engaged in, the shared and sometimes competing goals they may have for that practice, and the institutional and sociocultural context in which the practice is taking place. Recognizing the normative conversational ground rules that exist in the practices of L2 teacher education and making those ground rules explicit and/ or altering them appropriately is essential if teacher educator/teacher dialogic interactions are to support the development of L2 teacher/teaching expertise.

Intermental development zone

In exploring the quality and character of *responsive mediation* that emerges in the practices of L2 teacher education, we are most interested in what Mercer describes as "understanding the quality of *obuchenie* (teaching-learning) as an 'intermental' or 'interthinking' process" (2000, p. 141). Mercer proposes the construct of an *intermental development zone* (IDZ) to conceptualize how teachers and learners stay attuned to each other's changing states of knowledge and understanding, and we would add how teachers stay attuned to the learners' emotions, over the course of an educational activity. In other words, the concept of an IDZ is useful in explaining how dialogic interactions support *obuchenie*, the processes of teaching and learning. Mercer distinguishes the IDZ from Vygotsky's ZPD as offering a more dialogic, negotiated, and emergent view of the dynamics of conceptual development through collective dialogue and engagement in joint activity. In Mercer's own words, he claims:

> For a teacher to teach and a learner to learn, they must use talk and joint activity to create a shared communicative space, an '*intermental development zone*' (IDZ) on the contextual foundations of their common knowledge and aims. In this intermental zone, which is reconstituted constantly as the dialogue continues, the teacher and learner negotiate their way through the activity in which they are involved. If the quality of the zone is successfully maintained, the teacher can enable a learner to become able to operate just beyond his/her established capabilities, and to consolidate this experience as new ability and understandings. If the dialogue fails to keep minds mutually attuned, the IDZ collapses and the scaffolded learning grinds to a halt. (Mercer, 2000, p. 141)

We agree with Mercer that the IDZ and ZPD are constitutive of the same Vygotskian sociocultural theoretical foundation, but we are drawn to the idea that the IDZ is more adaptive to group instructional settings and to its dual focus on "observing the progress a learner makes with the support of a particular adult [and] . . . also observ[ing] how the adult uses language and other means of communicating to create an IDZ during the activity" (Mercer & Littleton, 2007, p. 22). Mercer's attention to what the adult is doing, or for us, what teacher educators are doing, is very compelling. A major aim of this book is to interrogate the activities and intentions of teacher educators as we jointly *think together* with the teachers with whom we work. This is not to neglect the contribution that our teachers make to our joint intellectual activity but to focus our attention on the IDZ as a shared communicative space in which to see how teacher educators and teachers stay attuned to each other's changing states of knowledge and understanding. We believe the co-construction of the IDZ becomes visible by examining the rhetorical and linguistic devices teacher educators draw on to create frames of reference for sharing their expertise with teachers and for teachers to express their emerging understandings with teacher educators. In other words, we are not only interested in how teacher educators and teachers orient to the minds of one another, but also how teacher educators make explicit their expert thinking about teaching and responsively adapt such expert thinking for the teachers with whom they work, especially in response to how their teachers respond.

While distinguishing between the IDZ and the ZPD may, for some readers, seem like splitting hairs, we are very cognizant of the differential power relationships and levels of expertise between teacher educators and teachers. And while we are drawn to the dialogic emphasis of the IDZ, we also agree with Miller (2011) who argues, also from a Vygotskian sociocultural perspective, that mediation and dialogue are not the same thing. In dialogue, according to Miller, meanings and understanding are exchanged whereas the ZPD "is concerned with the learning and teaching of new understanding in situations where prior or pre-understanding is inadequate" (p. 380). In the practices of L2 teacher education we are not just engaged in dialogue and activities with our teachers; we are not simply exchanging or even offering ideas about effective teaching. Given our expert knowledge and extensive experience, we have specific professional development goals in mind and as we interact with our teachers we may be attempting to accomplish any number of different goals with our teachers who will, no doubt, have their own goals. For example, we may be attempting to dislodge long-standing everyday notions about teaching and learning that are inadequate for how we expect our teachers to think about and carry out the activities of L2 teaching. We may be attempting to connect the *academic concepts* that we expose our teachers to in their coursework to their *everyday concepts* about what constitutes language teaching and learning. We may be attempting to enable our teachers to gain an expert's perspective on the subject matter they are expected to teach or the instructional practices they are attempting to carry out. Yet, our teachers may have the goal of simply getting through a lesson or being liked by their students. Accomplishing any one of these goals will be mediated through language within the metaphoric space where *obuchenie* takes place. Accomplishing any one of these goals will likewise be mediated by the emotions that are co-constructed in these interactions. So while the IDZ is a useful construct for exploring the dialogic interactions that emerge inside the practices of L2 teacher education, we trace the co-construction and preservation of an IDZ over the course of a professional development practice in order to highlight the unique contributions that teacher educators can make to teachers' conceptual development.

Sociocultural discourse analysis: Analyzing language as a social mode of thinking

Since our interest in this book lies in uncovering the educational value of teacher educator/teacher dialogic interaction while engaging in the practices of L2 teacher education, we are once again drawn to the work of Mercer (2004) and his colleagues and their use of *sociocultural discourse analysis* (SCDA) as a methodology for characterizing and exploring the nature of classroom talk and its educational significance (Littleton & Mercer, 2013; Mercer & Littleton, 2007; Mercer et al., 2004). Grounded in Vygotskian sociocultural theory, SCDA focuses on "how language is used as a social mode of thinking—language as a tool for teaching-and-learning, constructing knowledge, creating ideas, sharing understanding and tackling problems collaboratively" (Littleton & Mercer, 2013, p.13).

Littleton and Mercer (2013) distinguish SCDA from linguistic discourse analysis as being less concerned with the organizational structure of language in use and more with its content, specifically, "how it functions for the pursuit of joint intellectual activity and the ways in which shared understanding is developed, in social context, over time" (p. 13). SCDA can focus on lexical content because word choice and cohesive patterning represent ways that knowledge is being jointly constructed. However, SCDA also utilizes knowledge that is not explicitly invoked by speakers (unlike conversation analysis, i.e., Drew & Heritage, 1992; Schegloff, 1997), such as the historical, social, cultural, and institutional contexts in which interaction takes place. Most significant for us is the fact that Mercer's use of SCDA focuses on both the processes of education as well as their educational outcomes. He and his colleagues have spent more than two decades investigating the relationship between the ways that teachers talk with students and the learning that students can subsequently demonstrate (http://thinking-together.educ.cam.ac.uk). Utilizing a wide range of discursive techniques that teachers use to elicit knowledge from learners, to respond to what learners say, and to describe significant aspects of shared experiences, SCDA has proven to be a useful methodological tool for relating the content, quality, and temporal nature of dialogic interaction during joint activities to learning outcomes, such as the success or failure of problem solving or specific learning gains.

Moreover, like Lantolf and Poehner's (2014) *pedagogical imperative*, in the design and enactment of our teacher education practices we use the principles and concepts from Vygotskian and neo-Vygotskian sociocultural theory in order to intentionally promote the development of L2 teacher/teaching expertise through our practices as teacher educators. We are less interested in mere description and more in intentional, well-organized intervention. SCDA provides us with a methodological tool to trace teacher development, in essence, indicating the consequences of implementing concrete educational practices intentionally derived from Vygotskian sociocultural theory for teacher learning.

Specifically, in Chapters 5–9, we rely on SCDA as a methodology for conducting *microgenetic analyses* (Vygotsky, 1981) to uncover the development of new psychological processes as they unfold over the course of a particular L2 teacher education practice. Wertsch (1985) describes microgenesis as a "very short-term longitudinal study," making explicit the moment-to-moment revolutionary shifts that lead to the development of independent mental functioning (p. 55). Additionally, in line with SCDA, our microgenetic analyses operate simultaneously at three levels or "depth[s] of focus" (Littleton & Mercer, 2013, p. 21): (1) linguistic, the quality and character of teacher educator/teacher interaction as spoken and/or written text; (2) psychological, the analysis of teacher educator/teacher interaction as joint thinking and action; and (3) cultural, the institutional contexts, social settings, and shared cultural meanings embedded and valued within the contexts and settings in which teacher educator/teacher interaction takes place.

In Chapters 5–9 we use SCDA for analysis of the moment-to-moment, asynchronous, and at-a-distance teacher educator/teacher dialogic interactions (oral and written) that take place in five different practices that we have designed, repeatedly implemented, and subsequently collected data on in our own L2 teacher education programs. For each practice, we outline our educational goals and pedagogical procedures. We then situate each practice in the unique institutional and sociocultural context in which it occurred as well as provide sociohistorical information about the teachers who participated in these practices.

For each practice our analyses accomplish the following: (a) highlight the linguistic, rhetorical, and pragmatic characteristics of the teacher educator/teacher dialogic interaction; (b) trace the psychological processes that emerge as teacher educators and teachers engage in *interthinking*; (c) identify the emergence of cognitive/emotional dissonance as potential *growth points*; (d) follow the emergence and preservation of an IDZ over the course of the practice; (e) describe the quality and character of the *responsive mediation* that emerges; and (f) explore the consequences of *responsive mediation* on the ways in which teachers begin to think about and/or attempt to enact their instructional practices.

Finally, we have intentionally selected practices that by design create structured mediational spaces, tools, and activities that allow for teacher educators and teachers to engage in dialogic interactions that attend to the learning of teaching and, in particular, the interactional spaces, mediated through language, where *obuchenie* takes place. Our analyses of what happens inside these practices make the psychological processes of teacher educator mediation and teacher learning visible. Yet, we have been careful to focus our analytic lens on the unique characteristics of our teachers, our practices, and our teacher education programs, and thus offer these practices as illustrative rather than definitive. The educational value of analyzing our own practices, with our own teachers, in our own programs, we hope, is in enabling others to scrutinize their own practices, to hold themselves accountable to the teachers with whom they work, and to reclaim the relevance of L2 teacher education *in* and *for* the professional development of their L2 teachers (see Johnson, 2015).

References

Drew, P., & Heritage, P. (Eds.) (1992). *Talk at work: Interaction in institutional settings.* Cambridge: Cambridge University Press.

Johnson, K. E. (2015). Reclaiming the relevance of L2 teacher education. *The Modern Language Journal, 99*(3), 515–528.

Lantolf, J. P., & Poehner, M. E. (2014). *Sociocultural theory and the pedagogical imperative in L2 education.* New York: Routledge.

Littleton, K., & Mercer, N. (2013). *Interthinking: Putting talk to work.* London: Routledge.

Mercer, N. (2000). *Words & minds: How we use language to think together.* London: Routledge.

Mercer, N. (2004). Sociocultural discourse analysis: Analyzing classroom talk as a social mode of thinking. *Journal of Applied Linguistics, 1*(2), 137–168.

Mercer, N., & Littleton, K. (2007). *Dialogue and the development of children's thinking: A sociocultural approach.* London: Routledge.

Mercer, N., Littleton, K., & Wegerif, R. (2004). Methods for studying the process of interaction and collaborative activity in computer-based educational activities. *Technology, Pedagogy, and Education, 13*(2), 367–384.

Miller, R. (2011). *Vygotsky in perspective.* Cambridge: Cambridge University Press.

Schegloff, E. (1997). Whose text? Whose context? *Discourse and Society, 8*(2), 165–187.

Vygotsky, L. S. (1981). The genesis of higher mental functions. In J. V. Wertsch (Ed.), *The concept of activity in Soviet psychology* (pp. 144–188). Armonk, NY: Sharpe.

Wertsch, J. V. (1985). *Vygotsky and the social formation of mind.* Cambridge, MA: Harvard University Press.

PART III

Exploring Responsive Mediation in L2 Teacher Development

5
RECONCEPTUALIZING ENGINEERING STUDENT PARTICIPATION

"But I was too nervous to think of what's the right thing to do right now"

Video recall has been used as a tool in research on teacher cognition to study teacher learning, and in the practices of L2 teacher education to promote the development of L2 teacher/teaching expertise. Given the difficulty, if not impossibility, of accessing teacher thinking directly during the act of teaching, video recall, typically referred to as stimulated recall (Calderhead, 1981; Shavelson & Stern, 1981), represents a kind of introspective tool that has been exploited to assist teachers in expressing their thinking retrospectively. In L2 teacher cognition research, Borg's (2003) review provides an excellent reference for examples of research using stimulated recall. When conducting a stimulated recall, researchers typically instruct teachers to relive their teaching experience, and to stop the tape when they could recall their thoughts at a particular point in the lesson concerning whatever the research focus is, such as decision making. The teachers being able to control when they stop the video and talk through a systematic protocol is intended to control researcher subjectivity in the data collection process. Not surprisingly, concerns have been expressed about collecting data pertaining to interactive cognition after the fact via stimulated recall (Gass & Mackey, 2000; Keith, 1988; Lyle, 2003). Although researchers need to limit their own subjectivity within a stimulated recall procedure, teacher educators can bring something quite intentional to guide a reflective interaction with a teacher while watching that teacher's videotape in ways that make explicit expert teacher thinking.

In fact, over the last 35 years, the use of video recall feedback has evolved as a tool used in support of varied practices within L2 teacher education programs or professional development workshops. Beginning teachers enacting a stand-alone microteaching assignment might be videotaped and observe the video with a teacher educator who has established a specific agenda and expectations for interaction. Beginning teachers participating in the lengthier practicum might be videotaped and similarly engage in watching the video with a teacher educator one or more times as a way to gauge and support teacher learning (Schratz, 1992). In these cases, teacher educators play a pivotal role in the interactions during the viewing of the videotape, as they determine specific learning objectives and patterns of interaction to achieve those objectives, as well as provide expertise through their in-process appraisals of and feedback to teachers. Another option, *video study groups* (Tochon, 1999), includes a small group of teachers viewing and discussing together a teacher's instructional actions captured through the video. Because the goals for using videos for teacher development differ from those of teacher cognition research, Tochon (2008) has suggested that we abandon the term 'stimulated recall' for teacher learning purposes and proposed in its place "video-based shared reflection" (p. 425). The focus when using videos for teacher development shifts to reflection on whether teachers are enacting instructional practices that align with their beliefs and goals as teachers, and that promote student learning.

When used for teacher development, a video recording of what transpired in a class provides an objective account of what both teachers and students said or did during the lesson, and enables multiple replays for analysis (Richards & Lockhart, 1994). Rather than reconstructing a lesson based on memory or on how a teacher wished the lesson had gone, the instructional interactions materialized on the videotape open the teacher's activity to analysis, and thus, from a Vygotskian sociocultural perspective, to social influence and restructuring. If the interaction between the teacher educator and the teacher while watching the videotape is conceptualized as a teaching/learning (*obuchenie*) opportunity, the interaction between the more expert teacher educator and the teacher has the potential to become an *intermental development zone* (IDZ) in which the videotape becomes the object of analysis, the concrete resource through which the teacher educator and teacher talk through their jointly constructed analysis of the teacher's implementation of specific instructional activities in the observed class. This crucial point—through talk our thinking is made transparent and transformed—is what has led us to call these interactions surrounding the sense-making of the videotape *dialogic video protocols* (DVPs) (Golombek, 2011).

When the *dialogic video protocol* is conceptualized as a teaching/learning (*obuchenie*) opportunity within an L2 teacher education program, teacher educators must be able to articulate the motive behind and object of this practice in order to engage in *responsive mediation* with a teacher. The teacher educator needs to be able to explain motives and goals in using DVPs to the teacher, and the highly interactive, co-constructed nature of their participation. The teacher educator needs to assess the teacher throughout the interaction to identify 'lower' and 'upper' thresholds: to understand how a teacher is perceiving and feeling about certain interactions, to elicit the teacher's pedagogical reasoning, to problem-solve in the face of quandaries, and to push the teacher's thinking about alternative instructional responses in implicit and explicit ways, depending on the circumstances. Simultaneously, teacher educators can make their expert thinking transparent as a way to orient teachers to restructure their thinking about and their activities of teaching. In essence, if an IDZ is created and maintained throughout the DVP, the teacher is enabled to experience a kind of 'do over' in a 'safe zone,' an opportunity to 'mentally manipulate' (Lantolf & Thorne, 2006) thinking and doing that has already occurred in a particular place and time and co-construct new conceptualizations of and activities in teaching.

Creating this joint communicative space for *interthinking*, co-constructed on the foundations of shared knowledge, motives, and objectives, is cognitively and emotionally demanding for both the teacher educator and teacher because interaction within a DVP happens in real time. And while the teacher educator and teacher may work together to identify the teacher's internal cognitive/emotional struggles, the teacher educator fundamentally has the greater responsibility within the IDZ to create the spaces to address immediate needs and/or concerns of individual teachers and push them beyond their current capabilities. As in the other practices of L2 teacher education, we engage our teachers in DVPs to reconstruct their lived experiences in order to create conditions for the development of L2 teacher/teaching expertise.

In this chapter we examine engagement in the DVP between an ESL teacher named Abra and a teacher educator during a microteaching experience conducted as part of coursework in an MA TESL program. For this dialogic video protocol,[1] Abra was videotaped teaching an oral communication course for international teaching assistants (ITAs), and then she and the professor of the course (teacher educator) viewed the video together. In the transcripts from the DVP, we are able to identify how Abra and the teacher educator co-construct an IDZ in response to repeated instances of cognitive/emotional dissonance she experiences in terms of her *perezhivanie* and her inability to enact the pedagogical tool of *engineering student participation* in her teaching. We also identify how the teacher educator uses rhetorical choices to continually learn more and assess what Abra knows about this tool and how she perceives and feels about what is happening in her class, as well as to push her understanding of the analysis and articulation of it beyond what she can express alone. What the teacher educator and Abra uncover is that Abra knows more about *engineering student participation* than her performance indicates.

The dialogic video protocol within an American English phonetics course

Abra was enrolled in a core course in the MA TESL program, a course designed to develop student understanding of American English phonetics in order to integrate pronunciation, listening, and speaking holistically in a discourse-oriented approach to L2 instruction. As part of the course requirements, the students designed a lesson on connected speech, for example reductions or allophones of /t/, which concentrated on developing learners' listening abilities, and taught the lesson in a *practice teach*[2] to their classmates. Then, after revising their lesson on the basis of their *practice teach*, they were videotaped teaching that lesson in one session of a course offered by the ESL program overseen by the academic department in which the MA TESL program was housed. After they taught the lesson, the teachers engaged in a DVP with the teacher educator.

Before they began the DVP, the teacher educator explained to Abra that she could stop the videotape at any point and talk about what she found compelling for whatever reason. The teacher educator noted that she would do the same. She explained that the objective was not for her to tell Abra what to do, but to encourage Abra to articulate her feelings, understandings, reasoning, and evaluation of her instruction. The teacher educator explained that she would ask Abra numerous questions in order to prompt her thinking further, that she hoped to enable Abra to identify alternative instructional practices, and that she would guide her whenever necessary. In this way, the teacher educator explicitly set up the discursive norms, or conversational ground rules, of their interaction to establish an IDZ in relation to their real-time viewing of and talk about her videotaped teaching. Moreover, the teacher educator intentionally encouraged Abra to articulate her thoughts, feelings, understandings, and evaluations about specific events in her teaching in order to engage in *responsive mediation*.

Though the pedagogical tool of *engineering student participation*[3] is used to characterize the analysis presented in this chapter, it was not presented in a systematically organized formal manner as Vygotsky (1986) suggested, or as is done in Chapter 7, in the course Abra was taking. How to facilitate student participation was discussed at different points during the course, and Abra mentioned that she wanted to have meaningful student participation as she created her lesson plan with the teacher educator, which is discussed below. In setting up the microteaching assignment, the teacher educator focused on developing the *pedagogical content knowledge* (Shulman, 1987) needed to transform teachers' conceptual understanding of the *academic concept* of 'linking' into the material activity of teaching (i.e., the lesson plan and actual teaching). As Abra planned and taught her lesson on linking, it was clear as they watched the videotape that she had internalized the *academic concept* of 'linking' as a psychological tool. As a result, she and the teacher educator engaged in *responsive mediation* as they watched the video and a *growth point* emerged through their talking together. Thus, while we believe this chapter shows how invaluable the dialogic interactions orchestrated in/through the DVP can be for teacher educator and teacher engagement in *responsive mediation* and the development of L2 teacher/teaching expertise, we also believe it shows the shortcomings of only being able to enact a stand-alone microteaching assignment, a situation that may constrain many teacher educators. It also highlights the challenges of dealing with the extensive knowledge base needed to teach, especially in an initial teaching assignment, e.g., basic structuring of a lesson, adequate knowledge of subject matter, or *pedagogical content knowledge* (Shulman, 1987) to name a few. Given that teacher development requires teachers working through *academic concepts* introduced by the teacher educator, as well as sustained participation in the activities of teaching, we believe this chapter buttresses our argument that systematically organized formal instruction is crucial in the 'critical period' of L2 teacher education.

Abra's pre-understandings

Born in England, Abra moved to the northeast of the United States as a small child and attended public schools. She was raised in a deeply observant Muslim family, which was evident in her attire and in her interactions with others. When Abra entered the MA TESL program, she was technically not a beginning teacher. She graduated with a BA in education from a large public university in the Northeast, where she had also done a practicum; she thus had some teaching experience, though it was not with English language learners.[4]

Abra was highly motivated in her own learning as a student and sought to connect instruction to her personal life. The professor of this course, hereafter referred to as the teacher educator, had worked with Abra in two previous MA TESL courses, noting that she consistently asked to and adapted course assignments to meet her own needs and interests. For example, in another course with the teacher educator, Abra created a whole-semester reading curriculum that extended well beyond the three-week unit required in the course syllabus, so she could enable Muslim women to connect reading of the Koran and Koranic interpretations with English language learning. Abra consistently and actively shaped the nature of classroom interactions in the courses she attended as a student through her incisive questions and comments. She also frequently asked the teacher educator for explicit mediation, for example, to point out weaknesses in arguments she was making or explanations for course content. The teacher educator met with Abra outside class from time to time to discuss intellectual, professional, and personal issues. Abra often referenced Islam when discussing these issues, so the teacher educator understood how interconnected and grounded her personal and professional life was in her faith. In fact, throughout these interactions, Abra made it clear how important it was for her actions to align with her faith and to improve herself if they did not, as well as to treat others in a way she expected to be treated. These interactions enabled the teacher educator to glean the kind of deep personal, historical knowledge about Abra that is critical to *responsive mediation*. However, we recognize that teacher educators are not always able to establish relationships such as this for a variety of sociocultural (social hierarchies) and/or practical reasons (working with numerous teachers).

Creating the lesson plan

Abra first observed the class she was assigned to teach in order to familiarize herself with the nature of the class and the students. The class had 13 students, who were from the People's Republic of China, the Republic of China, and South Korea. As Abra developed her lesson plan for the lesson on linking, she repeatedly commented that she wanted to encourage meaningful student participation, especially as she valued it from her *perezhivanie*, which could be described as an emotional lens through which she interpreted new experiences in terms of how she lived up to her self-expectations (how she treated others) along with self-improvement (how she might better live up to those expectations). Her evaluation of herself and how she treated people was an emotional experience for her, resulting in her feeling bad if she had not lived up to her expectations and being quick to make amends (e.g., an email of apology if she felt she had mistreated you in any way). Given her pre-understandings and *perezhivanie*, Abra worked hard to create a detailed lesson plan and consulted with the teacher educator in the process, expressing that she wanted the students in the ITA class to engage with the material and participate actively. As a result, her lesson plan (her ideal) involved students constructing their understandings of linking through the prediction, listening, and debriefing activities she designed.

Abra could not only explain the *academic concept* of 'linking' in a student friendly way in the materials she created for her lesson, but could express the pedagogical reasoning behind the sequence of activities in her lesson plan. She focused on five kinds of linking from the course textbook (Celce-Murcia, Brinton, & Goodwin, 1996). In the creation of her lesson plan, she explained that students needed a conceptual understanding of linking and the various kinds of linking, so she began with an interactive lecture with verbal and visual definitions and examples (for example, CV linking = joining of last sound in a word when it's a consonant and first sound in next word when it's a vowel so it sounds like one word, sto**p** **i**t → stopit). She chose a scene from *Star Wars: Episode I – The Phantom Menace* (McCallum & Lucas, 1999), a movie that was one of her personal favorites, and created a transcript of the scene. The students were given the script in order to predict where linking would occur, which they would note on the transcript. In this way, Abra felt she could assess students' conceptual understanding of linking. Then, to assess their ability to perceive linking, she had students watch the scene several times and note on the transcript if their predictions proved accurate. They would then compare answers in a whole-class discussion, and discuss reasons why linking may not have occurred, for meaning-based reasons, in instances they had predicted.

Identifying Abra's cognitive and emotional dissonance

The data extracts selected for inclusion in this chapter highlight the quality and character of the collaborative teaching/learning relationships (*obuchenie*) that unfolded throughout the DVP and the role of the teacher educator in supporting Abra's identification of missed opportunities for her to engage students in meaningful participation, and then articulation of alternative instructional actions she could have taken to engineer student participation. Analyzed from an emic perspective using sociocultural discourse analysis (Mercer, 2004), the data extracts highlight (marked in bold font) the linguistic instantiations of how the teacher educator, while engaging in the DVP, sought to create the conditions for *responsive mediation* through which Abra could 'jump above' her teaching activity captured on the video. The data show how the teacher educator enabled Abra to express (1) some ideal conceptions of teaching concerning student participation, (2) her assessment of her instructional activity on the video through which a *growth point* emerges, and (3) alternative instructional responses to address her *growth point*. The data show how Abra's *perezhivanie* influences her assessment of her activity as well as how the teacher educator tries to be sensitive to Abra's emotions. Within the structured mediational space of the DVP, the teacher educator and Abra co-construct an IDZ in which they stay highly attuned to each other's knowledge and motives.

To review briefly, Abra first taught explicitly about linking through explanations and examples, had students predict where linking could occur on excerpts from the movie script, and then had them listen and then explain whether linking occurred. Then, Abra and the class went over the transcript together, a debriefing, to compare what they had predicted and heard. As Abra and the teacher educator watched the videotape, Abra expressed dissatisfaction several times with her attempts to foster student participation, which she felt often resulted in her answering her own questions. But it was during the viewing of the debriefing activity that Abra stopped the video to discuss her inability to respond to one student making a face and laughing in response to one of the examples of linking.

Excerpt 1

A: and then **one of the girls at that point laughed**

TE: hmm

A: like she was understanding and I wanted ta- **I wanted to take that and do something with it but I didn't know what so I just kept on going**

TE: yeah ( ) hmm

A: but **I saw her um respond like "oh my god that's so strange"**

TE: uh-hm

A: but **I didn't know what to do with it**

TE: uh-hm

A: I

TE: I saw her kinda go **["wo"]**

A: [yeah]

TE: too

A: yeah what-what **is there something I could've done to like um (.5) tap into that response? Or should I cause I felt like I just ignored it** I just

TE: uh-hm

A: kept going

TE: uh-hm

A: and **I didn't mean to**

TE: uh-hm

A: **completely ignore it**

TE: yeah

A: I wanted to acknowledge it like "yeah isn't that weird?" (1.0) and so I said (.5) so it sounds strange (.5) but that's how it is

TE: uh-hm

A: I said tha:t

TE: uh-hm

A: in hopes that that would address her (1.0) is that what I said?

((rewinds tape and replays))

Abra hones in on the student's laughter as suggesting an understanding of how the linking of words leads to unexpected pronunciation, one of the points of Abra's lesson, and, thus, as an opening to involve the student in her learning more explicitly. She begins to explain how this was a missed opportunity to respond to a student and engage her in meaningful participation, "*I wanted to take that and do something with it but I didn't know what so I just kept on going.*" It is interesting to note how Abra's struggle to take up and use student responses effectively to advance her instructional goals is such a common problem for beginning teachers (for example, see Kyla in Chapter 6). This interaction, between Abra and the student, signals a potential *growth point* that emerges during the DVP. In other words, a contradiction emerges between her ideal conceptualization of how teacher–student interaction should unfold and the critical role she believes she should play in it and the reality of what is captured on the videotape, or what Abra views as a missed opportunity to engage the student in meaningful participation. This realization is expressed in negative terms; she "*ignored*" the student's response, further indicating Abra's cognitive/ emotional dissonance as it 'comes into being.' This dissatisfaction is not surprising given her *perezhivanie* of continual self-improvement and her valuing of student engagement. Her sense of cognitive/emotional dissonance appears to be powerful enough that she directly asks the teacher educator for mediation, explaining how she "*didn't mean to completely ignore it* [the student's reaction]." She begins to confuse what she thought, perhaps wished, she had said with what she actually said. She rewinds the video and finds that what happened was indeed different from what she hoped had happened.

Excerpt 2

A: yeah well **all I did was I smiled**

TE: uh hm

A: that was my response to her (1.0) that was how I acknowledged her

TE: **Well I don't know.** I mean **think about it is there something- do you think there is something you could've done?** What could you have done? (3.5)

A: **I could have stopped and said yeah it sounds weird right**

TE: uh-hm

A: y'know an like to her yeah **it sounds wei:rd so that she knows**

TE: uh-hm

A: that I- **I noticed her response**

TE: uh-hm

A: and **that she's ri:ght to make that response**

TE: uh-hm (1.0) yeah (1.0) **I: no:ticed (1.0) you had a strong reaction**

A: yeah

TE: **How come?**

A: yeah

TE: yeah=

A: =**how come**

TE: yeah cause=

A: =**get her to (2.0) talk about it. Get her to think about it cause she obviously reacted and then she'll stop to think why did I react and whatever it was that went through her mind**

TE: uh-hm (.5) because (1.5) you know the first time what you said is you're automatically saying what it is that she thought. It is strange, y'know

A: yeah

TE: and **so I'm I guess what I'm saying is,** (.5)

A: **let her say it**

TE: let her say it

A: [yeah]

When the videotape confirms that she had not said anything, Abra expresses disappointment in herself with the minimizer 'all,' as in "*all I did was I smiled.*" Given Abra's emotional reaction to her lack of verbal response to the student, signifying a potential *growth point*, the teacher educator tries to create a space in which Abra could externalize her thinking about engaging student participation without the real-time cognitive demands of teaching: "*Well I don't know. I mean think about it (.5) is there something- do you think there is something you could've done?*" The teacher educator validates the difficulty of this situation by downplaying her own expertise, "*Well I don't know,*" and then reorients Abra to the situation in order to express her reasoning by saying, "*I mean think about it*," and then models the kinds of questions a teacher could ask herself when facing a lack of congruence between the ideal of engineering student participation and the reality of not achieving it to address this *growth point* with Abra, "*do you think there is something you could've done? What could you have done?*" The teacher educator's rhetorical choice to ask Abra a question rather than telling her what to do is meant to encourage her to articulate alternative actions that she could have taken in order to gauge whether Abra has the ability, without the cognitive demands of real-time teaching, to devise a response that aligns with her instructional values.

Abra reformulates what she could have done by responding "*I could have stopped and said yeah it sounds weird right*" and "*I noticed her response.*" The teacher educator builds on this part of Abra's response, "*I: no:ticed (1.0) you had a strong reaction*," but then explicitly voices what a teacher could say—"*how come?*" The expert-novice nature of their exchange is observable in that the teacher educator has attempted to focus Abra's thinking away from simply acknowledging the student's reaction to modeling a pedagogical strategy to elicit student participation. Abra stays attuned to the teacher educator's concrete suggestion by echoing "*how come?*" As the teacher begins to explain the reasoning behind this response with "*yeah cause*," Abra overlaps and provides the answer, "*get her to (2.0) talk about it. Get her to think about it cause she obviously reacted and then she'll stop to think why did I react and whatever it was that went through her mind.*" We see the emergence of a sense of intersubjectivity, in Wertsch's (1985) terms, *attunement to one's attunement*, as Abra begins to understand what an expert teacher might say and why, in order to engage students in their learning. The teacher educator reiterates what was problematic about Abra's initial response, and why she inserted the more direct "*how come*" question to the student. She sets up the gist of her expert reasoning by saying "*so I'm I guess what I'm saying is*," a rhetorical choice that sets up the kind of collaborative completion teachers use to check student comprehension (Hatch, 2002). Abra again exhibits a sense of intersubjectivity through her collaborative completion, "*let her say it.*" As a result of these two collaborative completions, the teacher educator has not only ascertained that Abra can articulate the pedagogical reasoning behind the teacher educator's instructional response in this specific instance of Abra's instructional activity, but also enabled her to 'jump above' her initial attempts to respond.

As Abra continued to talk about this interaction, her feelings about the interaction and disappointment with herself emerge.

Excerpt 3
> TE: oh you had a strong reaction
> A: yeah
> TE: I do this in class all the time

A: I know

TE: sure and **she did she made a really strong reaction**

A: yeah

TE: it really had an impact on her

A: yeah

TE: and so find out why:

A: yeah

TE: why did you respond that way

A: and **I feel like it was rude for me to ignore it an' just go on**

TE: hm

A: like it you'know. I don't know. **My my heart was not content with it** but I

TE: uh-hm

A: **but I was too nervous to think of what's the right thing to do right now**

TE: uh-hm

A: but now I know (.5) hopefully I'll do the right (3.0) so I'm verbalizing what I think was going on through her mind but it would've been nice if I let her say it

TE: uh-hm

((*They go back to watching video.*))

The teacher educator appears to be summarizing this interactional episode by recapping the main points she and Abra had discussed. Then, she reaffirms that the student's laughter did present an opportunity for Abra to respond instructionally, "*she did she made a really strong reaction.*" Abra exhibits a strong emotional response and further evidences that this interaction served as a potential *growth point* for her, as she negatively evaluates her inability to respond to the student's laughter, "*I feel like it was rude for me to ignore it an' just go on.*" She has violated her ideal sense of how she should treat people and expresses her dissatisfaction in a poetic way characteristic of her communication style, "*My my heart was not content with it,*" as well as a reason for why she could not have acted differently, "*but I was too nervous to think of what's the right thing to do right now.*" Abra's recognition of how cognitively and emotionally demanding teaching can be suggests the value of engaging in the activity of a DVP. In the 'safe zone' of the DVP, teachers are able to think about their conceptions of teaching, instructional objectives, student needs, abilities, and goals, and propose different instructional activity, and perhaps grow in confidence. Throughout this interaction, the teacher educator and Abra maintain their IDZ as Abra gains a heightened sense of *intersubjectivity* concerning a more expert notion of *engineering student participation* ("*but now I know*"), and the teacher educator gains more information about Abra's emotional/cognitive dissonance to guide her in their interactions.

Abra's continued lack of self-regulation in terms of engineering student participation

Once again, the preservation of the IDZ as attunement to Abra's enactment of meaningful student engagement is challenged. She transitioned the classroom activity from listening for instances of linking to discussing the instances they identified. On the video of her teaching, Abra asks the class a series of questions.

Excerpt 4

> A: So um who can tell (.4) who can tell us where they were able to detect what was going on with linking. Anywhere? Can you point to like a line, (.3) and what you thought (.1) was going on between those two words?

No one in the class responded. At this point, Abra stops the video and attempts to formulate what she could have done to elicit student participation.

Excerpt 5

> A: Okay, so when there was silence, **then I could've said**, (8.0)
>
> TE: So you said who could tell us, (1.0) you know (1.0) **sort of pick a line**=
>
> A: =yeah (.1) and then I could've said (.5) well do you: (2.0) di- okay (2.0) did any of the place you circled sound as if they were (.5) pronounced (1.0) separately? Sort of like
>
> TE: uh-hm
>
> A: physically going at it from the inverse=
>
> TE: =yeah
>
> A: instead of saying 'well did you hear linking?'
>
> TE: uh-hm
>
> A: Well did you hear it (.5) did you hear each (.5) word pronounced separately, (1.0) 'did you not hear linking' (1.0) so if they'd say 'no no no it wasn't separate here'
>
> TE: uh-huh=
>
> A: =y'know
>
> TE: **that may be going a step ahead of the game**=
>
> A: =yeah
>
> TE: **I don't know (1.0) what if you just simply said "okay let's look at line one together (.5) who can give me an example of linking here?"**
>
> A: okay
>
> TE: umm (.5) **it would be a way to specify the way that the thing is rather than like choosing one or (.5) whatever you're fo:cusing attention (.5)**

A: yeah=

TE: ="let's look at line one, (.5) does anybody have an example?" um (1.5) um

A: yeah

TE: that would be, that would be one way (1.0) um to do [that]

A: **['Did] anyone pick any- was anyone able to identify how: two words were being linked together in line one (1.0)**

TE: uh-hm

A: something like that

TE: I- I- think to draw their attention to line one ra[ther]

A: [yeah]

TE: than leaving it so: open (1.0)

A: yeah: (1.0)

TE: and **when things are so: open,**

A: **it's a little (.5) not so easy to figure out what to do**

TE: uh-hm (1.0) and so: you wanna help them know what to do. ((*undistinguishable talk*))

TE: But yeah: I think uh- (1.0) focusing them (.5) on: (1.0) especially you have these beautifully numbered lines

A: [laughs]

TE: why not why not use them [laughs]

A: yeah line one (2.0) line eight [both laugh]

The fact that Abra stopped the video after viewing Excerpt 4 shows her agency and understanding concerning student participation, as she is the one who identified an instance where she could have encouraged student participation. Abra attempts to rephrase the question she asked, "*then I could've said,*" but then stops. There is an eight-second silence during which the teacher educator gives Abra the space to think and create an alternative instructional response to elicit participation. But after the eight-second pause, the teacher educator makes a strategic choice to facilitate an explanation from Abra by initiating a possible response, including part of what Abra did say, "*who could tell us.*" By "introducing elements of the task's solution" (Vygotsky, 1987, p. 209), the teacher educator creates joint mental activity by trying to identify if Abra can articulate an alternative instructional response with some help, "*sort of pick a line.*" Abra picks up the teacher educator's assistance and provides an answer, what she calls "*physically going from the inverse,*" asking the students to consider where they had not heard linking. The teacher educator critiques Abra's response while staying cognitively and emotionally attuned to her; that is, the teacher educator uses the low certainty modal of 'may,' as in "*that may be going a step ahead of the game,*" uses hedges like "*I don't know,*" and begins with "*what if*" to voice what Abra could have said in more expert terms: "*okay let's look at line one together (.5) who can give me an example of linking here?*"

The teacher educator then explains her reasoning for what Abra could have said, "*it would be a way to specify the way that the thing is rather than like choosing one or (.5) whatever you're fo:cusing attention.*" Rather than simply mimicking the teacher educator's phrasing, Abra overlaps the teacher educator by *ventriloquating* (Bakhtin, 1981), or populating her own response with her own intentions, "*[Did] anyone pick any- was anyone able to identify how: two words were being linked together in line one.*" The teacher educator rephrases the reasoning behind her instructional response as it relates to engaging student participation—it focuses them—while indirectly noting what was problematic in Abra's response—it was too open-ended. Sensing from Abra's response that she did not completely understand what was problematic in her suggestion, the teacher educator explicitly mediates Abra by explaining why open-ended prompts to students are unlikely to result in student participation with the dependent clause "*and when things are so: open.*" But Abra again collaboratively completes the teacher educator's utterance, signaling that she does understand the reasoning. Once again, we see the preservation of an IDZ that is attuned to how Abra is experiencing this lesson, and her recognition of missed opportunities to engage meaningful student participation. However, at the same time, the teacher educator's mediation is responsive to Abra's emotional needs as the teacher educator attempts to expand Abra's understanding of instructional responses through modeling expert instructional talk intended to facilitate student participation. We also see how the teacher educator repeatedly replies with a few words that could initiate a longer, more explicit mediation and then stops to see whether and how the teacher can 'jump above' herself.

Conclusion

If we consider the dialogic interactions occurring throughout the dialogic video protocol in terms of *obuchenie*, the actions and intentions of the teacher educator are predicated on establishing a sense of Abra's *perezhivanie*. Abra perceived her teaching experience through her experiences as a learner in which self-improvement and being engaged with the instruction and content was paramount. She was concerned with how people treat each other in interaction, and she was critical of both her inability to engage students in meaningful action and her perceived mistreatment of them as people (being rude, ignoring them). This concern, especially how she failed to enact it in her interactions with a particular student, signaled a potential *growth point* for Abra, one that the teacher educator picked up on and directly targeted throughout their co-constructing an IDZ. The teacher educator first sought to elicit how Abra understood what she was viewing on the videotape. The teacher educator's mediation was emergent, contingent, and responsive to Abra's immediate needs in terms of how she described and evaluated the episodes discussed from the videotape, and then how Abra responded to her mediation. When Abra identified incidents in which she failed to engage students in meaningful participation, such as missed opportunities to ask questions or questions met with silence, Abra was quick to ask the teacher educator for explicit mediation. The objective of the DVP was to model expert teacher thinking concerning what an appropriate instructional response could be and why that response was appropriate, so the teacher educator initially mediated by asking Abra what she could have done differently. How Abra responded signaled to the teacher educator what kind of assistance she might offer, such as introducing part of a possible solution to the problem, or voicing what a teacher could say to engineer participation, resulting in a continuous interaction between the teacher educator and Abra as they stayed attuned to each other.

The teacher educator acknowledged Abra's expressions of emotions concerning her inability to engage students in meaningful participation, but the synchronous nature of the interaction during the DVP generates challenges in creating an IDZ for the teacher and the teacher educator alike. Even though doing the DVP is intended to model and encourage expert teacher thinking, a teacher, especially a beginning teacher, cannot help but feel vulnerable when engaging in even constructive criticism. The face-threatening nature of this interaction is tangible. This creates further challenges for the teacher educator, who is mediating in real time while trying to understand the teacher's thinking, to be mindful of the teacher's *perezhivanie* and the teacher's cognitive and emotional needs. We see that enacting mediation within an IDZ in real time requires the teacher educator to, as previously noted, be mindful of his/her purposeful intentions when interacting in and throughout the DVP in order to create conditions for mediation that are emergent, contingent, and responsive.

If we had observed or only watched the video of Abra's teaching activity in that particular class, we would have an inadequate understanding of what she knows about *engineering student participation* and of the kind of support she needs to develop her teacher/teaching expertise. Unfortunately, without immediate follow-up teaching activity, we do not have evidence of whether Abra can integrate, or is gradually internalizing, her emerging conceptions of meaningful participation in her actual teaching activity. From a sociocultural theoretical perspective, Abra needs to materialize this pedagogical concept in concrete goal-directed activity repeatedly. The findings in this chapter accentuate a central point of this book—teacher educators need to create multiple, integrated opportunities for authentic participation in the activities of language teaching, which open up multiple, assorted *structured mediational spaces* for *responsive mediation* to emerge throughout the learning-to-teach experience. Also necessary are ongoing opportunities to materialize *academic concepts* and pedagogical tools in authentic teaching experience so teachers can begin to use them as psychological tools to regulate their cognition, emotion, and activity of teaching. But before teachers can engage in such activities, teacher educators need to introduce the kind of systematically organized instruction that Vygotsky (1986) viewed as fundamental to the development of higher mental processes. Providing Abra with a conceptualization of some fundamental pedagogical tools, such as *engineering student participation*, would have, from a Vygotskian sociocultural theoretical perspective, provided a way for her to talk about what she had experienced through the concept to assist her internalization of it. For teacher educators, integrating *academic concepts* within the DVP allows teachers to connect them to their *everyday concepts* about teaching and to the concrete activity of what they are experiencing in their classrooms. Through *responsive mediation* co-constructed throughout DVP, teacher educators can identify teacher potentiality, so that the interactions in/through the DVP can lead teacher development.

Notes

1 Data extracts reprinted with permission from Routledge. Golombek, P. R. (2011). Dynamic assessment in teacher education: Using dialogic video protocols to intervene in teacher thinking and activity. In K. E. Johnson & P. R. Golombek (Eds.), *Research on second language teacher education: A sociocultural perspective on professional development* (pp. 121–135). New York: Routledge.
2 The teacher educator did not collect data on the *practice teach*, and thus cannot link these experiences. For an explanation of how a *practice teach* can be integrated more comprehensively into the learning-to-teach experience, see Chapters 6 and 9.
3 See Chapter 7. Operationally defined as "Don't assume students will know how you want them to participate. Arrange your activities so that students have opportunities to participate in different ways (individually, round-robin, pairs, small groups, large groups) and be explicit (meta-talk) about how you want them to participate" (course handout).
4 These details signal the problematic nature of labels used in teacher education, such as pre- and in-service teachers, or novice and experienced teachers, in which unhelpful binaries are set up according to Cartesian logic. See Chapter 10 for further explanation.

References

Bakhtin, M. M. (1981). *The dialogic imagination: Four essays by M. M. Bakhtin.* Austin: University of Texas Press.
Borg, S. (2003). Teacher cognition in language teaching: A review of research on what language teachers think, know, believe, and do. *Language Teaching, 36*(2), 81–109.
Calderhead, J. (1981). Stimulated recall: A method for research on teaching. *British Journal of Educational Psychology, 51*(2), 211–217.
Celce-Murcia, M., Brinton, D. M., & Goodwin, J. M. (1996). *Teaching pronunciation: A reference for teachers of English to speakers of other languages.* Cambridge: Cambridge University Press.

Gass, S. M., & Mackey, A. (2000). *Stimulated recall methodology in second language research*. Mahwah, NJ: Lawrence Erlbaum Associates.

Golombek, P. R. (2011). Dynamic assessment in teacher education: Using dialogic video protocols to intervene in teacher thinking and activity. In K. E. Johnson & P. R. Golombek (Eds.), *Research on second language teacher education: A sociocultural perspective on professional development* (pp. 121–135). New York: Routledge.

Hatch, J. A. (2002). *Doing qualitative research in education settings*. Albany, NY: SUNY Press.

Keith, M. J. (1988). *Stimulated recall and teachers' thought processes: A critical review of the methodology and an alternative perspective*. Paper presented at the Annual Meeting of the Mid-South Educational Research Association, Louisville, Kentucky.

Lantolf, J. P., & Thorne, S. (2006). *Sociocultural theory and the genesis of second language development*. Oxford: Oxford University Press.

Lyle, J. (2003). Stimulated recall: A report on its use in naturalistic research. *British Educational Research Journal, 29*(6), 861–878.

McCallum, R. (Producer), & Lucas, G. (Director) (1999). *Star Wars: Episode One – The Phantom Menace* [motion picture]. United States: Lucasfilm Ltd.

Mercer, N. (2004). Sociocultural discourse analysis: Analyzing classroom talk as a social mode of thinking. *Journal of Applied Linguistics, 1*(2), 137–168.

Richards, J. C., & Lockhart, C. (1994). *Reflective teaching in second language classrooms*. Cambridge: Cambridge University Press.

Schratz, M. (1992). Researching while teaching: An action research approach in higher education. *Studies in Higher Education, 17*(1), 81–95.

Shavelson, R. J., & Stern, P. (1981). Research on teachers' pedagogical thoughts, judgments, decisions, and behavior. *Review of Educational Research, 51*(4), 455–498.

Shulman, L. S. (1987). Knowledge and teaching: Foundations of the new reform. *Harvard Educational Review, 57*(1), 1–22.

Tochon, F. V. (1999). *Video study groups for education, professional development, and change*. Madison, WI: Atwood Publishing.

Tochon, F. V. (2008). A brief history of video feedback and its role in foreign language education. *CALICO, special issue, 25*(3), 420–435.

Vygotsky, L. S. (1986). *Thought and language* (A. Kozulin, Trans.). Cambridge, MA: MIT Press.

Vygotsky, L. S. (1987). Thinking and speech (N. Minick, Trans.). In R. W. Reiber (Ed.), *The collected works of L. S. Vygotsky, Vol. 3. Problems of the theory and history of Psychology* (pp. 37–285). New York: Plenum Press.

Wertsch, J. V. (1985). *Vygotsky and the social formation of mind*. Cambridge, MA: Harvard University Press.

6

RECONCILING ONE'S TEACHING PERSONA

"I was able to nicely balance my mellow and nice attitude with being the 'teacher.'"

The quintessential culminating experience in most L2 teacher education programs is the teaching practicum. Typified as 'finally in the field,' the practicum provides a mentored clinical experience where the doing of teaching and the learning about teaching are meant to come together in developmentally significant ways. Conceptualized as a teaching/learning (*obuchenie*) opportunity rather than for the evaluation of teaching performance, practicum teachers are typically eased into the day-to-day workings of classroom life. They may begin by simply observing or working with small groups of students, but then gradually take on greater responsibility for instruction, including planning, teaching, and assessing student learning. Mentor teachers (instructors of record) play a pivotal role in modeling, mentoring, and assisting practicum teachers as they take up and try out new repertoires of instructional strategies, make sense of subject matter content instructionally, and, in general, acclimate to the realities of classroom life. University supervisors (teacher educators) also play an important role in this process, although their involvement may be much more indirect: holding regular face-to-face meetings outside the practicum placement, conducting teaching observations, and holding pre- and post-observation conferences. While on the surface this might seem like a natural and neutral site for the learning of L2 teaching—a real classroom, a mentor teacher, a teacher educator, and an eager practicum teacher—the practicum experience is not as straightforward as it might seem. Practicum teachers typically find themselves navigating a maze of institutionally and socially negotiated roles, values, and standards of conduct as they learn the texture of classroom life, struggle to develop conceptions of themselves as teachers, and attempt to function as 'real' teachers before they have the necessary expertise and/or competence to do so (Crookes, 2003; Farrell, 2006; Flowerdew, 1999; Gebhard, 1990, 2009; Johnson, 1996; Smagorinsky, Cook, Moore, Jackson, & Fry, 2004).

With its dual focus on the doing of teaching and the learning about teaching, most practicum experiences require some sort of structured reflective component, usually in the form of a reflection journal (Bailey, 1990; Gebhard & Oprandy, 1999). Within L2 teacher education, teacher reflection, or the narrative reconstruction of experience, has long been thought of as a productive mechanism for teachers to not only make sense of their learning and teaching experiences but also to make worthwhile changes in their teaching practices (Borg, 2006; Burns & Richards, 2009; Johnson & Golombek, 2011). As we mentioned in Chapter 1, we have argued that engagement in narrative activity influences how teachers come to understand what they are narrating about, and this involves a complex combination of description, explanation, analysis, interpretation, and construal of one's private reality as it is brought into the public sphere (Johnson & Golombek, 2011). A potentially powerful feature of written teacher reflection is the concretization of teachers' thoughts, feelings, and understandings, an opening up of sorts, of the 'meaningfulness' of teachers' experiences to social influence, giving teacher educators access to teachers' internal cognitive/emotional struggles and creating spaces for *responsive mediation* to address their immediate needs and/or concerns.

In the early days of our work as teacher educators, that is before the widespread use of Internet-based communication, we asked our practicum teachers to keep handwritten reflection journals as a means of recounting and reflecting on the practicum experience. We read and responded to their journals periodically but the time delay between the doing of teaching and our discussions about their teaching was difficult to overcome. Today, the immediacy and dialogic nature of Internet-based communication forums, such as private, asynchronous blogs, creates the sense that we are 'right there, in the thick of things' with our practicum teachers. And while we recognize that blog entries, like the old-fashioned handwritten journals, represent the reconstruction of experience, how our teachers constitute themselves in 'story' has as much to do with the construction of self as it does with the purpose for and the specific time and place in which the story was constructed (Bakhtin, 1981; Holquist, 1990). Like their handwritten predecessors, practicum dialogic blogs represent 'small stories' (Georgakopoulou, 2006) and reflect the emotional, moral, and relational dimensions of how teachers hold and use their knowledge (Elbaz, 1983). For practicum teachers, the process of blogging about their practicum experiences imparts significance to particular instructional events and concretizes the meanings infused in those events. As mentioned above, this opens a window into their lived worlds and such access allows teacher educators to mediate and support their learning and development.

Of course, we recognize that there have been legitimate critiques of reflective journals as a means of fostering substantive teacher reflection and/or professional development (Akbari, 2007; Hobbs, 2007; Mann & Walsh, 2013; Strand, 2006), particularly when teachers' motives are simply to get a good grade or to tell the teacher educator what she thinks she wants to hear. However, we find educational value in the dialogic nature of blogging during the practicum experience. The blog creates an ongoing, co-constructed, shared communicative space for *interthinking* that is mutually built on the foundations of shared knowledge and motives. Each time a blog entry is entered into that space, the dialogue between the teacher and teacher educator gets reconstituted as they negotiate their way through whatever instructional event they are focusing on. In order to maintain an *intermental development zone* (IDZ), as Mercer (2000) argues, the teacher educator must provide mediation that creates conditions so that teachers can operate just beyond their current capabilities as well as consolidate their jointly reconstructed and/or rearticulated experiences into new abilities and understandings.

Today when we engage in dialogic blogging we are not only interested in how our practicum teachers are reconstructing their lived experiences, we are actively seeking to create conditions for learning and development. We do this in various ways: by providing *responsive mediation* directed at potential *growth points*, by linking lived experience (*everyday concepts*) with formal knowledge (*academic concepts*), by modeling expert teacher thinking, by framing our expert understanding of the subject matter content to be taught, and by offering a range of instructional resources to teach it. Furthermore, we want our practicum teachers to become consciously aware of what they are experiencing while simultaneously developing a future-orientated focus in their thinking, so they can become more purposeful when planning and enacting future L2 instruction.

In this chapter we examine engagement in private, asynchronous online exchanges via a blog between a novice ESL teacher and a teacher educator during a 15-week MA TESL teaching practicum.[1] We present the case of Kyla, who struggles to construct a teaching persona that will enable her to function successfully while teaching an oral communication course for international teaching assistants (ITA). Analyses of her blog entries highlight how she expresses this struggle through emotive language that shifts from overconfidence to deep disappointment. The blog exchanges between

Kyla and the teacher educator function as an important mediational space, providing Kyla with emotional support, offering her concrete instructional strategies, and modeling expert thinking, all of which work in consort to assist Kyla as she overcomes the dissonance she is experiencing between her imagined teaching persona and the instructional experiences she is attempting to create for the ITAs in her practicum placement.

The teaching practicum blog

As a requirement of the practicum, Kyla posted weekly online blog entries that were read and responded to by the practicum supervisor (teacher educator) (45 total posts). Kyla also met weekly with the teacher educator, who observed her teaching on two separate occasions, held pre- and post-observation meetings, and provided support and feedback throughout the practicum through both face-to-face meetings and the practicum blog. The blog data, while asynchronous in nature, are presented side-by-side to emphasize their dialogic nature. Each time Kyla posted an entry, the teacher educator posted a response. There were several occasions (12 total) when Kyla posted a follow-up entry to which the teacher educator responded again. In the data extracts presented below, the bold-faced text and connecting lines utilize the methodological techniques of sociocultural discourse analysis (Mercer, 2004) by capturing how language is being used as a social mode of thinking and illustrates the quality and character of *interthinking* on the linguistic, psychological, and cultural levels. The teacher educator (right column) takes up dimensions of Kyla's blog entries (left column), building a contextual foundation for their exchanges, guiding her thinking as they jointly reconstruct Kyla's understanding of her experiences, and assisting Kyla as she works to resolve the cognitive/emotional dissonance she is experiencing.

The practicum context

Kyla's practicum placement was a graduate-level English as a second language (ESL) oral language course for ITAs taught by an experienced ESL instructor (mentor teacher). All of the ITAs were highly accomplished in their academic fields of study, mostly from Asian cultures, and required to take this course because of their performance on a university-mandated oral language proficiency test. The ITA course was institutionally defined as an opportunity for ITAs to improve their overall oral language proficiency while coming to understand the psyche of American undergraduates and learn about the instructional norms for teaching discipline-specific large-enrollment general education courses. Kyla was fairly inexperienced in this instructional context, whereas the teacher educator held a great deal of knowledge concerning the goals and curriculum of this specific ITA program and research concerning ITA issues.

Kyla's pre-understandings

When Kyla entered the MA TESL program, she was technically not a novice teacher. She held a BA in elementary education and had limited experience teaching young boys who were labeled 'special needs' within an urban K–12 school setting. Interestingly, many of the boys were also English language learners whose learning difficulties were "wrapped up in who they are, their lack of English, and the impoverished neighborhoods they come from." Kyla described her undergraduate teacher education program as heavily front-loaded with "lots of theories and techniques about working with special needs children but very few opportunities to actually teach." She described her teaching philosophy as "connecting with the students, as people who were largely misunderstood by the institutional systems in which they found themselves." This social positioning Kyla related to her own experiences as a student in which she recalled screaming silently, "You don't know me! You don't know who I am!" upon hearing disparaging remarks made about her by her seventh grade teacher. She berated most of her own teachers for "placing labels on students" instead of attempting to see "the worth each brought into the classroom." She described herself as "a teacher that creates a safe environment where students could say what they want and be heard.... I want to create a space for each student where everything *they* believe in, and everything *they love* could be materialized so that it could be a source of motivation to their learning."[2]

Recognizing Kyla's pre-understandings

Atypical of the practicum experience, Kyla had an opportunity to teach a solo lesson quite early in the practicum because her mentor teacher was unexpectedly called away due to a family emergency. After the lesson, which Kyla describes in mostly emotive terms, she differentiates her teaching style from that of her mentor teacher, who in an earlier blog post she had described as "intimidating for students" and "as an authority figure rather than a peer." This blog post provides insight into Kyla's *perezhivanie*, or how she experienced this lesson, positioning herself as successfully facilitating greater student participation than her mentor teacher as a result of her 'relaxed and comfortable' teaching persona.

Excerpt 1

Kyla	**Teacher Educator**
I did some things differently than from what my master teacher would have done. I expected a lot of **participation from the students** and I did this by having **a very relaxed and comfortable environment for the students.**	Well, if it **felt good**, it probably **was good.**
	How do you **engage students** with the text in ways that highlight its essential features?
This class was **so mellow and fun that I completely forgot that I was teaching**... I don't know if that was bad or good, but this teaching experience **felt really good.**	Yes, you need to have **a clear goal in mind, model what you want them to do, create comfortable spaces for them to do it, and support them as they carry out the activities.**

In this blog exchange, the teacher educator validates Kyla's reported success, but then lays the groundwork for *interthinking* by encouraging her to consider the pedagogical reasoning behind her instructional activities and reiterating her instructional responsibilities as a teacher. In particular, her rhetorical choice to ask the question, "*How do you engage students with the text in ways that highlight its essential features?*" is directed at Kyla's rather underdeveloped reference to "*a lot of participation from the students.*" The teacher educator thus reorients Kyla's attention instead to the substance of student participation in relation to the content of the lesson in order to encourage her to express her reasoning through the particulars of this instructional event.

The teacher educator is responsive to Kyla's somewhat naïve claim of "*I completely forgot I was teaching*" by explicitly framing the way an expert might think about the responsibilities of a teacher, including a series of directives: "*have a clear goal in mind, model what you want them to do, create comfortable spaces for them to do it, and support them as they carry out the activities.*" The expert-novice nature of their exchange is obvious; Kyla focuses on how she felt about her first solo teaching experience while the teacher educator, in response, creates a more expert frame of reference by redirecting Kyla's attention toward considering the rationale and reasoning behind her actions, as well as offering her a more expert conceptualization of a teaching persona. The teacher educator's response to Kyla's blog post is also interesting since from her own *perezhivanie* regarding practicum teachers, she is well aware of the naiveté that novice teachers typically bring to the practicum experience: criticize the old, imagine yourself as better, assume good teaching is simply a matter of being friendly, and focus on how the lesson felt rather than on what the students may have learned. How Kyla takes up/does not take up this mediation is not readily evident in her subsequent blog entries.

Recognizing and responding to Kyla's perezhivanie

The following blog exchange occurred after the teacher educator's first observation. The lesson had not gone well, which Kyla describes once again in mostly emotive terms, as she struggled to, in her words, "*balance my mellow and nice attitude with being the 'teacher.'*"

Excerpt 2

Kyla

So, on Monday **I was really disappointed** in myself for doing such **a horrible job**. I noticed myself get **pretty nervous** while teaching... and it also didn't help when **I wasn't completely prepared.** Just because I was nervous, didn't mean I should have **jumped from one idea to the next.**
In reflecting back, I think I set off this frantic pace for myself in my head which made me want to keep rushing things. I realized that one of the things that I needed that day was **understanding what my purpose was...**

To tell you the truth, that was one of the criticisms that my mentor professor had given me in the past. She noticed how when I teach in the classroom. I have a tendency **to appear unsure of myself.** But by the end of that year, she said I was able to nicely balance **my mellow and nice attitude with being the 'teacher'.** I guess again I was **a bit disappointed in myself** because in the process of thinking of my students, I, in my rusty state of teaching, reverted back to my old ways.

Teacher Educator

No one expects you to be 'the perfect teacher' right off the bat – that's what the internship is for– so you can try some things out in a semi-real context, reflect on it, learn from it, and move forward.

It is one thing to relate to students as a fellow student but you need to establish **a teaching persona** in which you **look and sound like you know what you are doing.** Acting 'sheepish' or 'coy' or 'silly' may get a laugh out of them, but you need to establish **a sense of authority** in the classroom-I'm not talking domination here or a power trip, but developing a **strong sense of self**, that you **know what you are doing, you know where you are going, you know and care about them** as people, as future ITAs, and as L2 learners, and together you are **working toward a common goal.**

All lessons have some sort of **organization** – depending on what you are going to teach, where, to whom, why, and when... **so consider these issues** as you plan out your next lesson. Today's could have been as simple as *'Today we are going to focus on language that is used to get people to do things --- this sort of language is used all the time, in lots of different contexts, but it is especially important in teaching, because in teaching, ITAs and/or teachers are always trying to get students to do things--- so first we are going to do X, and then Y, and then I'm going to put you in groups and ask you to do Z, and then your groups will share ZZ with us ---'*

Kyla's emotional appraisal of her teaching activity is a critical move in her and the teacher educator's co-construction of the *intermental development zone* (IDZ). Kyla's highly negative emotions most likely point to an area of her cognition as a learner of teaching that needs to be developed. By being attuned to Kyla's emotional state, the teacher educator validates the normalcy of what she is experiencing by reminding her that she need not be *"perfect,"* that her learning to teach is part of the developmental purpose of the practicum itself. Moreover, by attuning to Kyla's emotional appraisals, the teacher educator can begin to ascertain the kind of mediation that is needed at this point. Kyla's highly negative self-appraisals are accompanied by comments that suggest a need for other-regulation in the IDZ: her nervousness was exacerbated by her lack of preparation and lack of understanding of her instructional purpose. The teacher educator's mediation is responsive to Kyla's very practically oriented emerging concerns, that is, struggling to enact her imagined teaching persona of being a mellow teacher while carrying out a well-organized and focused lesson. From the teacher educator's point of view, she is trying to initiate "new understanding in situations where [Kyla's] prior or pre-understanding is inadequate" (Miller, 2011, p. 380). Kyla's struggle with being a mellow and well-organized teacher is not surprising, as from her pre-understanding, mellow and organized may seem to be contradictions—organization being synonymous with rigidity. However, the teacher educator uses this contradiction as a potential *growth point* by offering an expert characterization of a teaching persona in which mellow and organized are analogues. She also responds to Kyla's realization that what was missing from her lesson was an *"understanding what my purpose was."* The teacher educator emphasizes the need for *"a sense of authority"* and *"a strong sense of self"* as being linked to characteristics of an expert teaching persona: *"know where you are going."* In addition, the teacher educator continues to stay attuned to Kyla's concern about jumping *"from one idea to the next,"* setting off at a *"frantic pace,"* and *"rushing things"* by emphasizing organization as a fundamental concept of good instruction and then modeling expert instructional talk that enacts how her lessons could have been organized. The teacher educator's voicing of how Kyla could have introduced the lesson frames a way to make her purpose and the organization of the lesson explicit for the ITAs. Once again, we see the teacher educator attuned to Kyla's *perezhivanie* and her recognition of a seemingly shattered idealized teaching persona and lack of self-regulation by responding with explicit mediation.

The teacher educator knows, from her own *perezhivanie* regarding practicum teachers, that Kyla has to bounce back emotionally and teach sufficiently well in the next class for the students' sake as well as for Kyla's emotional and professional well-being. Being too implicit in her mediation for Kyla, at this point in time, may simply be too frustrating for her. The teacher educator thus attempts to support Kyla as she works through the emotion connected to the contradiction existing between her idealized teaching persona and instructional behaviors/activities that align with enacting that persona. The teacher educator thus has a specific developmental goal in mind: to provide Kyla with a concretization of what a more expert teaching persona looks and sounds like. She does this by explicitly reiterating the characteristics of a more expert teaching persona while also modeling expert instructional talk for carrying out a more organized lesson with explicit instructional objectives.

Seeking assistance

Prior to her next solo lesson, Kyla and the teacher educator had collaboratively designed a lesson plan on ITA office hour interactions that they both believed would enable her to enact a more organized lesson and her imagined teaching persona. Unfortunately, as is often the case in real teaching, the ITAs had not completed the assigned homework, which left them unprepared for several of the activities Kyla had planned. In this blog exchange, Kyla expresses frustration and anxiety over their failure to participate in the lesson. She describes herself as "*slowly doing more of a monologic lecture,*" a teaching style that is contrary to her imagined teaching persona and which, in terms of her *perezhivanie*, she perceives in a highly negative light. In essence, her response to this lesson signals a loss of self-regulation. However, this time she makes a choice to ask a series of questions, and in doing so her motive is to explicitly seek assistance from the teacher educator.

Excerpt 3

Kyla

I guess I'm **really bummed** and **disappointed** with today, only because **I tried really hard to make the lesson meaningful for the students**, and **I felt I didn't fully do that**... But **what do you do when your students are not prepared for the material**? What happens then?... **What does a good teacher do with the lesson plan, when the students are unprepared**?

Kyla

When things aren't going exactly as planned, **I end up freezing up**, being **unable to think of other things I could do**. And in the attempt to come up with something, and having multiple thoughts racing through my mind, **I end up fumbling over my words** even more and **I start jumping from one thing to another**...

Teacher Educator

Well, believe it or not, **this happens all the time**...... so, **you could have** listed the different purposes of office hours on the blackboard (to ask a content question, to get help with a problem, to explain why something wasn't handed in, to contest a grade, etc) and then asked them to talk about what role the TA would have to play as the purpose changes...

You could have shared an experience you had in office hours (real or made up) and asked them how they would have handled it differently...

You could have asked them to speculate on what sort of small talk might be appropriate in office hours...

You could have had them make up a problem/issue that might be resolved in an office hours setting, present it to the class, and have the rest of the class come up with different ways to resolve the problem/issue...

Once again, the teacher educator begins by being responsive to Kyla's emotive response, offering emotional support that normalizes what she just experienced. However, the teacher educator then becomes highly explicit, as she recognizes Kyla's need for other-regulation. She answers Kyla's abstract question of what a 'good' teacher does when students are unprepared with concrete examples of what Kyla could have done in the lesson she just experienced, thus grounding her mediation in the particulars of Kyla's lived experience. Kyla responds in a follow-up blog post, by continuing to express frustration with her inability to "*think on my feet*." She repeats some self-characterizations presented in Excerpt 2 about "*jumping from one thing to another*," but whereas in the previous excerpt the jumping around occurred because she was unprepared, in this excerpt she was prepared but the students were not. Kyla begins to offer an explanation for *why* she is struggling to gain a sense of self-regulation over her teaching—when faced with the unexpected, she does not know how to respond instructionally. In a sense, Kyla has now come to realize what she does not know and explicitly seeks help. As the teacher educator and Kyla reconstruct their contextualized joint mental activity, or *interthinking*, in more expert terms, Kyla's exploration and realization of what she does not know and needs to know marks an important step in regaining a sense of self-regulation over her teaching.

Supporting the development of new understandings

In her final solo lesson, observed by the teacher educator, Kyla describes herself as consciously slowing down and feeling more comfortable with not completing the lesson as planned. She describes how the teacher educator's instructional strategies actually enabled her to regulate her own thinking while she was teaching. She evaluates her instructional activities and is able to say what she should have done, as well as what she did.

Excerpt 4

Kyla

Even while I was teaching on Wednesday, and I wasn't able to start on the activity as I had first intended, **I kept telling myself to slow down**, and be okay with continuing on Friday. While I was doing the first half of the lesson, **I started getting flustered** at one point because **things I thought weren't going as I planned in my head**, but **I purposely tried my best** to remain calm and still slow down. **I kept reminding myself** that it was OKAY to not have finished the class **as I had initially planned it**.

Today in class, we reviewed closings and most of **the students appeared to have grasped the essential elements** of closings. However, **I did realize that I should have been more concrete** with the students.

For Friday's class, **I'm very proud** of myself for **sticking with my objectives**. I think **before, I let the content rule over the objectives, when the content should have illustrated or supplemented my objectives**. This time around **I purposefully memorized my objectives** so **that it would be running through my mind as I taught**.

Teacher Educator

What **a pleasure** to watch you teach today!

You provided a **nice overview of the lesson**, you **situated it** nicely in what had come before, **why it is important**, and you provided **concrete and detailed directions** so that the students knew exactly what they would be asked to do.

At the end of the session it was clear to me that **they not only got what you were trying to teach them, they were able to do it**. You also **presented yourself as a confident, genuine, interested teacher** who is competent to teach them but also willing to work and learn with them.

Throughout this blog post, Kyla recounts the kind of *private speech* (Vygotsky, 1987) that she used to mediate herself and her tendencies to rush and jump around in her activity of teaching. She recalls, "*I kept telling myself...,*" "*I purposely tried my best...,*" "*I kept reminding myself....*" Compared to earlier posts in which her emotion reflected her lack of self-regulation, in this post she demonstrates her self-regulation through more expert pedagogical reasoning: "*it was OKAY to not have finished the class as I had initially planned,*" "*the students appeared to have grasped the essential elements,*" "*before I let the content rule over the objectives, when the content should have illustrated or supplemented the objectives.*" Kyla still expresses emotions, but they are positive ones of satisfaction, and they index cognitive/emotional congruence between her internal conception of teaching and her activity of teaching. The teacher educator positively evaluates what Kyla did and commends her for establishing a more expert teaching persona, "*confident, genuine, interested teacher,*" one that is more in line with what the teacher educator has all along been attempting to assist her in developing.

Obuchenie, responsive mediation, and Kyla's emerging development

If we consider these asynchronous exchanges in terms of *obuchenie*, the actions and intentions of the teacher educator are predicated on recognizing Kyla's *perezhivanie*. She does, in fact, acknowledge Kyla's expressions of cognitive/emotional dissonance and emphasizes the 'normalness' of what she was experiencing/feeling. However, she also provides expert characterizations of the contradictions Kyla is facing and offers concrete suggestions for how she might rethink and reenact her teaching practices. She pushes Kyla to restructure how she thinks about her imagined teaching persona. In maintaining an IDZ, the teacher educator's mediation is emergent, contingent, and responsive to Kyla's immediate needs, but she clearly takes on the role of expert-other, consistently soothing Kyla's emotional responses while gently pushing her to consider alternatives and then repeatedly reframing Kyla's novice characterizations of her teaching in more expert terms on both a practical level (i.e., *what to do*) and a conceptual level (i.e., *why she is doing what she is doing*).

For Kyla, she is able to bring into conscious awareness her understandings of and struggles with her imagined teaching persona. When her lessons do not go as planned, the resulting emotional turmoil leads to expressions of disappointment and a crisis of self-confidence. However, the co-constructed IDZ that emerged throughout their blog exchanges functions as a structured mediational space where she is able to make her tacit thoughts and beliefs explicit, create a sense of coherence out of the tension she is experiencing, and seek and receive *responsive mediation* from the teacher educator.

It is significant to note that in spite of the mediation that the teacher educator offered through the collaborative preparation of a lesson plan, Kyla, like many new teachers, struggled with the unanticipated aspects inherent in teaching. This reinforces the idea of how *responsive mediation* as part of the complex process of learning to teach is dependent on the particular practice in which we are engaged. The teacher educator's mediation of the lesson plan may have enabled Kyla to begin to understand what she was teaching as content and how to teach that content with instructional foci and activities in mind. Creating a lesson plan (the ideal) is one activity, but enacting that lesson plan (the material) is another, especially as the circumstances in which a teacher enacts a lesson plan can differ from what is anticipated when planning (e.g., students will read assigned readings) or be unanticipated. Because the realities of teaching are messy and unexpected, it is this dynamic enactment of teaching that teacher educators cannot mediate directly, and that makes the *when, where*, and *how responsive mediation* occurs matter in L2 teacher education.

In this chapter we have highlighted how dialogic engagement in a private, asynchronous practicum blog exposes the emergent nature of *responsive mediation*. Kyla's cognitive/emotional dissonance emerged out of the lived experience of teaching two lessons during the early stages of her practicum placement: the first, which, as she retells it, matched her imagined teaching persona, and the second, which did not. Yet blogging about the incongruence between these two lessons enabled the teacher educator to recognize this as a potential *growth point* for Kyla and target her mediation accordingly. It is also obvious that while assisting Kyla in understanding and developing a more expert teaching persona, other issues of quality instruction emerged: lesson organization, unanticipated (lack of) student engagement, articulating appropriate instructional objectives, and so on. This reminds us, as teacher educators, of the inherent complexities of teaching as well as the inherent complexities of learning-to-teach. Our mediation in this process must be emergent, contingent, and responsive to the immediate needs of our teachers, but it must also be directed at the upper limits during the ZPD, placing our teachers ahead of themselves while providing emotional, cognitive, and material support and expertise as our teachers work towards being and becoming more competent L2 teachers.

While an insider look into the practicum blog makes visible what teacher learning looks like as it is unfolding, and the role of *responsive mediation* in supporting teacher learning and development, we recognize that it remains very much a limited view. While we isolated our analysis to the practice of using practicum blogs, these blog exchanges were going on against a rich mediational backdrop, including but not limited to face-to-face meetings between Kyla and the teacher educator, Kyla's interactions with her mentor teacher, and obviously her daily interactions with the ITAs in her practicum placement. What is quite obvious in the practicum blog is the concretization of Kyla's lived instructional experiences, the meanings she associated with these experiences, the emotional/cognitive dissonance she experienced and the quality and character of the *responsive mediation* that emerges as Kyla and the teacher educator create and sustain an IDZ over the course of this particular practice of L2 teacher education.

Notes

1 Some data extracts reprinted with permission from Cambridge University Press. Johnson, K. E. & Golombek, P. R. (2013). A tale of two mediations: Tracing the dialectics of cognition, emotion, and activity in teachers' practicum blogs. In G. Barkhuizen (Ed.), *Narrative Research in Applied Linguistics* (pp. 85–104). Cambridge: Cambridge University Press.

2 All single-quote extracts were taken, with permission, from Kyla's *learning-to-teach history* and *portfolio*, requirements of her first-semester MA TESL methods course. The supervisor of her practicum was the same teacher educator who taught the methods course.

References

Akbari, R. (2007). Reflections on reflections: A critical appraisal of reflective practices in L2 teacher education. *System, 35*, 192–207.

Bailey, K. M. (1990). The use of diary studies in teacher education programs. In J. C. Richards & D. Nunan (Eds.), *Second language teacher education* (pp. 43–61). New York: Cambridge University Press.

Bakhtin, M. M. (1981). *The dialogic imagination: Four essays by M.M. Bakhtin*. Austin: University of Texas Press.

Borg, S. (2006). *Teacher cognition and language education: Research and practice*. London: Continuum.

Burns, A., & Richards, J. C. (Eds.) (2009). *The Cambridge guide to second language teacher education*. New York: Cambridge University Press.

Crookes, G. (2003). *The practicum in TESOL: Professional development through teaching practice*. New York: Cambridge University Press.

Elbaz, F. (1983). *Teaching thinking: A study of practical knowledge*. London: Crown Helm.

Farrell, T. C. (2006). *The first year of language teaching: Insights and perspectives for the first year*. London: Equinox.

Flowerdew, J. (1999). The practicum in L2 teacher education: A Hong Kong case study. *TESOL Quarterly, 33*(1), 141–145.

Gebhard, J. G. (1990). Interaction in a teaching practicum. In J. C. Richards & D. Nunan (Eds.), *Second language teacher education* (pp. 118–131). New York: Cambridge University Press.

Gebhard, J. G. (2009). The practicum. In J. C. Richards & A. Burns (Eds.), *The Cambridge guide to language teacher education* (pp. 250–258). New York: Cambridge University Press.

Gebhard, J. G., & Oprandy, R. (1999). *Language teaching awareness: A guide to exploring beliefs and practices*. New York: Cambridge University Press.

Georgakopoulou, A. (2006). Thinking big with small stories in narrative and identity analysis. *Narrative Inquiry, 16*, 122–130.

Hobbs, V. (2007). Faking it or hating it: Can reflective practice be forced? *Reflective Practice, 8*, 405–417.

Holquist, M. (1990). *Dialogism. Bakhtin and his world.* London: Routledge.

Johnson, K. E. (1996). The vision versus the reality: The tensions of the TESOL practicum. In D. Freeman & J. C. Richards (Eds.), *Teacher learning in language teaching* (pp. 30–49). New York: Cambridge University Press.

Johnson, K. E., & Golombek, P. R. (Eds.) (2011). *Research on second language teacher education: A sociocultural perspective on professional development.* New York: Routledge.

Mann, S., & Walsh, S. (2013). RP or 'RIP': A critical perspective on reflective practice. *Applied Linguistics Review, 4*, 291–315.

Mercer, N. (2000). *Words & minds: How we use language to think together.* London: Routledge.

Mercer, N. (2004). Sociocultural discourse analysis: Analyzing classroom talk as a social mode of thinking. *Journal of Applied Linguistics, 1*(2), 137–168.

Miller, R. (2011). *Vygotsky in perspective.* Cambridge: Cambridge University Press.

Smagorinsky, P., Cook, L. S., Moore, C., Jackson, A., & Fry, P. G. (2004). Tensions in learning to teach: Accommodation and the development of teaching identity. *Journal of Teacher Education, 55*(1), 8–24.

Strand, K. (2006). Learning to inquire: Teacher research in undergraduate teacher training. *Journal of Music Teacher Education, 31*, 29–42.

Vygotsky, L. S. (1987). Thinking and speech (N. Minick, Trans.). In R. W. Reiber (Ed.), *The collected works of L. S. Vygotsky, Vol. 3. Problems of the theory and history of Psychology* (pp. 37–285). New York: Plenum Press.

7

DEVELOPING PEDAGOGICAL CONTENT KNOWLEDGE

"How do I teach something I myself don't fully grasp?"

One of the most persistent challenges facing teacher education programs is overcoming the traditional theory/practice dichotomy. As longtime teacher educators, we are sensitive to claims that while teachers may value what they read, wrote, and talked about in their teacher education programs, they recall few opportunities to engage in the activities of actual teaching, sometimes not until the culminating internship/practicum near the end of their degree programs. In designing the practices in our teacher education programs we continually seek to address this challenge. And while we recognize the value of early field experiences (Anderson & Graebell, 1990; Maxie, 2001; Whipp, 2003), given our sociocultural theoretical stance, we are adamant that initial learning-to-teach experiences must be mediated by experts. Simply placing new teachers in classrooms as observers, tutors, or even instructors may do little to support the development of teacher/teaching expertise. As we have stated throughout this book, we believe that learning-to-teach is not, and should not be, a process of 'discovery learning' or 'learning by doing,' but rather learning that is intentional, deliberate, and goal-directed by experts who are skilled at moving teachers toward more theoretically and pedagogically sound instructional practices and greater levels of professional expertise. Therefore, by design our practices present relevant *academic concepts* to teachers in ways that bring these concepts to bear on their everyday experiences as learners, teachers, and learners of teaching. This involves making meaningful connections between *academic concepts*, *everyday concepts*, and their imagined enactments and identities as future language teachers as they participate in a range of authentic activities associated with language teaching.

It is our belief that the goal of any teacher education practice is to replace the traditional theory/practice dichotomy with the more fluid construct of *praxis* (Freire, 1970; Johnson, 2006) or "the integration of conceptual knowledge and practical activity with the goal of stimulating change or [concept] development" (Lantolf, 2009, p. 272). Ultimately, we believe it is this transformative process of making sense of everyday experiences through the theoretical constructs of the broader professional discourse community and vice versa that will radically change how teachers come to think about and carry out their work.

The practice that we highlight in this chapter, the extended team teaching project, began as an attempt to reconceptualize the traditional microteaching simulation in which teacher candidates plan and teach 'mini-lessons' in front of their peers as a component of a methodology course. Originating in the 1960s, microteaching emerged out of a technicist view of teaching with the promise of greater efficiency in the training of teachers. The Stanford Model (Politzer, 1969) ran novice teachers through a cycle of plan, teach, observe, and critique short micro lessons (5–10 minutes) followed by a new cycle of replan, reteach, reobserve, and re-critique. The content of each cycle consisted of a specific set of teaching behaviors that were first modeled, then practiced, critiqued, and then practiced again. At that time, teaching was conceptualized as consisting of a discreet set of behaviors that could be broken down into its smallest parts, studied, practiced, and mastered largely through imitation and repetition. In addition, microteaching was deemed to be a more efficient way of acclimating novices to the 'real world' of teaching, as opposed to the lengthy apprenticeship model of 'sink or swim' once they entered schools.

Even after a rejection of this technicist view of teaching and the emergence of the reflective teaching movement in the 1980s (Zeichner & Liston, 1996), the microteaching simulation remains a staple of most methodology courses. Its newer permutations include opportunities for systematic reflection that enable teacher candidates to move beyond instructional practices based on intuition or routine toward those that are guided by careful self-examination and critical reflection on the broader social and institutional contexts in which teaching takes place (Farrell, 2008; Richards & Farrell, 2005: Roberts, 1998; Wallace, 1996). And while these more progressive forms of the microteaching simulation are generally perceived positively by teacher candidates, both in the general education (MacLeod, 1987) and L2 teacher education literature (Burns & Richards, 2009; Farrell, 2008), the fact remains that the learners aren't real, the subject matter isn't real, and the context in which the microteaching is carried out isn't real. In this sense, microteaching does not simulate 'real' teaching, largely because the social, institutional, and historical factors that are endemic to 'real' teaching are simply not present. Void of the many factors that shape the complex nature of 'real' teaching, we believe the microteaching simulation, as a practice in L2 teacher education, is inherently flawed, though we recognize that for some teacher educators, it may be the only teaching opportunity that their local circumstances allow.

Within the context of a TESL methodology course, the extended team teaching project requires a team of three or four teachers to engage in a series of activities designed to prepare them to teach a 50- to 75-minute lesson in an actual English as a second language (ESL) class. Completed over a 15-week semester and counting for 40 percent of the overall grade, the project creates varied and multiple *structured mediational spaces* for the team to develop a sense of the instructional setting in which they will teach, to conceptualize and materialize the subject matter content to be taught, to enact an initial lesson *in*, *for*, and *with* their classmates and the teacher educator, to teach a revised lesson in the actual ESL class, and finally, through critical reflection and dialogic interaction, to become consciously aware of the theoretical and pedagogical reasoning for their instructional practices.

Before moving on to a detailed description of the project itself, it is important to revisit what we mean by *structured mediational spaces*. Mediation, as we discussed in Chapter 2, is central to our understanding of and support for the development of teacher/teaching expertise. Some have argued that simply by being in the world, one is mediated by it—a notion closer to the constructs of *acculturation* or *socialization* from social learning theory (Chaiklin & Lave, 1996; Lave & Wenger, 1991; Wenger, 1998). However, from our Vygotskian sociocultural stance, the quality and character of that mediation is critical. We do not want our teachers to simply experience teaching—we want to mediate their learning-to-teach experiences, support their attempts at enacting teaching by creating new circumstances, or *the social situation of development*, where the development of teacher/teaching expertise can occur. We seek to push them past their everyday notions of teachers and teaching and to accomplish instructional goals that are beyond their current level of development. *Structured mediational spaces*, in one sense, reflect the Vygotskian construct of *prolepsis*, or paraphrased nicely by van Lier (2004), "to create invitational structures and spaces for learners to step into and grow into" (p. 162). By design, the extended team teaching project assumes that our teachers know more than they actually know, and can do more than they actually can do. In fact, in end-of-semester ratings of teaching effectiveness, our teachers often comment that at the start of the semester they felt both terrified and excited by the prospects of teaching an actual ESL class, many claiming they had few clear ideas about how to prepare for or teach an actual ESL lesson. The *structured mediational spaces* embedded in the project and the teacher/teacher educator dialogic interactions that emerge in these spaces create opportunities for the team and the teacher educators to *think together*, and to stay attuned to each other's changing states of knowledge, emotions, and understanding in an *intermental development zone* (IDZ). During the IDZ, the teacher educator is able to provide the necessary assistance so that the team can 'step into' being L2 teachers while simultaneously consolidating their experiences throughout the project as new abilities and understandings. The IDZs that emerge in these *structured mediational spaces* create opportunities for the teacher educator to make explicit her expert thinking, and to responsively adapt to the team's immediate understandings, needs, and/or concerns.

As we mentioned in Chapter 2, these *structured mediational spaces* create 'safe zones' where teachers are able to 'play' with being and becoming L2 teachers. Therefore, by design, the extended team teaching project creates various and multiple *structured mediational spaces* in which teachers, with assistance, are asked to 'jump above' themselves as they 'play' in 'safe zones' and ultimately create rich experiences that can be reinterpreted for future teaching activity.

The extended team teaching project

The teachers who typically enroll in the TESL methodology course are first-semester MA TESL students, undergraduate TESL minors, or undergraduate College of Education majors seeking a state-endorsed TESL certificate. Over the past eight years, we have received permission from almost all of the teachers who have enrolled in this course to access the 'data' that was produced (described below) as a result of the project. For several teams, teaching different content, under different instructional circumstances, we have examined their data by tracing teacher learning and development as it unfolds throughout the various stages of the project. Additionally, we have been able to capture the quality and character of the teacher educator/teacher dialogic interactions that emerge at key stages of the project (see Johnson, 2015; Johnson & Arshavskaya, 2011; Johnson & Dellagnelo, 2013; Johnson & Worden, 2014). Below, we provide a brief description of each stage of the project followed by a description of the particular team we selected to analyze in this chapter.

Initially, the team observes one session of the ESL class they will eventually teach in order to develop an understanding of the instructional setting, including required assignments and assessments, as well as the students' L2 proficiency, goals, and motivation. For many of our teachers, this is their first entrée into the world of teaching ESL and their reactions often become rich fodder for discussion and consideration as they begin to prepare the initial lesson plan. Many expect instruction to focus on the more traditional approaches that focus on the language itself (i.e., grammar, pronunciation, vocabulary) rather than language as constituted in subject matter content (content-based) or as social practice (Gee, 1999; Halliday, 1985; Johnson, 2009). Some are intrigued, while others are intimidated by the vast array of languages and cultures represented in an ESL versus an English as a foreign language (EFL) or foreign language (FL) instructional context.

Early in the semester, each team member participates in six one-hour tutoring sessions with an ESL student who is enrolled in the assigned ESL class. This activity creates an opportunity for extensive informal tutor/tutee interaction in which they provide assistance on relevant course assignments and/or other L2 learning priorities identified by the ESL student. The tutoring experience has proven to be critical in both planning and teaching the eventual lesson because team members gained invaluable information about the ESL course from their interactions with their tutees and they are assured of at least one familiar face in the ESL class that they will eventually teach. A three- to four-page final reflection paper is required in which they reflect on what they learned about L2 learners, L2 learning, and L2 tutoring at the conclusion of the tutoring experience. The teacher educator reads and responds substantively to the tutoring reflection papers.

During the lesson planning stage, the team has both face-to-face and virtual meetings with each other, the instructor of the ESL class, and the teacher educator as they co-construct an initial lesson plan. The content of the lesson plan reflects what is listed on the course syllabus for the day they are scheduled to teach. This often creates tension, as the team typically needs to negotiate their collective understanding of the subject matter content they are expected to teach and then materialize it in the form of a lesson plan. Typically, the initial lesson plan is comprised of a set of procedures and/or activities, but often lacks a coherent conceptual understanding of the subject matter content to be taught or appropriate instructional strategies to teach it. These issues typically become the focus of much of the teacher/teacher educator dialogic interaction during the co-construction of the initial lesson plan.

The team then participates in a one-hour video-recorded *practice teach* in which they teach their lesson in the TESL methodology course. The *practice teach* allows the team to not only enact the lesson but also to externalize their conceptualization of the lesson and thus lay it open for social mediation. This occurs as the teacher educator and fellow classmates regularly halt instruction in order to ask questions, provide feedback, and/or make suggestions. Moreover, since evaluative comments invariably creep into this activity, their classmates are prompted to focus on how they experienced the lesson as students, rather than what the team could or should have done. The dialogic interaction that emerges in this activity is instrumental in assisting the team as they reconceptualize their lesson plan to better meet the instructional goals they had envisioned and to align their instructional activities with how their classmates experienced their lesson.

A week later the team teaches the revised lesson plan in the actual ESL class. During the *actual teach* the team typically makes many in-flight decisions as they realize that in the activity of actual teaching they need to alter and/or adjust their plans according to how the ESL students respond to and engage in their instructional activities. The teacher educator attends and video records the lesson but does not intervene.

Within 48 hours, the team participates in an audio-recorded *stimulated recall session* in which they watch and discuss the video-recorded *actual teach* with the teacher educator.[1] Team members are encouraged to stop the recording whenever they want to comment on the lesson. The teacher educator also stops the recording to ask questions, to allow the team to reflect on critical moments in the lesson, and to offer suggestions. Once again, this activity allows for extensive externalization of the team's thinking, and often of their emotional struggles and triumphs as well. More often than not, the team engages in a collective 'in-hindsight' reconstruction of the lesson or articulates new insights about themselves as teachers and the activity of actually teaching. The *stimulated recall session* also creates opportunities for the teacher educator to provide mediation that is intentional and deliberate, with the goal of enabling the team to gain an expert's perspective on the subject matter content they taught and/or the instructional practices they were attempting to carry out in the lesson.

Finally, after receiving digital copies of the *practice teach*, the *actual teach*, and the *stimulated recall session*, each team member is required to write a five- to seven-page reflection paper about the project, paying particular attention to what they have learned about themselves as teachers, about the activity of L2 teaching, and about this series of initial learning-to-teach experiences. The teacher educator reads and responds substantively to the final reflection papers.

Teaching parallelism in an ESL freshman composition course

In this chapter, we chronicle the experiences of four novice teachers as they experienced the extended team teaching project. The team—all American undergraduate students enrolled in a TESL minor: Deb (elementary education), Annie (international studies), Josh (Italian literature), and Ryan (English)—was taking the TESL methodology course as a requirement of their program of study. The team was assigned to teach a 75-minute lesson in a freshman ESL composition course that focused on the literary concept of *parallelism* and its uses in academic writing. Data from the team's extended team teaching project included broad transcriptions of (1) the video-recorded *practice teach*, (2) the video-recorded *actual teach*, (3) the audio-recorded *stimulated recall session*, and (4) the final reflection papers.[2]

The data extracts selected for inclusion in this chapter highlight the quality and character of the collaborative teaching/learning relationships (*obuchenie*) that unfolded throughout the project and the role of the teacher educator in providing *responsive mediation* that supported the teachers' emerging conceptualizations of and initial attempts at enacting L2 teaching. Analyzed from an emic perspective using sociocultural discourse analysis (Mercer, 2004), the data extracts highlight (marked in bold font) the linguistic instantiations of how engagement in the project exposed what these teachers brought to this learning-to-teach experience (*pre-understandings*) as well as how they were experiencing what they were learning (*perezhivanie*). The data also signal a potential *growth point*, where a contradiction or a sense of instability emerges, and capture the emergent, contingent, and responsive nature of the teacher educator's mediation. Within the *structured mediational spaces*, IDZs emerge as the team and the teacher educator co-construct new understandings in situations where their pre-understandings were inadequate. IDZs are maintained as the teacher educator assists the team in gaining an expert's understanding of the subject matter content being taught and appropriate pedagogical resources to teach it. In other instances, mediational means are offered but not taken up by the team, or taken up in unique ways as the team makes in-flight decisions in response to immediate instructional needs. Finally, through dialogic interaction and critical reflection, the team becomes consciously aware of the theoretical and pedagogical reasoning for their instructional practices.

Enacting *obuchenie*: Structured mediational spaces and responsive mediation

The team's pre-understandings of parallelism

All four teachers admitted in their reflection papers that initially they did not know what parallelism was or how to teach it. Their reflections expose their *perezhivanie* about having to teach unfamiliar content that, as native speakers of English, they had an intuitive (*everyday*) understanding of but lacked any sort of academic (*scientific*) knowledge about or pedagogical expertise to teach it. This quandary is captured nicely in the opening paragraph of Annie's reflection paper.

Excerpt 1
When I first got the email saying we'd be teaching parallelisms, half of me groaned and the other half breathed a sigh of relief. On one hand, I was happy to be teaching something with substance and something that mattered and would be new to the students, but on the other hand, **teaching parallelism was new to *me*.** When I looked up parallelisms, I realized it was something I'd grown up using, and although I was never formally taught about them, I use them all the time just naturally. This brought up the challenge of **"how do I teach something I myself don't fully grasp?"** Until we sat down to plan our lessons, parallelisms were one of those **"I'll know it if I see it" type of things.**

Josh also expressed negative emotions about teaching an academic concept that he initially perceived as unfamiliar to him, although his *perezhivanie* is expressed in terms of the images he holds about formal schooling and teachers as holders of all knowledge. His 'panic' is eased after seeking out an online resource that enabled him to both recognize and name the concept of parallelism as something with which he was actually quite familiar.

Excerpt 2
When we found out what our topic was going to be, **I started to panic** a bit again. Our topic was parallelism and **I had no clue what it was.** I thought, **how did I get through school this long without knowing what parallelism was? And what kind of indication was this about the teacher I was going to be in that one ESL lesson? If there were questions would I even be able to answer them?** After reading about parallelism on the Purdue OWL website, I learned that it was a simple concept and that **I had actually known about it all along,** but never really thought about it or knew of a name for it. From that point on **I felt pretty good** about the project.

The practice teach: Reconceptualizing parallelism

As they planned the lesson, the team admitted they relied heavily on open access websites, such as the Purdue Online Writing Lab, for formal definitions and examples of sentences with parallel structure. In fact, at the start of the *practice teach*, Josh essentially read a definition of parallelism taken directly from the Purdue OWL.

Excerpt 3

Josh: Great. So, what is parallelism? U:m basically **parallel structure is using the same pattern or words or similar grammatical structures to show that two or more ideas ha:ve the same level of importance and this could happen in three ways, it could happen at u:m with words, phrases or clauses.** U:m the easiest and most frequent way to join parallel structures is with the use of **coordinating conjunctions such as and (.) or or. (.) That's from Purdue OWL our savior.** So, (.) just kidding ((*laughs*))

Josh's characterization of parallelism as "grammatical structures" as defined by the Purdue OWL website served as the conceptual frame through which the team proceeded to teach the concept of parallelism. In fact, the introductory portion of their *practice teach* lesson entailed presenting examples of sentences with parallel structure and highlighting the different grammatical forms they may take (e.g., use of gerunds, infinitives, prepositional phrases). In the following excerpt, Annie, Josh, and Deb each present an example sentence by foregrounding its grammatical structure and offering rather vague (*everyday*) explanations for its parallel structure (e.g., "*it flows,*" "*consistency*").

Excerpt 4

Annie: So you can see here we've used **prepositional phrases to create (.) a syncopated rhythm** that you know adds to the flow of the sentence and (.) it it just makes it a **more balanced sentence and you know i-it just it flows a lot better**. (.)

Josh: Right. (.) U(h)m a:nd you can also **use it in a clause** "The GPS told us that we <u>should</u> make a right, that we <u>should</u> get on to I-84, and that we <u>should</u> drive for a 199 miles." Um, an incorrect form would be "The GPS told us that we <u>should</u> make a right, <u>that</u> we should get onto I-84, and <u>to drive</u> for 199 miles." So once again **it just doesn't flow as well**.

Deb: Basically consistency is key and like you were mentioning earlier like going from **–ing to like the infinitive like driving <u>to</u> drive you have to make sure it's consistent throughout the entire sentence**.

In preparation for the team's first application activity, which Deb jokingly refers to as 'parallelisms gone wrong,' she provides an additional example of faulty parallel structure, once again noting its grammatical structure (infinitive vs. gerund) and stressing the importance of being consistent. Interestingly, this is the first occasion where the team indicates that there may be more than one way that these 'faulty' sentences might be corrected. It also reflects a focus on language as form rather than social practice, which as we noted earlier, is the typical pre-understanding of language of these teachers.

Excerpt 5

Deb: So, a faulty parallelism would be "My uncle likes to <u>eat</u> in expensive restaurants and visiting museums." So as we can see here, in the very beginning **"to eat" is the infinitive** but then it switches the next verb **to the –ing form** which **is not consistent** as we said earlier. So there are **two ways that you cou:ld go about fixing this**. Uh, you could **keep it in the infinitive** and say "My uncle likes <u>to</u> eat in expensive restaurants and <u>to</u> visit museums." Uh, or you could **go the –ing route** and say "My uncle likes <u>eating</u> in expensive restaurants and <u>visiting</u> museums." Uh, a second example- Yes?

Immediately following Deb's explanation, the teacher educator picks up on the notion of *multiple correct answers* and praises the team for building this into their application activity. She links their decision to encourage *multiple correct answers* to her own expert insights about the mindset of ESL students, explaining how ESL students tend to conceptualize language learning as having 'right or wrong' answers. She also uses this opportunity to emphasize the educational value of thinking about language as having *multiple correct answers*.

Excerpt 6

TE: I was just gonna say **I really like the fact that you gave multiple (.) correct answers.** Because **I think ESL students are often (.) treated as "Here's the right answer, here's the wrong answer."** But there's often multiple ways stuff can be written. So **I really like** that you have "It can be done this way, or it can be done this way." And I think that's a- that's **a really good way for students to think about these kind of grammatical structures, there <u>isn't</u> one right way that it can be done**. (.) So, kudos.

Despite the teacher educator's explicit mediation regarding the pedagogical value of encouraging *multiple correct answers*, neither the team's intuitive pre-understandings of parallelism nor information gleaned from the Purdue OWL website prove to be adequate during the application activity in which they asked small groups of their classmates (CM) to correct a series of sentences that contained inappropriate and/or missing parallel structure. In the following exchange, the teacher educator prompts the team to discuss the corrected sentences, indicating that there might be *multiple correct answers*.

Excerpt 7

Annie: Okay. I mean do you guys want to actually go over them?

TE: **Maybe one or two because I think there are (.) more than one right answer?**

Annie: [Sure. And you can direct your answers to our error master, Mr. Ryan. (.)

Josh: Yeah.

TE: What did you guys think of (.) number one, your group?

CM1:   Uh, ( ) says that, "The runner says that his new shoes are lighter, faster, and more comfortable."

Ryan: **Y:es.**

TE: [(((*laughter*))

Annie: [Good

TE: **Y:es.**

Ryan: **[Good [job. (.) It flows beautifully.**

Annie: [Sounds g[ood.

Deb: **[That's one way-**

TE: **[(h)(.) And will you ask- will you ask them (.) wh:y?**

Ryan: Yeah, why? Why d- Why do you think-

Class: ((*laughter*))

Ryan: I could do that. Why do you think it sounds best?

In this exchange, Ryan's emphatic single word response ("*Y:es*") to his classmate garners a good deal of laughter but it is challenged by the teacher educator, who prompts him to explore the reasoning behind his classmate's choice. Interestingly, Deb attempts to interject the notion of *multiple correct answers* ('[*That's one* way-') but is overlapped by the teacher educator who continues to press Ryan to ask his classmates why they corrected this sentence as they did.

Before CM1 is able to respond to Ryan's question, another classmate, CM3, offers an alternative answer, to which Ryan struggles to articulate any sort of academic explanation of what parallelism is or why writers might use it.

Excerpt 8

CM3:   I also thought, maybe it "feels better." (.)

TE: Ah, whatdya think Ryan?

Ryan: What's that?

CM3:   What if the last one ( ) "feels better" rather than "more comfortable"?

Ryan: **"Feels better?" I mean I guess that- that works with it.**

CM3: I'm trying to keep- trying to keep the -er rhythm.

Ryan: **Yeah [it's like- it's**

TE: [Oh, bett<u>e:r</u>. Mmm?

Ryan: **I mean, it- it keeps the ending going (.) all the way through-out, (.) that's- that's a parallelism.**

We highlight Excerpts 7 and 8 as signaling a potential *growth point*, at least for Ryan, who, given his emphatic single word response "*Y:es*," was clearly not expecting to be asked to explain why CM1's contribution was or was not an appropriate use of parallel structure. The shared laughter and Ryan's sarcastic mimicking of the teacher educator's prompt, "*Yeah, why?*" signal the emergence of a contradiction, or a sense of instability at being asked to assess CM1's contribution without having the necessary competence to do so. This contradiction continues in Excerpt 8 where, once again, Ryan uses very tentative language, ("*I mean I guess that- that works with it*") and vague explanations ("*it keep the ending going (.) all the way throughout*") as he attempts to assess the appropriateness of CM3's offer of "*feels better.*"

Sensing that the team may be struggling to assess unanticipated answers from their classmates, the teacher educator provides *responsive mediation* that builds on Annie's earlier reference to syncopated rhythm and CM3's reference to trying to keep the rhythm by modeling a pedagogical strategy that assists the team in determining if the corrected sentence has an appropriate parallel structure.

Excerpt 9

TE: **Well let's- lets try it. (.) "The runner says that his new shoes are lighter, faster, and feel better." How's the rhythm?**

CM4: Or just "better." ((*short laugh*)) Cause I-

TE: Better? (.)

Josh: Yeah, cause I (think)-

TE: Oh, how about that, "lighter, faster, and better." (.)

Then Annie, addressing the class as if they were actual ESL students, connects the teacher educator's references to *multiple correct answers* to the notion of *conveying one's message*. The teacher educator builds on this connection, emphasizing again that the team is likely to get *multiple correct answers*, and then reframes parallelism as a *rhetorical strategy* for conveying a writer's message (*effect on the reader*). The teacher educator mediates responsively in three ways: by revoicing how a teacher might ask questions to get at the rhetorical effect of parallel structure, by providing a rationale for why writers choose to use parallel structure, and by inserting the academic definition that parallel structures in academic writing function as a rhetorical strategy.

Excerpt 10

Annie: So we see, **there's lots of different ways to answer this**. That's one of the beauties with this, is that **there is no exact right way**, it can really come down to, **what message you most strongly want to convey.**

TE: So that's another suggestion. (.) Cause I suspect **you'll get different answers**, so: you could ask the class, **"So, when I say it this way, what's the impression you get? When I say it another way, what's the impression you get?"** Because **all:: of this has to do with the <u>effect</u> this has on the reader**. Right? What- as a writer, what <u>effect</u> do I want this to have on my reader? And that's when you're trying to figure out (.) how to use this as **a rhetorical strategy**, <u>that's</u> what you want your writers to focus on. So that you can ask, if they give you different answers, **"Well, so, how did, what's the <u>effect</u> of that on the reader?"** (.)

Through this series of interactions an IDZ emerges and a more robust understanding of parallelism begins to take shape. This is accomplished as the team build this understanding by *thinking together*, simultaneously engaging in the activity of teaching in this mediational space where they are expected to play the part of being a teacher, try out their instructional ideas, and receive supportive feedback, all the while consciously and collectively analyzing their own thinking and activities. The emergent nature of their understanding of parallelism is striking. They pick up on each other's incidental references to critical notions that begin to reframe the concept of parallelism as much more than grammatical structures. This is led by the teacher educator who mediates responsively with repeated emphasis on *asking why*, *multiple correct answers*, and *effect on the reader*.

The practice teach: Engineering student participation

In addition to working to reorient the team's understanding of the concept of parallelism, there were several instances during the *practice teach* when the teacher educator focused the team's attention on instructional strategies that garner greater levels of student participation. Clearly not preplanned, these moments of *responsive mediation* emerged at different points throughout the *practice teach* as the team attempted to enact the various components of their lesson plan. For example, during the second application activity the team asked their classmates to listen to American president John F. Kennedy's 1961 inaugural address and use a transcript to identify instances of parallelism. After listening to the speech and following along on the transcript, Annie's open-ended question, *"All righty, who heard some parallelisms in there?"* was met with three seconds of silence and scattered laughter from the class. Deb's follow up attempt, *"Would anybody like to point out one that they found?"* was also met with silence. At this moment, the teacher educator interrupts the flow of the activity and asks the team about the level of student participation in the ESL class they observed. (Readers are reminded of Abra's similar types of questions to encourage participation in Chapter 5.)

Excerpt 11

> TE: Um, does this group tend to participate quickly and easily or **do you have to engineer it a little bit?** (.)
>
> Ryan: She like- when I-
>
> TE: Like when you guys observed.
>
> Ryan: Whenever I observed they were kinda (.) they were kinda like mellowed out [they really weren't- they really weren't saying to much
>
> Class: [((*scattered laughter*))
>
> TE: Okay well the reason I ask is that you can ask that open-ended question "Can anybody find a parallelism?" but you often get (.) silence **so one way is to say "Can you find one in the first paragraph? Can you find one in the second paragraph? Can you find one in the third paragraph?" and then ((***snaps three times***)) they'll go like that.** So then it's again it's just (.) you may not need to do that, not all groups need that, but if they do, think about that.
>
> Ryan: **That's what happened. She she like asked the question and after ten seconds of silence she called on someone.**
>
> TE: Yeah. **So you can engineer it that way if you want** or (.) but often times **when you ask that open-ended question (.) It's not that people don't want to answer it's like "Okay I need to think, I need to look" it takes a little time, you know. (.) And it also allows you- your your students to say "Okay I'm not looking at the <u>whole</u> thing but I'm looking at (.) a piece of it." So cognitively it's less complex to do.**
>
> Annie: And we could **also mix it up** by saying you know (.) **"Morgan there's a parallelism in the second paragraph, can you tell us why?"** [And so **we might do some questions like that if we're getting some blank silence. (.)**
>
> TE: There you go.

During this interaction, Ryan confirms that the ESL instructor also struggles with getting the ESL students to participate. Addressing this concern, the teacher educator revoices how to ask a question that can lessen the cognitive load by focusing ESL students' attention on a single paragraph from the speech. She also provides the team with insight into how ESL students might struggle when faced with broad, open-ended questions. Twice in Excerpt 11, the teacher educator uses the term 'engineer' when talking about student participation. Their shared understanding of this term and its contextualized meaning originates from a handout the teacher educator had previously distributed in the class that contains a series of pedagogical tools that teachers can use to foster greater levels of student engagement and partic) ipation. On the handout, *Engineering Participation* is defined as:

> Don't assume students will know how you want them to participate. Arrange your activities so that students have opportunities to participate in different ways (individually, round-robin, pairs, small groups, large groups) and be explicit (meta-talk) about how you want them to participate.

Thus, a pedagogical tool from the course handout, which began as a material tool, reemerges during the *practice teach* as a mediational means for how to think about formulating more targeted and less open-ended questions. The teacher educator references this pedagogical tool and reiterates its pedagogical value in garnering greater levels of student participation. Interestingly, Annie projects this pedagogical tool into the future by revoicing how she might reorient her questions if, in fact, the ESL students are reluctant to participate during the *actual teach*.

Overall, the *responsive mediation* that emerged throughout the *practice teach* included various mediational means. The teacher educator sometimes revoiced how a teacher might talk to accomplish a particular instructional goal. There were multiple instances when the teacher educator provided an explicit rationale for enacting a particular pedagogical strategy or emphasized a more sophisticated, more nuanced definition of the subject matter the team was expected to teach. Other times, she modeled particular pedagogical strategies and in doing so provided insight into the mindset of the ESL students that the team would eventually teach. Ultimately, the quality of her mediation was emergent, dynamic, and contingent on the moment-to-moment dialogic interactions that occurred throughout the *practice teach*. As we will see in the next section, the consequences of this *responsive mediation* plays out in interesting ways during the *actual teach*.

The actual teach: Mediational means enacted as pedagogical strategies

While the content and structure of the team's initial lesson plan did not change significantly from the *practice teach* to the *actual teach*, how they carried out each segment of the lesson and how they talked about the concept of parallelism did. And while all four teachers continued to make references to 'grammatical structures' throughout the *actual teach*, these were supplemented with instances where the team took up the mediational means of *multiple correct answers* and *asking why* as pedagogical strategies.

In the following excerpt, Deb, Annie, and Ryan all ask if other groups had alternative answers, in essence, signaling to the ESL students that more than one right answer is desirable.

Excerpt 12

> Deb: Could you read the whole sentence please? (h)sorry.
> S2:   "The runner says that his shoes are lighter, faster, and more comfortable."
> Deb: Great. Now, that **is one way you could do it. Is there another way** that you think– I mean, most of these, you can do in a **multitude of ways**, so does any other group have **something other than that?** (4.0) Anyone?
> S7:   They use– (.) Or, they like what–
> Ryan: They said "lighter, faster, and more comfortable."
> S7:   Ah, okay.
> Annie: Which, they got it right, but we were [just curious **if there's any other** ( )
> Ryan: [Yeah, it's like I told you guys, **there's a couple different ways you can write these.**
> S7:   We– we said, "The runner says the– that his shoes are light, fast, and feel more comfortable." Or just "comfortable."
> Ryan: Comfortable, yeah.

This pedagogical strategy of asking for *multiple correct answers* repeatedly opened up spaces for the ESL students to participate, by both contributing alternative answers and asking questions about the appropriateness of their choices. This happened most often when the team used the pedagogical strategy of *asking why*, as is evidenced below where the ESL students elaborate on their choices and demonstrate their understanding of parallelism.

Excerpt 13

> Deb: U:h, ((*pointing to S7 and S8*)) boys in the back, could you do the next one?
> S8:   Yeah. (.) U:h "So we ran to my car, sat in our seats, and drove away?"
> Deb: **Okay, why did you choose "sat"?**
> S8:   **Uh, it sounded like (.) the proper thing.**
> S7:   **The proper tense.**
> S8:   **Yeah.**
> S7:   **Cause it's past.**
> Deb: Past? "Ran" and "drove," exactly. (.) A:nd ((*pointing to S9 and S10*)).
> S9:   **"We were just riding along at a safe, responsible, and controlled speed." Uh, this word describes the speed and they are adjectives.**
> Deb: Perfect.

Thus, an important instructional consequence of the shift in the team's conceptual understanding of parallelism from 'grammatical structure' to allowing for *multiple correct answers* is greater levels of ESL student participation and engagement in the lesson.

Interestingly, the mediational means that emerged in the *practice teach* did not simply operate as isolated pedagogical strategies in the *actual teach*, but instead were sometimes combined and expressed uniquely by individual teachers. In the following excerpt, the ESL students had just listened to Kennedy's inaugural address and were asked to use the transcript to identify instances of parallelism. Annie's framing of parallelism contains hints of rhythm (*"natural pauses"*) that she links to effect on the reader (*"let the message sink in"*) as a rationale for why parallelism is used as a rhetorical strategy (*"another reason why we use parallelism"*).

Excerpt 14

Annie: All right so that one was chock full of parallelisms and another thing you'll notice you're looking at a written version of it but you can even hear them as he speaks there's **natural pauses** in his (.) in his speaking and **that's another (.) really big clue** and that's **another reason why we use parallelisms because by using them it gives you a place to naturally pause and let the message sink in**.

Ryan also demonstrates a more nuanced understanding of parallelism during a segment of the *actual teach* in which he uses the example of résumé writing as a real-life context in which appropriate use of parallelism can affect how an employer might perceive an applicant. While he continues to rely on rather vague language to describe parallelism, he is, for the first time during the project, linking the concept of parallelism to the effect it may have on a reader (employer).

Excerpt 15

Ryan: And uh **a practical way to <u>use</u> this** where you're actually uh **gonna need it in real life one day down the road is a résumé** ... So uh a wrong way to make a list of your accomplishments would say "Responsible for editing copy, supervised layout, three years experience as a news writer" (.) Uh, that's switching tenses back and forth (.) it doesn't look good (.) it doesn't sound right. The correct way to say it would be uh "edited copy one year, supervised layout for two years, wrote news for three years." (.) **They're all in the same tense, it looks good, and you (.) you've shortened it up enough that they can read it briefly and give them a good idea of what you know how to do. (2.0) Parallelisms.**

Additionally, there were multiple instances during the *actual teach* when the team appeared to make in-flight decisions regarding ways to engineer student participation. During the team's final application activity they asked the ESL students to complete a Mad Lib: a comical story-like structure in which each of the five sentences had a parallel structure where either the first, second, or third word was left blank. During the *practice teach*, the team had asked their classmates to complete the entire Mad Lib. However, during the *actual teach*, Deb assigned one sentence to each pair, stating explicitly to "*just focus on <u>one</u> sentence*," which would "*make sure that you're looking at the structure and the form that we've been talking about all day.*"

Excerpt 16

Deb: . . . you're gonna work in your same pairs you've been working on **a:nd if you could just focus on <u>one</u> sentence** so if you ((*pointing at S1 and S2*)) could just work on the first blank, if you ((*pointing at S9 and S10*)) could do the second blank sentence, if you ((*pointing at S5 and S6*)) could do the third, ((*pointing at S7 and S8*)) fourth, and ((*pointing at S3 and S4*)) fifth blank. U:m so **we just want you to do one sentence** u:m so you want to **make sure that you're looking at the structure and the form that we've been talking about all day** a:nd then we're going to come together and we're going to read them aloud a:nd uh if we have time talk about uh (.) why they're awesome. Okay.

While lessening the cognitive load of the activity, assigning a single sentence to each pair allowed the follow-up discussion activity to flow smoothly because the ESL students could anticipate the order in which they would be expected to participate.

However, there were other instances where the mediational means offered by the teacher educator during the *practice teach* were not taken up by the team during the *actual teach*. For example, as she did during the *practice teach*, after the Kennedy inaugural address listening activity, Annie proceeded to ask the same open-ended question, which was met with silence. However, instead of giving the ESL students an opportunity to answer or reorienting her question, Ryan quickly jumps in, asks for volunteers, and then almost immediately calls on S8. This interactional pattern continues throughout this activity as Annie takes up this same strategy, directly calling on other pairs to participate.

Excerpt 17

Annie: **So can we just quickly get some people to (.) you know put forth some of the parallelisms that they found?** (2.0)

Ryan: **Any volunteers?** (1.0) **((*pointing at S8*)) You sir.**

S7:   U:m second paragraph (.) or no the first one "As well as a beginning" and then it goes on "as well as change." (.) Could that be a parallelism?

Annie: Yep, that definitely is.

Ryan: Yes it is. (.)

Annie: So "as" is your clue thing.

S7:   Yeah.

Annie: We're using as to set up both of them and then we follow with something different. (.) **Alright how about another. ((*pointing to S3 and S4*)) Can we get you guys in the corner to give us one?**

S9:   Uh the third (.) the third paragraph, start from "let the word go forth" and (.) "born in this century, tempered by war" and uh to: (.) yeah.

Interestingly, even though Annie failed to take up the teacher educator's suggestion to ask less open-ended questions, during the *stimulated recall session* she not only becomes consciously aware of her inability to self-regulate the form of her solicitations, she also recognizes how one of her teammates was able to do so and thus successfully engineered student participation.

The stimulated recall session: Conscious awareness develops

The *stimulated recall session* functioned as an additional *structured mediational space* for the team to become consciously aware of their emerging understanding of parallelism as well as various pedagogical strategies to teach it. In the excerpt below, the teacher educator prompts the team to reflect, once again, on the notion of *multiple correct answers*.

Excerpt 18

TE: One of the questions I wanted to ask you- This could have been done in multiple ways, right? I mean, they could have corrected it differently.

Josh: **Oh sure. I mean, there wasn't (.) just one right answer.**

TE: But did they pretty much all do them the same?

Deb: I'm trying to remember.

Josh: **Um, well I know a couple people had different ones because I think- (.) I think we said, "Does anyone else have anything-" I mean, we might've [said "Does anyone else have anything-"**

Deb: [Um, (.) like we went arou:nd. Um, Annie said the back group had some- I think it was ( ). **They had something different.** So what um what we did is we called on someone else, but when we asked "Does anyone else have anything?" they were a little timid but **we kn:ew that they had something different, and that it wasn't wrong,** so we felt okay to like- I think- I think we called on them or they felt confident enough to do that, but um I think walking around we kind of saw where everyone was at and **kind of saw differences and then we wanted to make sure we highlighted that it could all be different.**

Josh: Yeah, cause people in the back had- **cause we had our own answer sheet with just one answer on it and I think that's why Annie wanted to call on them because they had something different than our answer. (.) And it was pretty unique.**

[BREAK]

TE: Do you remember what they- what they were struggling with?

Ryan: Uh, they uh- it was the one about the shoes that were "lighter, faster, and felt (.) felt comfortable." They said "Would more comfortable work here?" or "felt better." **[Yeah. It was- it was (.) interesting cause it was one that, like, I didn't have written down on like the answer sheet, like one of the possible ones but it worked.**

TE: Yeah, yeah. Which is good. I mean that shows them that- And I think (.) either Deb or Annie or maybe both of them said, **"There's multiple ways you can do this. There's not a right answer, but there is a right pattern."** And that, I think- I think they got that. I think that was pretty clear.

For Deb, the notion of *multiple correct answers* becomes a motivating factor for choosing to call on other groups, opening up the floor for greater levels of student participation. Thus, in the activity of the *actual teach*, the mediational means offered by the teacher educator during the *practice teach* become linked up and emerge in the rationale that Deb uses to justify her instructional decisions. For both Josh and Ryan, an unexpected answer (not on their answer sheet) is portrayed as desirable. Throughout this interaction the teacher educator repeatedly focuses the team's attention on *multiple correct answers*, allowing them to externalize not only *how* they asked questions during the lesson but also *why* they chose to encourage *multiple correct answers*. The teacher educator's targeted yet open-ended questions create mediational spaces for conscious awareness to develop.

In another instance, Annie praises her teammate's consistent use of *asking why*, which allows the teacher educator to make explicit the pedagogical reasoning behind this particular strategy.

Excerpt 19

Annie: And she did a good job of (.) pulling apart each of them and **asking why** they got it. I think (.) if I had been leading this I would have just been so caught up in getting through the activity that **I would have forgotten to ask why but she did a good job of remembering for everyone.**

TE: Because **the more you ask them to explain why they made the choice the more conscious they get of the concept.** So.

And finally, despite the fact that during the *actual teach* Annie failed to take up the teacher educator's suggestion to ask less open-ended questions, she is consciously aware that she did not do this, but was able to see how her teammate, Deb, had accomplished this during the final application activity. Such conscious awareness, Vygotsky (1987) argues, is necessary for designing and carrying out future actions. Additionally, Annie's recognition of this pedagogical strategy gave the teacher educator an opportunity to reinforce its pedagogical value and revoice not only how a teacher might accomplish this but also what ESL students might be thinking as a result. Interestingly, both Annie and the teacher educator engage in revoicing, a mediational means that appears to be emerging as a psychological tool for Annie to reimagine her teaching in the future.

Excerpt 20

Annie: One thing we could have done, and Deb definitely did it with her Mad Libs, and (.) **I knew we should have done it** but **I got so caught up in teaching and it just slipped my mind is warn them ahead of time**, you know, **"Okay, we're gonna do this and you guys are going to find the first, the first uh parallelism"** um you know **to reduce the cognitive load** and also just give them a heads up, **"We are going to call on you in a minute or two."**

TE: Exactly. And that's that whole thing I was talking about **making your instruction predictable by engineering participation.** So it's all that meta-talk about ((*in sing-song voice*)) **"what we're gonna do and why I'm asking you to do it, and when you're done, by the way, you're gonna do this"** and you are **much more likely to get participation** if you do that because then they know ((*less pronounced sing-sing*)) **"Okay, I'm gonna get number two, and I'm gonna have to answer it, so I'm gonna be ready"** and they may still be a little (.) reluctant, but it, but it does help, so absolutely (.) absolutely.

Overall, the team's conscious awareness of the academic concept of parallelism and how to teach it emerges as the teacher educator probes the team's new understandings by grounding it in the activity of teaching they just experienced and then emphasizing its pedagogical appropriateness.

Reflection papers: New realizations about teaching ESL

The team's reflection papers provide rich evidence that they had begun to make broader connections between teaching the lesson on parallelism and the teaching of ESL in general. Each acknowledged a gap between their intuitive knowledge of English and inadequate knowledge of how to teach it. They also expressed an emerging view that teaching is contingent on understanding content, students, context, and purpose. More importantly, each attributed the process of collectively planning, practicing, enacting, and reflecting on the lesson as enabling them to reach these new realizations. As just one example, Ryan sums up this new realization in his final reflection paper.

Excerpt 21

One of the main factors I learned about ESL teaching through this assignment was that we as native English speakers use these language techniques on a daily basis and **do not realize the difficulty level that nonnative speakers are faced with when we go to teach them something.** As I mentioned in the recall **I was not really sure what the function of parallel structure was**, but after a brief review of it, I realized that I use it on a daily basis. And although the concept and the use of the literary element seemed simple and logical to me, **it was not until we as a group were deciding how to explain it to the students that [we realized] the students might have trouble understanding what it is and why they should use it.**

Obuchenie, responsive mediation, and the team's emerging development

Considering the dialogic interactions that emerged throughout the various *structured mediational spaces* of the project in terms of *obuchenie*, the actions and intentions of the teacher educator were predicated on recognizing the team's pre-understandings of the concept of parallelism and how they were attempting to teach it, which were evident in both the reflection papers and the *practice teach*. As the teacher educator became attuned to this she worked dialogically to insert specific mediational means that pushed the team to consider a broader understanding of the concept. Yet her mediation was contingent and dynamic—it built off of the team's attempts to enact the lesson while simultaneously pushing them to broaden their understanding of the concept, with an emphasis on its pedagogical value and explicit modeling of how this could be accomplished instructionally. When the team enacted the *actual teach* these mediational means became some of the very pedagogical strategies that the team used to talk about and teach the concept of parallelism. And through guided reflection on the activity of teaching, the team became consciously aware of these new understandings and to some extent was able to articulate a more nuanced understanding of the unique nature of teaching ESL. Over the long term, of course, such new understandings would need to be repeatedly materialized in the activities of being and becoming a teacher in order for these externalized dialogic interactions with this teacher educator to become internalized psychological tools that support these teachers' developing teacher/teaching expertise.

In this chapter we have highlighted how engagement in the extended team teaching project created opportunities for authentic participation in the activities of language teaching, opening up varied and multiple *structured mediational spaces* for *responsive mediation* to emerge throughout this initial learning-to-teach experience. As is often the case with beginning teachers, the team, perhaps some members more than others, lacked sufficient knowledge of *what* they were expected to teach or *how* to teach it. Providing mediation that is responsive to the immediate needs of each individual teacher within the team can be quite challenging, and perhaps only through micro-level retrospective analysis, as we have done here, can teacher educators recognize signals of teachers' pre-understandings, their past and present *perezhivanie*, or potential *growth points*, and then calibrate their mediation so it is maximally beneficial to both the individual and the team.

For the extended team teaching project showcased in this chapter, it was the *structured mediational spaces* and the *responsive mediation* that emerged in those spaces that created opportunities for the teacher educator and team members to build a fuller, more conceptual understanding of the content they were teaching and to teach it in ways that fostered greater student engagement and participation. It is our contention that it was the simultaneous attention to content (parallelism) and pedagogy (e.g., *multiple answers, asking why*), the teacher educator's *responsive mediation*, and multiple opportunities to verbalize, materialize, and enact the teachers' emerging understandings of both content and pedagogy, which worked in concert to foster the development of greater levels of teacher/teaching expertise. By tracing teacher development as it is in the process of formation, we are able to see the interdependence between content and pedagogy; in essence, the what and how of teaching are united, develop in relation to one another, and lay the foundation for the development of conceptual thinking, the basis of teacher/teaching expertise.

Notes

1 We recognize the stimulated recall session as the same activity as the digital video protocol detailed in Chapter 5; however, in this particular project this phrasing was used throughout.
2 Some data sets reprinted with permission from Wiley. Johnson, K. E. (2015). Reclaiming the relevance of L2 teacher education, *The Modern Language Journal, 99*(3), 515-528.

References

Anderson, N. A., & Graebell, L. C. (1990). Usefulness of an early field experience. *The Teacher Educator, 26*(2), 13–20.

Burns, A., & Richards, J. C. (Eds.) (2009). *The Cambridge guide to second language teacher education*. New York: Cambridge University Press.

Chaiklin, S., & Lave, J. (Eds.) (1996). *Understanding practice: Perspectives on activity and context*. New York: Cambridge University Press.

Farrell, T. C. (2008). Promoting reflective practice in initial English language teacher education: Reflective microteaching. *Asian Journal of English Language Teaching, 18*, 1–15.

Freire, P. (1970). *Pedagogy of the oppressed*. New York: Seabury Press.

Gee, J. (1999). Learning language as a matter of learning social language within discourses. In M. Hawkins (Ed.), *Language learning and teacher education: A sociocultural approach* (pp. 13–31). Clevedon, UK: Multilingual Matters.

Halliday, M. A. K. (1985). *Introduction to functional grammar.* London: Edward Arnold.

Johnson, K. E. (2006). The sociocultural turn and its challenges for L2 teacher education. *TESOL Quarterly, 40*(1), 235–257.

Johnson, K. E. (2009). *Second language teacher education: A sociocultural perspective.* New York: Routledge.

Johnson, K. E. (2015). Reclaiming the relevance of L2 teacher education. *The Modern Language Journal, 99*(3), 515–528.

Johnson, K. E., & Arshavskaya, E. (2011). Reconceptualizing the micro-teaching simulation in an MA TESL course. In K. E. Johnson & P. R. Golombek (Eds.), *Research on second language teacher education: A sociocultural perspective on professional development* (pp. 168–186). New York: Routledge.

Johnson, K. E., & Dellagnelo, A. (2013). How 'sign meaning develops': Strategic mediation in learning to teach. *Language Teaching Research, 17*(4), 409–432.

Johnson, K. E., & Worden, D. (2014). Cognitive/emotional dissonance as *growth points* in learning to teach. *Language and Sociocultural Theory, 2*(1), 125–150.

Lantolf, J. P. (2009). Knowledge of language in foreign language teacher education. *The Modern Language Journal, 93*(2), 270–274.

Lave, J., & Wenger, E. (1991). *Situated learning: Legitimate peripheral participation.* New York: Cambridge University Press.

MacLeod, G. (1987). Microteaching: Modeling. In M. J. Durkin (Ed.), *The international encyclopedia of teaching and teacher education* (pp. 720–722). Oxford: Pergamon.

Maxie, A. (2001). Developing early field experiences in a blended teacher education program: From policy to practice. *Teacher Education Quarterly, 28*(1), 115–131.

Mercer, N. (2004). Sociocultural discourse analysis: Analyzing classroom talk as a social mode of thinking. *Journal of Applied Linguistics, 1*(2), 137–168.

Politzer, P. (1969). Microteaching: A new approach to teacher training and research. *Hispania, 52,* 244–248.

Richards, J. C., & Farrell, T. C. (2005). *Professional development for language teachers.* New York: Cambridge University Press.

Roberts, J. (1998). *Language teacher education.* London: Arnold.

van Lier, L. (2004). *The ecology and semiotics of language learning: A sociocultural perspective.* Boston: Kluwer Academic.

Vygotsky, L. S. (1987). Thinking and speech (N. Minick, Trans.). In R. W. Reiber (Ed.), *The collected works of L. S. Vygotsky, Vol. 3. Problems of the theory and history of Psychology* (pp. 37–285). New York: Plenum Press.

Wallace, M. (1996). Structured reflection: The role of the professional project in training ESL teachers. In D. Freeman & J. C. Richards (Eds.), *Teacher learning in language teaching* (pp. 281–294). New York: Cambridge University Press.

Wenger, E. (1998). *Communities of practice: Learning, meaning, and identity.* Cambridge: Cambridge University Press.

Whipp, J. L. (2003). Scaffolding critical reflection in online discussions: Helping prospective teachers think deeply about field experiences in urban schools. *Journal of Teacher Education, 54*(4), 321–333.

Zeichner, K., & Liston, D. (1996). *Reflective teaching: An introduction.* Mahwah, NJ: Lawrence Erlbaum Associates.

8

REIMAGINING TEACHER
IDENTITY-IN-ACTIVITY

"I wanted to create a synergism between Genre Analysis and the institution's teach-for-test grammar."

In most L2 teacher education programs, coursework is the most visible and recurring professional development activity through which teachers are exposed to and construct their understandings of the knowledge base of L2 teacher education. The universality of coursework in an L2 teacher education program, however, conceals how diverse the experience of taking a course can be for teachers. The nature of courses differs depending on numerous factors, such as competing conceptions of language and language learning shaping a program and/or individual professors, and the academic home of the program (e.g., college of education or liberal arts). This array of factors converges in some fashion, resulting in core courses intended to provide foundational knowledge that the program deems essential to being able to teach a second language, and electives reflecting the vision of the program or the academic strengths of its professors. Courses differ in terms of academic content undoubtedly, but also in terms of how they are taught, providing both opportunities and constraints for teacher learning. In our experience, teacher candidates can unhesitatingly identify courses and professors they found invaluable in their development, and those they did not.

What constitutes the knowledge base of language teaching has been subject to vigorous debate since Freeman and Johnson put forward their reconceptualization in 1998 (Bartels, 2004; Freeman & Johnson, 2004, 2005; Tarone & Allwright, 2005; Yates & Muchisky, 2003). Research on language teacher cognition has heightened these discussions as the field has come to understand L2 teachers as actively constructing and enacting their understandings of teaching and learning, based on their sociohistorical experiences/activities as learners, learners of teaching, and teachers in diverse instructional contexts. Moreover, research on language teacher cognition has deepened our understanding of teacher learning as emerging in and through social practices and interaction, especially the cultural practices of language learning and teaching. In spite of this 'sociocultural turn' in language teacher education (Johnson, 2006), Freeman's (1989) critique of the normative practices of L2 teacher education still remains pertinent: more than a few programs equate knowledge of research in second language acquisition and applied linguistics with knowledge—and abilities—to teach language and to develop as teachers. We can critique such programs from a sociocultural perspective as detaching the *academic concepts* (Vygotsky, 1935/1994) to which teachers are exposed from the meaningful goal-oriented activities of actual teaching. Teachers may exhibit *empty verbalism* (Vygotsky, 1935/1994), meaning they are able to mechanically reproduce *academic concepts*, yet those concepts have not become internalized as psychological tools for thinking, which then can be used to (re)shape what they do in classrooms. Because teacher cognition cannot be removed from the activity of teaching, indeed "*what is learned* is fundamentally shaped by *how it is learned*, and vice versa" (Johnson & Golombek, 2011, p. 3, emphasis in original). *What* we teach in coursework, and *how* we teach it, and *how* we mediate our teachers in the process, are at the core of what we do as teacher educators. And this applies to all professors involved in the coursework that makes up L2 teacher education programs, regardless of whether or not they have conceptualized themselves and their work as being about supporting the learning of teaching and the development of teacher/teaching expertise.

Activities/assignments in L2 teacher education courses, when conceptualized as a teaching/learning (*obuchenie*) opportunity rather than as an evaluation of teachers' specific academic or content knowledge, can provide the kind of systematically organized formal education that Vygotsky (1986) envisioned as being the leading activity for introducing *academic concepts* and then engaging in what he described as *ascending from the abstract to the concrete* (see Chapter 1). Activities/assignments in L2 teacher education programs, by providing interaction of *everyday* and *academic concepts* in goal-oriented activities that a teacher might undertake in a 'located' teaching context, can help bridge the theory/practice divide and thus promote *praxis* (Freire, 1970). This notion is crucial because even teachers who are conceptually committed to a certain instructional approach may still struggle with implementing activities in their classrooms that align with that approach for various reasons, eventually reproducing the very practices that they had hoped to change. The dominant cultural practices of a particular institution and culture can override how a teacher has learned to conceptualize teaching in a teacher education program (Smagorinsky, Cook, Moore, Jackson, & Fry, 2004). For example, a teacher in a Japanese language classroom used English to establish classroom order and Japanese as a means to enhance English literacy skills in the face of institutional and political demands rather than using teaching practices theorized in the field of language teaching and learning, such as communicative language teaching (Cross, 2006; Cross & Gearon, 2007).

When thinking about coursework as supporting teacher learning in L2 teacher education programs, we need to consider several interrelated dimensions: the professors who teach them (their views on second language acquisition, language, and how they position themselves), the subject matter content (what they teach), the activities they create to teach that content (how they teach), and what teachers take from participating in those activities (teacher learning). From our Vygotskian sociocultural theoretical perspective, we see classroom activities and/or course assignments (how professors teach) as cultural practices and artifacts that create mediational spaces for teacher candidates to engage with that content and manipulate relevant linguistic, cultural, pedagogical, and interactional resources so that teachers may ultimately support student language learning. In other words, the activities/assignments (materials tools) are not a kind of *responsive mediation* in and of themselves, but how teachers interact with those tools can most certainly mediate their thinking and teaching activity. Teacher educators have to think purposefully about what their activities/assignments are designed to accomplish, how they will connect theory and practice, what kinds of mediational spaces they create, and the role that they will play as these activities/assignments are carried out. Professors, as teacher educators, thus play a pivotal role in both designing and implementing classroom activities and course assignments that create the conditions for *responsive mediation* to emerge.

Such activities/assignments, moreover, are not intended to simply transfer knowledge. Rather, the teacher educator engages teachers in developing their *teacherly thinking* (Golombek, 2011) as they situate these activities/assignments in terms of their local context, including learners' abilities, needs, and goals, and the student learning objectives of the institution. Classroom activities/assignments as cultural practices and artifacts similarly function as material tools that are used to direct teacher thinking through social interaction with peers, the professor, the teacher him/herself, and the teacher's students (if teaching while taking coursework). The *object* of these activities within coursework then is to provide that initial 'safe zone' for teachers to grapple, or play, with their understanding of *academic concepts* through social activities, engaging in the kind of sustained participation with these concepts that they can internalize gradually while addressing their own students' abilities, needs, and goals through curriculum and instruction. Readers are reminded that Chapter 7 provides another example of a course assignment, the extended team teaching project, which offers multiple structured mediational spaces that provide opportunities for *responsive mediation* to emerge.

Engagement in narrative activity

To create a 'safe zone,' teacher educators have progressively exploited the value of teachers engaging in narrative activity, oral and written, as a form of professional development as their learning-to-teach "experience is literally talked into meaningfulness" (Shore, 1996, p. 58). As we mentioned in Chapter 1, we have explored how narrative functions as a mediational tool, both distinctively and interactively, to support teacher learning by opening up teacher thinking, feeling, and doing to expert guidance (Johnson & Golombek, 2011). When teachers articulate their perceptions and experiences concerning their learning-to-teach experience, *narrative as externalization* may unearth what is often tacit—understandings, beliefs, emotions, values, and assessments. *Narrative as verbalization* functions as a way to regulate the thinking process through the intentional insertion of *academic concepts* (Vygotsky, 1986), whether the teacher articulates such concepts her/himself and/or the teacher educator mediates through concepts as psychological tools to support understanding. *Narrative as systematic examination* functions to make explicit the interface between the how and what: how teachers work through narrative activity will fundamentally shape what they learn. Engaging in narrative activity and inquiry within L2 teacher education provides a conduit for teacher introspection and sense-making, as well as teachers' explanation in their own words for "how, when, and why new understandings emerge, understandings that can lead to transformed conceptualizations of oneself as a teacher and transformed modes of engagement in the activities of teaching" (Johnson & Golombek, 2011, p. 490). Engagement in narrative activity often exposes teachers' emotional and cognitive dissonance, a critical issue that we discussed in Chapter 3, which may lead to the emergence of *growth points*, through which *responsive mediation* could then emerge.

When we discuss classroom activity/assignments in coursework from a sociocultural perspective, thus, we are arguing for a radically different understanding of how teacher educators approach their classroom teaching: one that integrates authentic cultural practices of teachers in 'real' teaching within a 'located' instructional context; one that promotes *praxis*; and one that encourages verbalization of cognition, emotion, and activity. This understanding requires teacher educators to create learning opportunities that are intentional, deliberate, and goal-directed; to be able to 'see' teachers' thinking and development unfold as they engage in these activities (Johnson & Golombek, 2003); and to be able to calibrate their mediation in and through these activities/assignments to support the expression and development of L2 teacher/teaching expertise. We suspect that many teacher educators, ourselves included, will automatically say, "I already do that in my teacher education practices." It is thus, we reiterate, not the practices themselves that inherently lead to *responsive mediation* but what we intend and do in our practices and in or relationship with teachers that enable us to 'see' a teacher's thinking; to identify the constellation of a teacher's emotion, cognition, and activity; and to facilitate teacher reciprocity, so we can work with teachers at the 'ceilings' of their potential (ZPDs).

We admit from our own experiences as teacher educators that we have not always fulfilled this ideal in our own practices (e.g., Golombek, 2015). True to what we advocate with the teachers with whom we work, we have, in the writing of this book in particular, systematically investigated our practices and our mediation on the social plane to support our own development as teacher educators. Our engaging in dialogic interaction about the *motives* and *objects* of our activities, how we mediate individuals within those activities, and the consequences of our mediation has enabled us to become more transparent about our own *motives*, *objects*, and *pedagogical reasoning*, as well as more coherent in what we do and why we do it. It has pushed our thinking and doing outside the 'simulating teaching' box to imagine ways, undoubtedly with challenges, to create authentic teacher development practices for particular students with particular objectives in particular classrooms in particular institutions. It has also pushed us to bring a heightened level of mindfulness to the challenges of dynamic, emergent *responsive mediation*.

In this chapter we examine the concept and enactment of *responsive mediation* in a distinct manner from the other chapters. We have so far primarily detailed the moment-to-moment and asynchronous oral and written interactions between teacher educators and teachers within the cultural practices in which they occur, where teacher educators gauge where teachers are and calibrate their mediation responsively in order to enhance the professional development of L2 teachers. In this chapter, we consider how activities and assignments in a graduate-level course can function holistically as material tools mediating a beginning teacher through a trio of dynamics: (1) the teacher educator's mediational intent behind the activities/assignments in this particular course, which include the material tools designed for the course, or teacher educator mediation 'at-a-distance'; (2) the teacher's taking up of the tools, that is, how the teacher enacts the activities and assignments in a graduate-level course on genre; and (3) students' influence, how the teacher's new understanding of his students' motives, as well as the affordances and constraints embedded within his teaching context, reshaped his understanding of teaching grammar, and his *identity-in-activity* (Cross, 2006). To explain how this trio interacts, we first describe three instructional activities/assignments embedded in a graduate-level course on genre that function as material tools, and then the teacher educator's mediational intent behind them. Next, we present the case of Patrick,[1] an ESL teacher facing a contradiction, a *growth point*, in his teaching of grammar, and how he enacted these activities/assignments in that graduate course, connecting them as material tools to his current, past, and future (imagined) teaching context. Though the material tools and how Patrick enacted them no doubt created opportunities for moment-to-moment and asynchronous *responsive mediation*, our focus in this chapter is on how the activities and assignments functioned as *structured mediational spaces* and how Patrick took them up at-a-distance, and thus illustrates the evolution of his professional development.

The graduate course context

The course syllabus described in this chapter was a graduate-level course that examined "*different theoretical approaches to the concept of genre and how it has informed approaches to second language teaching*," focusing on both written and spoken genres.

The teachers were introduced to the history and conceptions of genre and genre analysis, especially in terms of three major schools of genre (Hyon, 1996), including English for Specific Purposes, Systemic Functional Linguistics, and New Rhetoric; other relevant constructs; and common instructional practices of each approach. Greater emphasis was placed on the first two schools of genre given their explicit focus on genre as an organizing principle in instruction. Teachers read seminal pieces from each of the perspectives; conducted genre analyses from the first two approaches, such as move analysis (Swales, 1990) and relational perspectives, that is semantic relationships between structural elements in texts (Paltridge, 1995, 2001) on genre analysis; conducted discourse analyses of different spoken genres (e.g., McCarthy, 1998); designed and critiqued genre-based activities; and designed a genre-based curriculum unit as a final project.

The class met one day per week for three hours. This time frame facilitated teacher candidates undertaking of genre/discourse analysis of short excerpts in class, as well as sufficient time for discussion of their analyses and implications for instruction. Attending the course were eight graduate students (five from a Department of Linguistics and three from a College of Education), one undergraduate majoring in Linguistics, and one visiting scholar, an English professor from China. Five of these teacher candidates were in a position to design a curriculum unit in the genre course that they could implement in their teaching context during the next semester.

Teacher educator mediation 'at-a-distance': Sample class activity and course assignments

In this section, we describe a typical classroom activity and several of the major assignments for the graduate course. First, we provide the guidelines and description of a classroom activity, the genre analysis assignment, the genre-based instructional activity and curriculum unit, and the *narrative inquiry* assignment. We then describe the teacher educator's mediational intent behind these course activities/assignments, functioning as material tools, as a way to capture teacher education mediation 'at-a-distance.'

Tense/aspect discourse analysis activity

The teacher educator designed numerous activities done in the regular day-to-day unfolding of this course in order to interweave the subject matter knowledge (*genre and genre analysis*), general pedagogical knowledge of classroom practices (*how to teach from a genre stance*), and the pedagogical content knowledge (Shulman, 1987) of teaching specific subject matter in genre- and discourse-based ways (see Chapter 1 for discussion of kinds of teacher knowledge). One exemplar of a classroom activity intended to interweave these kinds of knowledge was the 'tense/aspect activity 1' (TAA1). The handout for TAA1 (see Appendix A at end of the chapter) includes a set of guiding questions and four selected data excerpts, each with a different tense/aspect focus that realizes a specific communicative function in a different genre: functions of 'used to' and 'would' in reminiscing narratives, differences between 'will' and 'be going to' in different spoken and written contexts, a use of past perfect in conversation, and a use of present perfect and simple present in newspaper articles. The teacher educator asked teachers to name the tense and aspect focus, as well as the genre, and how that tense and aspect combination helped the speaker/writer to achieve a specific communicative function or intention. Teachers were allowed to work on their own and/or with a partner. The teacher educator checked in with individuals and pairs to mediate their answering of the questions responsively. After approximately 10 to 15 minutes, the teachers participated in a whole class discussion to share answers, which allowed for multiple expressions of similar ideas and clarifying of understandings. Each of the four sections was done separately in this manner so that the teachers could build on what they experienced in each section.

This first set of data excerpts illustrating 'used to' and 'would' in reminiscing narratives is a variation of an activity suggested by both McCarthy (1998, pp. 96–100) and Celce-Murcia and Olshtain (2000, pp. 66–67). The teacher educator, however, added a fifth prompt to this activity—identify a context in which this excerpt might be spoken (the written ones are more obvious)—so teachers could imagine a context in which each reminiscing narrative might be told and why a speaker might tell such a narrative. If only the first four questions of this activity are discussed, the activity risks addressing reminiscing narratives as form only, rather than achieving a speaker's intention, or *illocutionary force* (Austin, 1962). For example, the teachers examined Excerpt 1 from the handout.

Excerpt 1

The bad thing was they **used to** laugh at us, the Anglo kids. They **would** laugh because **we'd** bring tortillas and frijoles to lunch. They **would** have their nice little compact lunch boxes with cold milk in their thermos and **they'd** laugh at us because all we had was dried tortillas. Not only **would** they laugh at us, but the kids **would** pick fights. (Suh, 1992, as cited in Celce-Murcia & Larsen-Freeman, 1999, p. 169)

The teachers identified the speaker in the first narrative as trying to build solidarity with an interlocutor who may have just described discrimination s/he experienced. By adding the fifth prompt, the teacher educator wanted to highlight how discourse activities can unwittingly reduce a genre example to form, and thus, to push teachers to imagine how instructional activities could be contextualized to integrate speaker intention in the language learning classroom.

In setting up this activity as individual/pair problem-solving and then whole class discussion, the teacher educator sought to create a *structured mediational space* for dialogic interactions to emerge so that the teachers and teacher educator could *think together* about the meaning and function of the grammar in the genre. The teacher educator's intention behind creating this activity was to enable the teachers to connect their intuitive understanding of the grammar focus of 'used to' and 'would,' their *everyday concepts*, with a more systematic understanding, *academic concepts*, about the genre and relevant grammatical features. Simultaneously, this activity was designed to position the teachers to think as teachers from a student perspective in order to perceive the challenges and benefits ESL students might experience when analyzing a piece of discourse. From a Vygotskian sociocultural perspective, this is meant to push the development of their *teacherly thinking* by simultaneously mastering the subject matter and connecting it to student needs, abilities, and emotions, what some models of teacher development, such as Fuller and Brown (1975) and Katz (1972), associate with later stages of teaching expertise.

Throughout the activity, the teacher educator needed to stay attuned to the teachers' changing states of knowledge of the grammatical focus as they answered the questions and participated in the whole-class discussion, resulting in their emerging understanding in an *intermental development zone* (IDZ) (Mercer, 2000). Whereas Celce-Murcia and Olshtain's (2000) instructions to ESL students asked "Which form establishes a frame or topic?" (p. 67), the instructions given to the teachers were less directive in that they were expected to try to identify the function of the verbs themselves. The teachers varied greatly in their ability to analyze discourse because of their sociocultural histories, so the teacher educator needed to mediate responsively throughout this activity. For example, if a teacher could answer this question, the teacher educator would then move on to the next question. If this question proved difficult to answer, the teacher educator might mediate responsively by asking a leading question such as "Look at where 'used to' appears in the excerpt. What role might 'used to' play in that position?" or "How does the information in the first sentence differ from those that follow?" In this way, the teacher educator could gain a sense of each teacher's abilities to analyze discourse within a genre, and thus mediate responsively while also modeling the kinds of questions that the teacher might ask him/herself when encountering new genres or facilitating such a discussion. Disclosing these latter two objectives explicitly is important, as teachers do not necessarily discern teacher educators' objectives intuitively. Furthermore, because teachers may feel insecure when explaining grammar because they may only have or lack an intuitive understanding of the grammar focus, the teacher educator also needs to stay attuned to their emotional states, for example by reiterating how normal it is to experience barriers to articulating tacit knowledge or how doing the activity in this manner may help to build that intuitive sense.

By focusing on content (specific tense/aspect in specific genres) and pedagogy (through a guided discourse analytic activity), teachers have an opportunity to verbalize and hear others' verbalizations of which tense/aspect was being used and for what purpose, a kind of "talk through the concept and not about the concept"

(Negueruela, 2008, p. 211). From a Vygotskian sociocultural perspective, however, we know that doing such an activity in class does not mean that teachers have internalized their understandings so they can use them as psychological tools and integrate them into their instructional activity (see Chapter 9 for an example). At a minimum, this activity provides an initial concrete example of how a teacher can enact a genre- and discourse-based approach to language teaching. However, teacher educators still need to build on this experience by creating new circumstances, or *the social situation of development*, where the development of L2 teacher/ teaching expertise can be supported and evolve.

Linking of assignments: Genre analysis, genre-based instructional activity, and genre-based curriculum unit

The teachers then undertook a series of purposefully sequenced assignments having distinctive yet interconnected goals. They first selected a genre that they might/would teach for a 'located' teaching context and then conducted a genre analysis (adapted from Hood, Solomon, & Burns, 1996, as presented in Paltridge, 2001) that included individual analysis of at least three exemplars of the selected genre and then a cross-case analysis to identify key linguistic, grammatical, structural, and rhetorical features across examples, which could become instructional foci concerning the selected genre. After conducting their genre analysis, to which the teacher educator responded in writing to the results of the analysis, the teachers played in a 'safe zone' with, or connected, their understandings of their genre analysis with *academic concepts* of genre-based instruction that had been introduced in the course by instantiating their understandings in a one-hour instructional activity assignment (see Appendix B for assignment).

The teachers informally presented what they had constructed to the class, and received feedback from both the teacher educator and classmates. This one-hour instructional activity, and the feedback received in class, was then followed by teachers extending their understanding through the creation of a genre-based curriculum unit, the final project in the course (see Appendix C for assignment). The instructions, required elements, and format were fundamentally the same as for the one-hour instructional activity, though the time frame was expanded to six hours of sequenced, coherent instruction. In addition, the teacher educator provided several examples of genre-based curriculum units online, so teachers would have a template for how to format the unit, a practical concern of many, while also having an exemplar for how to integrate linguistic, grammatical, and pragmatic elements of a genre in goal-oriented activity. Teachers handed in drafts of the final project, and received written feedback, as well as face-to-face feedback if desired. They presented their projects on the last day of class, receiving feedback from classmates and the teacher educator, and handed in final projects two weeks later.

In essence, the teacher educator intended this sequence of assignments as *prolepsis* (van Lier, 2004), "invitational structures and space for learners to step into and grow into" (p. 162). The teacher educator's mediational intent for each of these assignments overlapped at times yet also differed. The teachers, by identifying a 'located' teaching context and an appropriate genre for instruction, had the concrete experience of identifying an appropriate genre for instruction for a 'located' teaching context, and then doing a genre analysis of the data samples—activities that they might do to create instruction in their current or future classes. The intention behind these activities, beyond the day-to-day coursework, was to provide that initial 'safe zone' for teachers to play with their emerging understanding of *academic concept* of 'genre' through authentic teaching activities, engaging in the kind of sustained participation with concepts that they can begin to internalize gradually in order to better support their own students' abilities and needs, and achieve their goals in their classrooms. The one-hour instructional activity allowed candidates to play with/through their understanding of the *academic concept* of 'genre' by first materializing the subject matter content to be taught to enact a lesson, and then receiving oral feedback from classmates and the teacher educator. For example, classmates or the teacher educator might question the pedagogical reasoning behind an activity, or suggest a particular pedagogical strategy to achieve a certain objective. Within the *structured mediational space* of designing the one-hour activity, IDZs could emerge as the teachers, along with their classmates and the teacher educator, co-constructed new understandings when *everyday concepts* concerning genre-based instruction were inadequate. For example, if teachers focused only on the form of a genre, they might receive feedback on tying the form to speaker intention. Teachers then had another 'safe zone' in terms of the curriculum unit in that they could play with their understandings in and through the more complex, extensive final project, the genre-based curriculum unit. The teacher educator intended for the teachers to implement this curriculum unit in their actual, 'located' teaching context. These multiple spaces created opportunities for the teacher educator and teachers to build a fuller conceptual understanding of the genre they were teaching, as well as how to construct genre-based instruction, through *responsive mediation.*

Narrative inquiry assignment

Two of the students in the class also did a *narrative inquiry* as a way to connect requirements from the Linguistics major with what they were learning in the course on genre (see Appendix D for assignment). In other work, we have defined *narrative inquiry* as "systematic exploration that is conducted *by* teachers and *for* teachers through their own stories and language" (Johnson & Golombek, 2002, p. 6, emphasis in original). The teacher educator's mediational intent behind assigning the narrative inquiry was connected to this definition and the functions of narrative detailed earlier in this chapter. By making the teachers' tacit thoughts, beliefs, knowledge, fears, and hopes explicit as they expressed their day-to-day understandings of their instructional contexts, the teacher educator anticipated that contradictions might emerge. The teacher educator intended that the teachers would work through the *academic concept* of 'genre' as a way to address any cognitive and emotional dissonance in their teaching in order to support any particular *growth point* that might emerge. By providing some parameters for self-inquiry, the teacher educator intended that the activity of inquiry would shape what and how teachers learned as a way to push their professional development. The teacher educator, with access to the teachers' internal cognitive and emotional struggles, as well as their activity of teaching, could thus attempt to mediate responsively.

A case study: Patrick's enactment of the activities/assignments

In this section, we recount the experiences of Patrick, who took the genre-based graduate course during the final semester of his MA program in Linguistics. After graduating with a BA in Linguistics and BS in Business, Patrick taught English as a foreign language (EFL) to junior high school students in Shenzhen, China, where he received four weeks of intensive training in teaching EFL. After teaching in China for two years, he returned to his undergraduate university to pursue his Masters in Linguistics, through which he hoped he would obtain substantive teacher professional development (Klager, personal communication, March 28, 2015).[2] Because he was independently teaching a low-advanced grammar class at the English Language Institute (ELI) five days/week simultaneously with attending the genre course, Patrick was able to design a genre-based curriculum unit for an authentic teaching context, and in fact, implemented it later in the semester as a review unit.[3]

We focus on how Patrick identified and developed his *identity-in-activity* through the activities/assignments of his formal learning context. The construct of *identity-in-activity* (Cross, 2006; Cross & Gearon, 2007) has been proposed as a way to unify identity as concrete practice in the classroom (what a teacher does) and discursively constructed practice by larger sociocultural, institutional, economic, and political forces (what macrostructures say a teacher should do). The data for this chapter include Patrick's *narrative inquiry* and his genre-based curriculum unit. Analyzed from an emic perspective using sociocultural discourse analysis (Mercer, 2004), the data from the narrative inquiry extracts highlight (marked in bold font) the linguistic instantiations of how Patrick expressed and played with his *identity-in-activity*, the contradiction between his idealized conception of his language teacher identity, his *identity-in-activity* originating in his activity/experiences as a language assistant, and the *identity-in-activity* he feels is being constructed for him as a grammar teacher with these particular students in this particular instructional setting. The contradiction represents a *growth point*, which Patrick addresses within the *structured mediational spaces* of the narrative inquiry and the final project for the genre class, the genre-based curriculum unit. The data from the genre-based curriculum unit show linguistic instantiations of Patrick's transformation of his *identity-in-activity* both conceptually and materially, tracing his development as a teacher through his engagement in these cultural practices of L2 teacher education.

Patrick's pre-understandings

Prior to the genre-based course, Patrick had taken two graduate courses with the teacher educator: Applied English Grammar, a pedagogical grammar course focusing on discourse-based approaches to grammar and grammar teaching, and TESL Materials and Methods, a praxis-driven course focusing on *multiliteracies* (The New London Group, 1996) and discourse analysis as a tool for understanding language in use in order to design curriculum for language teachers, and as a way to engage students in their language learning, especially when they leave the classroom. Because both of these courses shared the conceptualization of language as choice/resource for making meaning across a variety of interactional contexts, they provided a foundation for the conceptualization of genre in the graduate course.

Patrick held a strong pre-understanding of language learning as communication from his experience as a language assistant (LA). During his undergraduate studies, Patrick worked at an English Language Institute (ELI) in a paid position as an LA. Though language assistants meet with a teaching supervisor, make lesson plans, and are observed once per semester, they are expected to act as 'friends' rather than teachers by creating games or entertaining communicative activities for the students. They typically meet outside around picnic tables, adding to the informal language learning environment. In his *narrative inquiry*, Patrick recollected the joy he experienced working with English language learners as an LA.

Excerpt 2
When I taught my first IEP English class 4 years ago, I was **instantly entranced** with teaching English (much different than present-me). I **was hooked** because it is a truly **amazing experience** to watch non-native English speakers, from different parts of the world, communicating in English. The only way that these non-native English speakers could communicate with each other was by using English, **and it feels good as a teacher to help facilitate this communication. From my first classroom interaction, I was convinced that learning and teaching English served the purpose of communicating.** (Klager, 2013, p. 2)

Patrick's *identity-in-activity* as an LA was as a teacher who facilitates communication, and this identity reveals his pre-understandings *"that learning and teaching English served the purpose of communicating."* He describes his feelings about what he was doing as an LA facilitating communication (*"feels good"*) through playful, somewhat magical images that suggest being bewitched: *"instantly entranced,"* *"hooked,"* and the *"amazing experience."*

However, Patrick's pre-understandings stood in stark contrast to what he was experiencing in his teaching of the advanced grammar class. In the graduate course on genre, he regularly expressed frustration to the teacher educator and his classmates that his students only wanted to know the rules of grammar and do de-contextualized fill-in-the-blank exercises. He wondered out loud in class whether and how he could integrate anything he was learning in the genre class in his teaching. Because the teacher educator was also Patrick's MA advisor, she recommended that he conduct a *narrative inquiry* for his final MA project in order to investigate the dissonance, a potential *growth point*, he was experiencing. Through his *narrative inquiry*, Patrick discovered that his pre-understandings were a part of the dissonance he was experiencing in his teaching of grammar; yet, his pre-understandings shaped his response to his dissonance as well, as we will see as we delve further into his *narrative inquiry*.

Playing in and through narrative inquiry: Patrick's identity-in-activity as 'the grammar inquisitor'

Patrick worked through his frustration about his own and students' activity in the grammar class he was teaching through the writing of his *narrative inquiry*. As he described his students' and his classroom activity in the introduction to his narrative, Patrick played with his conception of himself as the teacher, his *identity-in-activity*, through the image of *"the grammar inquisitor"*:

Excerpt 3
The clock turns to 11:45 am, the students begrudgingly file into their seats, still tired and exhausted from the day before. They **take out their homework and look to the board, silently beginning the grammar warm-up, which consists of five sentences where either will or be going to is omitted**. Once they have finished, the students know and fear what awaits them next: the future perfect and progressive tenses. The **students silently and meticulously take notes as the grammar inquisitor writes decontextualized rule after rule** ...

1. Use *will* or *be going to* in the independent clause and the simple present in the dependent clause when talking about two separate actions in the future.
2. Future perfect progressive = S + *will have been* + V(-ing) + O
    a. EX: I *will have been torturing* myself with English grammar for 8 months by the time I take the TOEFL.

... on the board, seemingly with no end. After thirty minutes, **tortured by their boredom and lack of comprehension,** the students let out a collective sigh of relief as the final rule of the future perfect tense used in conjunction with *by the time*-phrases is written on the board—which is now completely obscured by rules they have yet to comprehend. (Klager, 2013, p. 1)

Patrick describes his teacher *identity-in-activity* through the exaggerated and monstrous image of *"the grammar inquisitor,"* who writes *"decontextualized rule after rule"* until the board is full, while students copy the rules and complete form-based, sentence-level exercises. He interprets how students feel about their activity by expressing negative, even harmful, emotions: resistance as they *"begrudgingly file into their seats,"* and *"fear"* as they anticipate what follows the opening warm-up activity. They are *"tortured by their boredom and lack of comprehension."* Patrick's expression of his tacit thoughts, fears, and frustration as he playfully storied his and his students' day-to-day activity functioned as *narrative as externalization* as suggested in an email he sent to the teacher educator.

Excerpt 4

... the 'grammar inquisitor image' basically made me realize that my approach to teaching was wrong, even if the students did claim to want it. It basically led me to the conclusion that I needed to '**give them what they want**' but do it **through my own means**. I was able to use the analogy of the grammar inquisitor (**a torturer of sorts**) to help me realize that I was unhappy, as well as the students. (Klager, personal communication, April 11, 2015)

Patrick's conception of himself and his teaching as *"the grammar inquisitor,"* an emotionally painful representation of *"a torturer of sorts,"* pointed to emotional and cognitive dissonance in his activity of teaching. Patrick's use of this grotesque image coincides with Vygotsky's (2004) suggestion that fairy tales act like a psychological tool for children, enabling them to self-regulate and act with increasing control over their worlds. Playing with this image and its associated activity in his *narrative inquiry* (see Chapter 2 on play and imagination) helped Patrick to recognize both his unhappiness and what he perceived as student unhappiness. Recognizing and naming this unhappiness motivated Patrick to explore what his students' *object* for learning grammar in his class was. In response, Patrick designed a short questionnaire to determine what his students thought about grammar and why they were studying English. This marks a move to Patrick asserting his agency, as he hopes to find a way to address their *object* (*"give them what they want"*) but *"through my own means."*

Patrick's reconceptualization of his students' reasons for studying grammar

The questionnaire had six questions, including asking whether students liked to study grammar, what the purpose for learning grammar was, and what their purpose for studying English was. Patrick's findings are not unexpected for many ESL/EFL teachers. Students overwhelmingly characterized "the purpose of grammar class is to learn English grammar to do well on a test, like the IELTS or TOEFL, or to write a paper for class" and learning grammar as "through rules and memorizing" (Klager,

2013, p. 4). The top two reasons for studying English—"to get a degree then return to my country" and "to do well on IELTS/TOEFL" (p. 4)—contradicted Patrick's pre-understandings of learning language for communication. The findings from the questionnaire provided Patrick with a kind of reality check for students' goals in his grammar class and their preferred method for learning grammar. That is, what Patrick learned about his students' conceptions of grammar and their *objects* for studying grammar from the questionnaire mediated his understandings of the grammar curriculum he was teaching at the ELI through the genre-based approaches he was learning about in the graduate course. Patrick's undertaking of classroom-based research, inspired by his *narrative inquiry*, mediated his understandings of what his students wanted from the grammar class, their *objects* from a Vygotskian sociocultural perspective, and deepened his understanding of his students.

Creating a new identity-in-activity: Synergy

Patrick's students thus mediated his understandings of their *object* for learning grammar and his *object* for teaching it, and moved him towards a new conceptualization of curriculum. However, he still needed to grapple with his understanding of the *academic concept* of 'genre' and genre-based instruction, by engaging in sustained participation with them through the cultural activities of teaching. He began internalizing these concepts, using them as *psychological tools*, when he played through the design of his genre-based grammar unit. Patrick's *narrative inquiry* demonstrates how he used his imagination to recreate his past experiences of teaching grammar as '*the grammar inquisitor*' and his experiences as an LA when he focused on teaching language for communication in the design of his seven-hour curriculum unit. As a result of the curriculum unit assignment, Patrick had a 'safe zone' to play with these concepts for his particular instructional context. He identified the grammatical features that form the student learning objectives required by the ELI that students must pass to move on to the next level. Then he imagined, that is, recreated his past experiences as an LA and a grammar teacher in his *narrative inquiry*, by creating a plan of action, what Ilyenkov (1977) has identified as a uniquely human ability.

Excerpt 5
What I plan to do is develop a curriculum that follows the following sequence of events:

1. Use the textbook for the teach-for-test grammar objectives that are required by the IEP.
   This needs to be done first because you are still trying to meet the motivations and needs of your students and institution. Not meeting these needs might make the students **disengage from your class and teaching**.

2. Find spoken and written texts for analysis that cover specifically the objectives required by the IEP.
   Use these spoken and written texts for your students to analyze **to reinforce the teach-for-test grammar as well as address the communicative purposes of the grammar.** (Klager, 2013, p. 6)

Patrick's 'plan,' identified by imperative voice, is to design a curriculum uniting students' and his *objects* for the grammar class. In bullet point number 1, he concisely states how he will use the textbook to fulfill student expectations, and then provides his pedagogical reasoning (*"This needs to be done first because you are still trying to meet the motivations and needs of your students and institution"*). If he does not do this first, he believes students will *"disengage from your class and teaching."* In number 2, he directs himself to find texts containing the specific grammatical features required by the program. His pedagogical reasoning demonstrates how he can further address point 1 while also attending to *"the communicative purposes of grammar."* Point 2 and his reasoning represents one way that Patrick is working through the *academic concept* of 'genre,' finding authentic examples of discourse that includes the grammatical items that are part of the student learning objectives at the ELI, but that can be used for communicative purposes. In articulating his pedagogical reasoning, he is assuming greater agency by asserting increasing control over his activity, and assigning "significance" (Lantolf & Thorne, 2006, p. 143) to his activity.

Patrick's writing in his *narrative inquiry* as he describes what he is doing in his genre-based grammar unit and why functions as *narrative as verbalization*.

Excerpt 6

For my approach to synergizing a teach-for-test grammar system with a communicative and contextualized grammar approach, Genre Analysis will need to be implemented into the classroom. It will need to be implemented in a way that it reinforces and further elaborates the grammar in the current teach-for-test system. Genre Analysis is appealing for a number of reasons, but most importantly because it is highly adaptive. **Being able to learn the skills for analyzing genres will provide students with skills that can be transferred to other components of their learning**. You aren't teaching specific grammar rules and abstractions, but rather are **teaching a process for learning and analyzing authentic discourse**; teachers can select texts that represent the specific grammar rules they are required to convey by the institution in a contextualized and spoken manner. This is critical for reinforcing the notion that grammar can be used for communication purposes and not only teach-for-test purposes. It is critical because Genre Analysis can convey the communicative benefits of the grammar in a way that the textbook cannot. Rather than teaching abstract rules with abstract exceptions from a textbook, **genre analysis will contextualize**

these grammatical abstractions in a meaningful and communicative way. (Klager, 2013, p. 5)

Patrick's instructional unit represents his new *identity-in-activity*, "*synergizing a teach-for-test grammar system with a communicative and contextualized grammar approach*," in which genre analysis will play a major role ("*Genre Analysis will need to be implemented into the classroom*"). He notes that he will revisit the previously taught grammatical features that he presented as rules from the student textbook by comparing those rules with student findings from their genre analysis activities in class. Patrick's reasoning for students doing genre analysis mirrors that of the teacher educator and her instantiation of the *academic concept* of 'genre.' He uses genre analysis as a kind of psychological tool for his students ("*Being able to learn the skills for analyzing genres will provide students with skills that can be transferred to other components of their learning*"). He moves away from teaching rules, "*teaching a process for learning and analyzing authentic discourse*." By having students unite the student learning objectives they learned through the rules of the textbook with a contextualized way of '*synergy*,' he hopes students will understand grammar in "*a meaningful and communicative way*."

The first two days of lesson plans from Patrick's genre-based curriculum unit further evidence how the activities and assignments in the graduate class mediated his understanding of curriculum, leading to his transformed *identity-in-activity* as '*synergism*.' Patrick appropriated some of the texts and instructions from TAA1, modifying them for his students' proficiency levels, as a means to implement his object in the grammar classroom. Patrick gave his students some authentic examples of reminiscing narratives, different from those in the graduate class, in which 'used to' and 'would' were used for the discourse-level functions discussed in the graduate class. He provided more explicit directions to guide students' genre analysis of these texts. For example, he had them circle all instances of 'would' and 'used to' in blue marker, and identify the location in the text where they occurred ('used to' functioning as a discourse frame would typically occur in the first sentence). This suggests that he has internalized the concept of 'genre' because he was able to take what he experienced in the graduate class and alter it so that it is appropriate in his instructional context while still enacting his conceptualization of language learning as communication. For a homework assignment, he asked them to use their analysis from class to answer the questions in the following excerpt.

Excerpt 7
1. What tenses are used in these excerpts?
   a. When does the author use these tenses?
   b. What purpose does the tense serve?
2. Look at all the instances of *Would* and *Used to* (blue circles). What is the author trying to do with *Would* and *Used to*?
   a. Is there a pattern?

3. Think back to our text-based rules we learned for *Would* and *Used to* earlier this semester. Are the authors in these excerpts using *Would* and *Used to* the same way as our text-based rules?
   a. How are they being used the same way?
   b. How are they being used differently?

After having students focus on form by identifying the tense, Patrick asks the students to think about the function of the tense with two related questions ("*What purpose does the tense serve?*" and "*What is the author trying to do . . . ?*"). For question 3, Patrick has students distinguish and compare the rules they were exposed to in the textbook ("*Think back to our text-based rules we learned*") to the contextualized discourse excerpts he presented ("*Are the authors in these excerpts using Would and Used to the same way as our text-based rules?*"). Moreover, Patrick created a material framework in the form of a chart for students to write the rules from the book, and then to externalize their discourse-based understandings of the grammar form appearing within a particular genre (see Appendix E).

The chart that Patrick created is a concrete representation of his imagination, or re-creation of his past experiences as a grammar teacher and LA, and a kind of resolution of the dissonance he was experiencing. In fact, the chart is material evidence of Patrick's development as a teacher. The chart embodies his '*teach-for-test grammar and Genre Analysis synergism*,' with the left column representing the former and the right, the latter. As a result of materializing the image of '*synergy*' through his genre-based curriculum unit, Patrick supports the development of his *growth point*, changes both what he and students do in the classroom, and transforms his *identity-in-activity* and his conception of curriculum. He engages students in different kinds of activities, such as doing discourse/genre analysis, and then thinking together and articulating the 'why' behind their findings about grammar in use in relation to the textbook rules. Patrick likewise engages in different activities in the classroom, such as mediating students' understandings while they do the discourse/grammar analyses. By playing with the *academic concept* of 'genre' through the creation of his genre-based grammar unit and writing his *narrative inquiry*, we find evidence that Patrick uses 'genre' as a psychological tool to transform his understanding of curriculum, of grammar teaching in his 'located' instructional setting, as well as his *identity-in-activity* when he implemented the curriculum.

Conclusion

Patrick's *narrative inquiry* functioned as *narrative as externalization*, in which he explicitly articulated thoughts and feelings about teaching, enabling him to express, and play with, his frustration as '*the grammar inquisitor*' and detail his 'rich experiences' (Vygotsky, 2004) as a teacher and LA. Patrick's playing with the image of 'the grammar inquisitor' exposed a *growth point* that he was able to address. Patrick's undertaking of *narrative inquiry* required inquiry into his students' *objects*, so that his new understanding of students mediated his 'play' with the *academic concept* of 'genre,' in a 'safe zone' in which he could 'jump above' himself as he designed his genre-based grammar unit. This linked activity of *narrative inquiry* and curriculum design for his specific teaching context fostered *narrative as verbalization*, especially as he described the *pedagogical reasoning* behind the instructional activities he designed for the unit and as he appropriated activities from the graduate class for his own class. In the process of linking activities and assignments from the graduate class with and through his *narrative inquiry*, Patrick elicited *narrative as systematic examination*, through which his engagement in narrative activity fundamentally shaped what he learned. Within the *structured mediational spaces* provided by the activities and assignments of the graduate course, Patrick (re)imagined his experiences and transformed his understanding of curriculum through the image of 'synergy' and materially through his development of the genre-based grammar unit. Patrick's new *identity-in-activity* as 'synergy' would next need to be implemented in his grammar class at the ELI.

This chapter has highlighted the value of *obuchenie* as portraying the actions and intentions of teaching *and* learning, the interconnection between the teacher educator and the teacher (as teacher and learner). *Obuchenie*, because of its focus on the instructional side of expert/novice interactions, requires teacher educators to think critically and deliberately about what they do in coursework in L2 teacher education. We saw in this chapter how the teacher educator mediated 'at-a-distance' by deliberately creating a sequence of activities/assignments that required teacher candidates to engage consistently with their understanding of *academic concepts* through increasingly demanding goal-directed activities, especially those focused on a 'located' instructional setting in which they would teach. In fact, the focal teacher in this chapter appropriated the teacher educator's activities for his own class. We are reminded that what we teacher educators do in coursework matters, to the detriment and/or benefit of teachers. We need to create multiple opportunities for authentic participation in the activities of language teaching, because our classes, not just the teaching practicum, are the exemplary 'safe zones' that can offer varied and multiple *structured mediational spaces* for *responsive mediation* to emerge within L2 teacher education. By focusing on a 'located' teaching context, this sequence of assignments also provided a 'safe zone' for the teacher candidates to deal with the kind of cognitive and emotional dissonance that often occurs when teacher candidates try to implement the *academic concepts* they have learned within teacher education in a real-world setting. By sequencing a number of purposefully created activities/assignments, we provide the kind of sustained participation in the activities of teaching that can support teacher development and allow us to trace that development as it is in the process of formation. Moreover, this chapter has demonstrated how students' motives in a real teaching context can mediate teacher conceptualizations to better meet learner expectations.

Appendix A: Tense/aspect activity

<u>Directions:</u>

Each section focuses on a certain tense/aspect combination that occurs within certain genres to help convey specific communicative intentions. We will go through each section and work through a series of questions in order to identify the focal tense/aspect and genre, but even more importantly, how the particular focal tense/aspect function in the genre to enable the speaker/writer to convey intentions beyond the descriptive rules of the grammar.

1. Identify the verb/tense aspect that is bolded. There may be more than one, which we'll contrast.
2. Identify the genre.
3. Recall our understandings of the grammatical explanation of the focal tense/ aspect combination.
4. Explain how the tense/aspect is functioning in the genre. What meaning/ intention do you think the speaker/writer is trying to convey through this combo? Or, how does the grammar function within this contextualized discourse to achieve particular communicative aims?
5. Identify a context in which this excerpt might be spoken (the written ones are more obvious).

Excerpt 1
The bad thing was they **used to** laugh at us, the Anglo kids. They **would** laugh because **we'd** bring tortillas and frijoles to lunch. They **would** have their nice little compact lunch boxes with cold milk in their thermos and **they'd** laugh at us because all we had was dried tortillas. Not only **would** they laugh at us, but the kids **would** pick fights. (Suh, 1992, as cited in Celce-Murcia & Larsen-Freeman, 1999, p. 169)

Excerpt 2
I **used** to phone my wife three, four times every trip. In Calcutta **I'd** wait five hours to get a phone call through. If I didn't get it through one night, **I'd** call again and wait three, four hours the next morning. Finally, just hearing her voice, **I'd** stand and actually choke up on the phone. (Celce-Murcia & Olshtain, 2000, p. 66)

Appendix B: Genre-based instructional activity

The purpose of this assignment is for you to take the results from your genre analysis and create a lesson plan based on your own analysis of that genre. You will determine appropriate instructional goals and objectives, and create a lesson for a 60-minute class. In addition to the lesson plan, you should include directions, activities, materials, assessment measures, activities, handouts, and/or homework.

Whatever is highlighted in **bold** must be included in the lesson plan. SEE ME if you have questions.

Instructional Context: Write a ½ to 1 page description of who your students are, their proficiency level, their goals and needs, the setting, and any other pertinent information. Explain whether your unit is for ESL or EFL.

Goals and Objectives: Your genre unit **must include appropriate goals and objectives.** They MUST be written as SWBATs—Students Will Be Able To XXXX. AND you MUST use the Bloom's taxonomy of verbs found on Sakai. Goals are general statements of the overall, long-term purposes of the course. Objectives express the specific ways in which the goals will be achieved. Thus, the goals represent the destination of the unit, while the objectives represent various points that chart your unit toward that destination (Graves, 1996). Your goals and objectives must address the questions: What are the purposes and intended outcomes of the unit (GOALS)? What will my students need to do or earn to achieve these goals (OBJECTIVES)?

Organization of Content and Activities: Your lesson plan must embody a coherent organization and sequence of activities. In your mind, you should address the questions: How will I organize the content and activities? Does the sequence of activities make sense? Do the activities build on each other and lead students towards the instructional objectives and goals? **BE SURE TO INCLUDE ALL HANDOUTS THAT YOU WOULD GIVE STUDENTS OR MATERIALS USED IN CLASS (E.G., POWERPOINTS, IN-CLASS TASKS).**

Evaluation: Your lesson plan must explain how you will assess student learning. Your lesson plan must address the following question: How will I know that students have learned what I wanted them to learn about genre? Your evaluation does not have to be in the form of a test. It could be, for example, through something students hand in as a result of a classroom activity.

Appendix C: TSL 6172 genre analysis instructional unit

The purpose of this project is for you to learn how to create an instructional unit focusing on a particular genre, based on your own analysis of that genre. If you have changed your mind since doing your genre analysis, you may need to do a new genre analysis. You will determine appropriate instructional goals and will sequence a number of activities that create a **cohesive 6-day unit**. Your instructional unit should have overriding goals and specific instructional objectives for each day of instruction. Each class should last 50–60 minutes. Your instructional unit should reflect a series of activities that include directions, activities, materials, assessment measures, activities, handouts, and/or homework. **Whatever** is highlighted in **bold** must be included in the unit. SEE ME if you have questions.

Instructional Context: Write a ½ to 1 page description of who your students are, their proficiency level, their goals and needs, the setting, and any other pertinent information. Explain whether your unit is for ESL or EFL.

Goals and Objectives: Your genre unit **must include appropriate goals and objectives.** They MUST be written as SWBATs—Students Will Be Able To XXXX. AND you MUST use the Bloom's taxonomy of verbs found on Sakai. Goals are general statements of the overall, long-term purposes of the course. Objectives express the specific ways in which the goals will be achieved. Thus, the goals represent the destination of the unit, while the objectives represent various points that chart your unit toward that destination (Graves, 1996). Your goals and objectives must address the questions: What are the purposes and intended outcomes of the unit (GOALS)? What will my students need to do or learn to achieve these goals (OBJECTIVES)?

Selecting/Adapting Materials and Activities: Your genre unit must articulate how you will select/adapt materials and the nature of the activities that will make up the learning experiences of your unit. These can be represented by core materials and activities and/or a sequence of course assignments. Your course project must address the questions: How and with what will I teach the course? **Explain in about one paragraph why these materials/activities are relevant for your target class.**

Organization of Content and Activities:

LESSON PLANS: This is the major part of your project. Your genre unit must exemplify a coherent organization and sequence of activities. In your mind, you should address the questions as you create your lesson plans: How will I organize the content and activities? Does the sequence of activities make sense? Do the activities build on each other and lead students towards the instructional objectives and goals? **BE SURE TO INCLUDE ALL HANDOUTS THAT YOU WOULD GIVE STUDENTS OR MATERIALS USED IN CLASS (E.G., OVERHEADS).**

For your lesson plans, use the following format:
General Goal(s): Can be stated once in your project
Specific Objectives: SWBATs should be enumerated with each daily lesson plan.
Required Materials:
Anticipatory Set (Lead-In): (How will you introduce your topic?)
Step-By-Step Procedures: AGAIN, INCLUDE ALL MATERIALS INCLUDING POWERPOINTS, ACTIVITES AND DIRECTIONS, ROLE PLAYS, ETC.
Closure (Reflect Anticipatory Set): (How will you end your lesson?)
Assessment Based on Objectives: (How will you as the teacher know if the student learned anything?) Your lesson plan must address the following question: How will I know that students have learned what I wanted them to learn about genre? Your evaluation does not have to be in the form of a test. It could be, for example, through something students hand in as a result of a classroom activity.

Appendix D: Narrative inquiry instructions

One of the goals of narrative inquiry in language teacher education is to enable teachers, or narrators, to bring together the disparate elements of their learning-to-teach experience (emotional, conceptual, social, practical, technical, etc.) through a systematic, reflective **process** of narrative writing and the **product**, the narrative. As such, in drafting your narrative, you may wish to review the variety of teaching-related artifacts you've been engaged in, including your journal, your dialogic video protocol, records of classroom observations, your teaching philosophy, as well as our email exchanges, and any reflections or documentation related to our individual or group meetings. There are no page minimums or limits—you should write your story as you see fit and in your voice. Your narrative inquiry can take the form that makes the most sense to you as you sort out and reflect upon your learning experience, and you may want to:

Identify aspects of your teaching experience that you experienced as surprising, challenging, or unsatisfying, and that you want/ed to better understand: *What dissonance did you want to understand?*

Explain the characteristics and context of those aspects of your teaching, and how they affected you (emotionally, personally, conceptually, instructionally, interactionally): *What was the nature of this dissonance? Who was involved?*

Explain any "research" or steps you took to understand and address the *dissonance: What did you do to address this dissonance?*

Connect and Story how thinking about those aspects of your teaching have led to new understandings of yourself as a teacher, of your teaching philosophy, of your teaching practice, etc. *How do you understand these different experiences as being connected to dealing with this dissonance create a growth point for you?*

Detail any new conceptual understandings, and/or instructional practices that embody these new understandings of who you are as a teacher: *What specifically do you think and/or do that represents how you've dealt with this dissonance? How have you taken your new understandings into your practice?*

Appendix E: Patrick's chart from his curriculum unit

With a partner, the students need to write down the text-based rules of *Would* and *Used to*. After students have done this with a partner, come back together as a class. On the board, the teacher should make a chart and divide it in two sections. On the left, the teacher should write all the text-based rules; on the right, the teacher will write the results of the class' contextualized analysis (to be done later). The board should look something like this once the class is finished giving you all the text-based rules:

This chart will be used again after the students have performed their contextualized analysis.

TABLE 8.1

Text-Based Rules	*Contextualized Analysis*
• Show habitual actions that happened in the past but are no longer true.	
• *Used to* and *would* are similar in meaning when they express past actions.	
• Only *used to* can show past location, state of being, or possession. EX: I used to live in Florida. (Location) EX: She used to be a doctor. (State) EX: Tom used to have a dog. (Poss)	

Notes

1 Some data sets reprinted with permission from Ilha do Desterro. Golombek, P. R., & Klager, P. (2015). Play and imagination in developing language teacher *identity-in-activity. Ilha do Desterro, 68*(1), 17–32.
2 Patrick's situation in which he taught for two years (not a true beginning teacher) with ostensibly no formal education (one month of 'training') points to an inherent problem in labeling teachers (novice, pre-service, etc.), as well as makes our case for the systematic formal education that L2 teacher education can offer.
3 Detailing the consequences of his implementation of the curriculum unit would undoubtedly be informative but is beyond the scope of this chapter.

References

Austin, J. L. (1962). *How to do things with words.* Oxford: Oxford University Press.
Bartels, N. (2004). Linguistic imperialism. *TESOL Quarterly, 38*(1), 128–133.
Celce-Murcia, M., & Larsen-Freeman, D. (1999). *The grammar book: An ESL/EFL teacher's coursebook (2nd ed.).* Boston, MA: Heinle & Heinle.
Celce-Murcia, M., & Olshtain, E. (2000). *Discourse and context in language teaching: A guide for language teachers.* Cambridge: Cambridge University Press.
Cross, R. (2006, November). Identity and language teacher education: The potential for sociocultural perspectives in researching language teacher identity. In *Teaching and Education at the Australian Association for Research in Education Annual Conference: Engaging Pedagogies* (pp. 27–30).
Cross, R., & Gearon, M. (2007). The confluence of doing, thinking and knowing: Classroom practice as the crucible of foreign language teacher identity. In A. Berry, A. Clemans, & A. Kostogriz (Eds.), *Dimensions of professional learning: Identities, professionalism and practice* (pp. 53–67). Rotterdam, Netherlands: Sense Publishers.
Freeman, D. (1989). Teacher training, development, and decision making. *TESOL Quarterly, 12,* 27–47.

Freeman, D., & Johnson, K. E. (1998). Reconceptualizing the knowledge-base of language teacher education. *TESOL Quarterly, 32*(3), 397–417.

Freeman, D., & Johnson, K. E. (2004). Common misconceptions about the "quiet revolution": A response to Yates and Muchisky. *TESOL Quarterly, 38*(1), 119–127.

Freeman, D., & Johnson, K. E. (2005). Response to 'Language teacher learning and student language learning: Shaping the knowledge base.' In D. J. Tedick (Ed.), *Language teacher education: International perspectives on research and practice* (pp. 25–32). Mahwah, NJ: Lawrence Erlbaum.

Freire, P. (1970). *Pedagogy of the oppressed.* New York: Seabury Press.

Fuller, F., & Brown, O. (1975). Becoming a teacher. In K. Ryan (Ed.), *Seventy-fourth yearbook of the National Society for the Study of Education* (pp. 25–52). Chicago: University of Chicago Press.

Golombek, P. R. (2011). Dynamic assessment in teacher education: Using dialogic video protocols to intervene in teacher thinking and activity. In K. E. Johnson & P. R. Golombek (Eds.), *Research on second language teacher education: A sociocultural perspective on professional development* (pp. 121–135). New York: Routledge.

Golombek, P. R. (2015). Redrawing the boundaries of language teacher cognition: Language teacher educators' emotion, cognition, and activity. *The Modern Language Journal, 99*(3), 470–484.

Golombek, P. R., & Klager, P. (2015). Play and imagination in developing language teacher *identity-in-activity*. *Ilha do Desterro, 68*(1), 17–32.

Graves, K. (1996). *Teachers as course developers.* New York: Cambridge University Press.

Hood, S., Solomon, N., & Burns, A. (1996). *Focus on reading.* Sydney: NCELTR.

Hyon, S. (1996). Genres in three traditions: Implications for ESL. *TESOL Quarterly, 30*, 693–722.

Ilyenkov, E. (1977). *Dialectical logic. Essays on its history and theory.* Moscow: Progress Press.

Johnson, K. E. (2006). The sociocultural turn and its challenges for L2 teacher education. *TESOL Quarterly, 40*(1), 235–257.

Johnson, K. E., & Golombek, P. R. (Eds.) (2002). *Teachers' narrative inquiry as professional development.* New York: Cambridge University Press.

Johnson, K. E., & Golombek, P. R. (2003). "Seeing" teacher learning. *TESOL Quarterly, 37*(4), 729–738.

Johnson, K. E., & Golombek, P. R. (2011). The transformative power of narrative in second language teacher education. *TESOL Quarterly, 45*(3), 486–509.

Katz, L. (1972). Developmental stages of preschool teachers. *Elementary School Journal, 73*(1), 50–54.

Klager, P. (2013). A narrative inquisition: High-grammar inquisitors of institutionalized grammar teaching methods. Unpublished masters project, University of Florida, Gainesville, FL.

Lantolf, J. P., & Thorne, S. (2006). *Sociocultural theory and the genesis of second language development*. Oxford: Oxford University Press.

McCarthy, M. (1998). *Spoken language and applied linguistics*. Cambridge: Cambridge University Press.

Mercer, N. (2000). *Words & minds: How we use language to think together*. London: Routledge.

Mercer, N. (2004). Sociocultural discourse analysis: Analyzing classroom talk as a social mode of thinking. *Journal of Applied Linguistics, 1*(2), 137–168.

Negueruela, E. (2008). Revolutionary pedagogies: Learning that leads (to) second language development. In J. P. Lantolf & M. E. Poehner (Eds.), *Sociocultural theory and the teaching of second languages* (pp. 189–227). London: Equinox.

Paltridge, B. (1995). Analyzing genre: A relational perspective. *System, 23*(4), 503–511.

Paltridge, B. (2001). *Genre and the language learning classroom*. Ann Arbor, MI: University of Michigan Press.

Shore, B. (1996). *Culture in mind: Cognition, culture and the problem of meaning*. London: Heinemann.

Shulman, L. S. (1987). Knowledge and teaching: Foundations of the new reform. *Harvard Educational Review, 57*(1), 1–22.

Smagorinsky, P., Cook, L.S., Moore, C., Jackson, A., & Fry, P. G. (2004). Tensions in learning to teach: Accommodation and the development of teaching identity. *Journal of Teacher Education, 55*(1), 8–24.

Suh, K. H. (1992). Past habituality in English discourse: *used to* and *would*. *Language Research, 24*, 857–882.

Swales, J. M. (1990). *Genre analysis: English in academic and research settings*. Cambridge: Cambridge University Press.

Tarone, E., & Allwright, D. (2005). Language teacher-learning and student language learning: Shaping the knowledge-base. In D. J. Tedick (Ed.), *Language teacher education: International perspectives on research and practice* (pp. 5–23). Mahwah, NJ: Lawrence Erlbaum.

The New London Group (1996). A pedagogy of multiliteracies: Designing social futures. *Harvard Educational Review, 66*(1), 60–93.

van Lier, L. (2004). *The ecology and semiotics of language learning: A sociocultural perspective*. Boston: Kluwer Academic.

Vygotsky, L. S. (1935/1994). The development of academic concepts in school aged children. In R. van der Veer & J. Valsiner (Eds.) (1994). *The Vygotsky reader* (pp. 355–370). Oxford: Blackwell.

Vygotsky, L. S. (1986). *Thought and language* (A. Kozulin, Trans.). Cambridge, MA: MIT Press.

Vygotsky, L. S. (2004). Imagination and creativity in childhood. *Journal of Russian and East European Psychology, 42*, 7–97.

Yates, R., & Muchisky, D. (2003). On reconceptualizing teacher education *TESOL Quarterly, 37*(1), 135–147.

9

CONCEPTUALIZING TEACHING IN/THROUGH REFLECTING ON TEACHING

"I was perpetuating the teacher-centric classroom model that I was trying to break away from."

In this chapter, we look at *responsive mediation* through several sequenced and interconnected cultural practices that we have already discussed in previous chapters. More specifically, we examine engagement in *structured mediational spaces* between a teacher educator and a beginning ESL teacher named Arya during her teaching internship. We begin this chapter by describing the teacher educator's mediational intent behind the selection and sequencing of each of these practices in the internship, specifically because it is the capstone course of a TESL certificate program. As we described in Chapter 6, the teaching journal is an invaluable tool through which a teacher educator can learn about a teacher's *perezhivanie*, the subjective significance of lived experiences contributing to the development of one's teaching personae. The teacher educator needs to develop some understanding of each teacher as an individual, so the journal entries provide a space for teachers to express their cognition (idealized conception of teaching) and emotion (anxieties and strengths in regards to teaching) before they even begin actual instruction. After the teachers begin teaching, the teaching journal serves as a place for them to externalize their thinking, doing, and feeling about their interactions with students and their activity of teaching, and, thus, for the teacher educator to have some sense of how the teachers are experiencing their instruction and where they need support. The relationship and understanding developed through the written interactions in the journal help to shape the moment-to-moment oral interaction between the teacher educator and each teacher in a dialogic video protocol (DVP). As we described in Chapter 5, the DVP provides a materialization of the instructional interactions that took place in real time in a given class, and thus, opens up the teacher's thinking and activity to analysis, mediation, and restructuring. By enacting the DVP, the teacher educator can identify each teacher's potentiality and work with him/her at his/her 'ceilings,' encouraging teachers to reflect on whether and how their activity of teaching aligns with their conceptions of teaching. If not, the DVP provides a 'safe zone' in which teachers can play with and imagine alternative instruction. The DVP also provides teachers with concrete instructions/activities that they can take into their teaching, and then reflect on in their teaching journals. After the teachers complete their teaching, they once again reflect on their thinking and doing of teaching but in retrospect, revisiting the various forms of mediation in which they were engaged in the process, through the writing of a *narrative inquiry*. *Narrative inquiry*, as discussed in Chapter 8, can help teachers to organize, articulate, and make sense of what they experience emotionally and cognitively in their day-to-day teaching, and through the process, possibly gain increasing control over their thinking and doing of teaching as they re-story their learning-to-teach experience in their own words and minds. We remind readers that in spite of similar cultural practices being used and described throughout Chapters 5–9, each interaction between a more expert teacher educator and a less experienced teacher will take shape and unfold in distinctive ways because each teacher and each teacher educator has a unique sociocultural history and *perezhivanie*, and motive.

The reflective teaching journal dialogic video protocol, and narrative inquiry

The internship context

Arya's internship placement was in a language program offering eight-week speaking/listening courses for visiting scholars at the university. The visiting scholars have completed or are in process of completing a PhD or MA degree, and are largely from China, Brazil, and Turkey. The scholars voluntarily participate in the free English classes, and are awarded a certificate of participation on the basis of attendance and requirements. Given the scholars' age and professional accomplishments, the teachers, as undergraduates and often first-time teachers, are initially intimidated by this instructional context, so they generally teach with a partner. Arya co-designed and co-taught an advanced listening and speaking course with Mark.[1]

The mediational intent of the teacher educator who designed the program is made overt to teachers as they design the syllabus for their classes. The teacher educator begins by explaining the instructional goals and student needs for the different levels in general, so teachers can design an initial syllabus, and then expand it as they interact with their students. The teacher educator also suggests specific instructional foci for the first weeks of teaching to focus teachers' instructional thinking and alleviate feelings of being overwhelmed by too many possibilities. Teachers can thus create instruction that is relevant to students' needs and goals, providing some sense of beneficial instruction/interaction for teachers and students alike. Also, by revising previous interns' lesson plans for the initial weeks of instruction, teachers can play in a 'safe zone,' imitating others' ideal conceptions of implementing content through the artifact of a lesson plan. As teachers overcome their initial teaching anxieties, they are then expected to design their own lesson plans in order to address what they have identified as instructional objectives through their interactions with students. Through her mediational intent at-a-distance, the teacher educator is creating a structure for *intermental development zones* (IDZs) to emerge by facilitating play and imitation that is supported in a 'safe zone' for a group of students, and pushing teachers at their 'ceilings' as they are increasingly expected to design and implement instruction, still with support as needed, to meet their specific students' needs and abilities.

As a requirement of the internship, Arya wrote seven reflective journals (three with prompts from the teacher educator and four to reflect on her actual teaching) to which the internship supervisor (teacher educator) responded. The first two journal prompts targeted cognitive and affective issues on an abstract level, asking teachers first to describe their ideal class (what the learning activity of the classroom would look like), and second to describe their strengths and challenges as beginning teachers. The teachers also did a *practice teach* (see Chapter 7), presenting a concept that they would be teaching in one of their initial classes as a way to get feedback in a 'safe zone' from the teacher educator and fellow teachers. After completing the lesson plan, Arya wrote a third journal entry in which she identified important lessons and/or personal goals from doing the *practice teach*, allowing for *growth points* to emerge. These three journal entries provide invaluable information about Arya's conception of teaching, perceived strengths, affective concerns, and abilities that helped the teacher educator attune her mediation. Arya taught four weeks of the eight-week internship, so she wrote four journal entries externalizing how she was experiencing her classroom teaching. She participated in the internship requirements (teaching journal, DVP, meeting with teacher educator, *narrative inquiry*) according to her own needs. For example, she met weekly with the teacher educator to touch base and sometimes go over lesson plans. She was videotaped teaching during her third week of teaching, and she and the teacher educator participated in a DVP the following day. At the end of the semester, she reflected on her learning-to-teach experience and wrote a *narrative inquiry* (see Chapter 8), including a draft and a final version that were commented on by the teacher educator.

We follow a similar procedure with these data as we did in Chapter 6. In the data extracts presented below, the bold-faced text and connecting lines utilize the methodological techniques of sociocultural discourse analysis (Mercer, 2004) by capturing how language is being used as a social mode of thinking and illustrate the quality and character of *interthinking* on the linguistic, psychological, and cultural levels. The teacher educator (right column) takes up dimensions of Arya's journal entries (left column), building a contextual foundation for their exchanges, guiding her thinking as they jointly reconstruct Arya's understanding of her experiences, and supporting Arya as she works to develop instructional activities that align with her conception of teaching, thereby resolving the cognitive/emotional dissonance she is experiencing.

Recognizing Arya's pre-understandings

A Linguistics major, Arya was in the last semester of her senior year at the university when she participated in the internship. She was simultaneously enrolled in a graduate-level course that focused on genre-based approaches to language teaching. The teacher educator for the internship was also the instructor for this graduate-level course. Arya was also working in a paid position as a language assistant (LA) at the English Language Institute (ELI) at the university. As an LA, she worked with a partner to create and implement communicative activities for the same group of language learners four times per week. Though the ELI does not characterize language assistants as teachers, they engage in many typical practices of language teachers, such as making lesson plans, giving directions for activities, and encouraging and responding to student participation.

The first three teaching journal entries, for which the teacher educator provided organized prompts, revealed some elements of Arya's pre-understandings and her *perezhivanie*. In the first journal entry, the teachers answered the following prompt: What does your idealized classroom look like?

Excerpt 1

Arya

My idealized classroom, whether it was grammar or listening/speaking or what have you, focus strongly on the **socially relevant functions of language.** I would want the main focus of the class to be the analysis of texts. Basically, I would want my ideal classroom to consist of **students doing guided analyses of texts in which they would come to understand not only how semantic choices are functioning with in the text, but also how the text is functioning with in a larger context.** I would want my students to not only focus on linguistic relationships with in the text, I would want them to **be aware of what speech act is occurring and how those linguistic relationships are contributing to it.**

Teacher Educator

Okay, you have a specific vision of what you want to happen in your class Arya. **Can you explain WHY you think this is important? How this will result in student learning?** It's important to be able to justify what you're saying as well. So in a sense, I'm asking you to bring your specifics into a more abstract level of how you think students learn language in the classroom. **Why do texts matter? What do they show? Why does being able to understand how linguistics relationships work in a particular genre help someone to learn a language?** Now you can imagine that I agree with you. But that's not sufficient for your purpose. **YOU need to make your argument for others** so they would understand what you are trying to accomplish in your classroom and why. Make sense?

Arya's journal entry to this prompt put forth her ideal conceptualization of how she wanted teaching and learning to occur in her classroom, to which the teacher educator returned consistently when they engaged in *interthinking* about how Arya was experiencing her actual teaching. In Arya's ideal class, students are actively constructing their understanding of language by "*doing guided analyses of texts*" through a discourse-based approach through which students understand "*how semantic choices are functioning within the text.*" She also describes a genre-based approach as students understanding "*how the text is functioning within a larger context.*" She describes how linguistic features are contextualized using the academic concept of a "*speech act,*" and her goal seems to be to enable students to communicate effectively in their daily lives abroad.

To foster an environment for *interthinking*, the teacher educator praises how specific Arya's ideas concerning student activity are, punctuating this with an exclamation point. She then lays the groundwork for an IDZ by asking Arya "*WHY*" she thinks it is important to focus on the socially relevant functions of language. She asks Arya to go beyond describing what they will do to describing the consequences of this kind of student activity on students' language development: "*How this will result in student learning?*" With this question focusing on the impact of instruction on learning, the teacher educator is orienting Arya's thinking to a central purpose of teaching, but one that typically emerges after much more teaching experience. Though Arya describes her conception of teaching using academic concepts such as "*speech acts,*" the teacher educator does not want Arya's cognition to remain at what Vygotsky (1988) described as a level of mimicry, an important but insufficient aspect of teacher development. She supports Arya's *teacherly thinking* by modeling a series of questions, for example a direct question getting at the rationale behind her instructional approach: "*Why does being able to understand how linguistics relationships work in a particular genre help someone to learn a language?*" In fact, the teacher educator, who understands Arya's conceptualization, encourages her to express her rationale for others ("*YOU need to make your argument for others*"). By modeling a series of questions that Arya could be asking herself, the teacher educator is pushing Arya to provide the pedagogical reasoning behind her instructional activity.

In the second teaching journal, the teacher educator asks teachers to describe areas in need of improvement and strengths in order to gain some understanding of how each teacher perceives her/himself.

Excerpt 2

Arya	Teacher Educator
I would say that my biggest weakness in teaching is the same as my biggest weakness in general. I often lack confidence, even if I am sure of what I am saying. Through I do a better job of faking it in the classroom (no statements ending with question intonation) I do think that **I need to work on becoming more confident in myself as a teacher.**	**If I had one goal for you in both classes, it would be for you to grow in confidence**... I like to use **self doubt as fuel for what I need** to do though. It points me in the direction I need to go. **What am I doubtful about? Okay, then I have to build my knowledge** about that.

Arya's lack of self-confidence, her *"biggest weakness,"* created a lens of *perezhivanie* through which she perceives herself *"in teaching"* and *"in general."* This journal entry confirmed what the teacher educator had inferred from previous interactions with Arya as she often unnecessarily apologized for ideas she expressed. By acknowledging her lack of self-confidence, Arya also reveals a personal attribute to which the teacher educator will need to be sensitive if she is to mediate her responsively. The teacher educator commented in Arya's journal by confirming that she had similar hopes for Arya (*"If I had one goal for you in both classes it would be for you to grow in confidence"*). The teacher educator also validates Arya's affective concern by sharing her own experience with and response to self-doubt, noting she uses it *"as fuel for what I need to do."* In doing this the teacher educator corroborates the value of *feeling-for-thinking* (Golombek & Doran, 2014), that is, explicitly integrating the catalytic function of emotion in teacher professional development. She models self-talk, voicing the question-response she would ask herself—*"What am I doubtful about? Okay, then I have to build my knowledge about that."* This interaction thus provides the teacher educator and Arya with a shared understanding of Arya's fledgling confidence and the goal of building her self-confidence that can guide them as they co-construct an IDZ.

When describing her strengths as a teacher, Arya noted her love of teaching and willingness to work diligently outside class to prepare lessons and to grow. She wrote what we see in Excerpt 3.

Excerpt 3

Arya

To me the majority of a teacher's work should be done outside of a classroom before class. I think that learning should be **mediated self-discovery**... Also, a quick note based on the last journal. I guess the **why behind what I'm saying is that students remember better what they discover for themselves**. They take more home from an activity in **which they were challenged to discover a pattern rather than when the pattern is spelled out for them**. The more control a student has over the journey he takes to learn a language, the more in control he feels over the language at the end.

Arya ties her own willingness to work hard outside class with her conception of student learning: *"mediated self-discovery."* Arya ended this journal entry by taking up the teacher educator's invitation in the previous journal to *"tease out"* her pedagogical reasoning for what she would like to do in her class. Arya's taking up in her second journal entry of the teacher educator's mediation from the first journal entry, that is, across journal entries, enables them to stay attuned to each other's thinking in an IDZ. Arya's use of the phrase *"mediated self-discovery"* to characterize student learning is something to which the teacher educator, given her understanding of Karpov's (2003) critique of discovery learning as inefficient and misleading (see Chapter 1), responds. Rather than write in the margin comments as she typically does, the teacher educator critiques discovery learning at the end of Arya's journal entry, and this is replicated here in a similar manner.

Excerpt 4

I feel the need to respond in text rather than in margin on this. **Discover a pattern rather than have it spelled out for them.** Okay, now I understand. Enabling your students to discover a pattern requires a great deal of skill on the teacher's part. After all, you don't want to waste precious class time and you want to lead to good discoveries. It's interesting that you say this **because I believed this myself as a teacher. As I started to read about concept based instruction, which is based on sociocultural theory (the theory I use in my teaching and research), I had this idea of discovery challenged**. Now I think the issue is the semantics of the word "discover," so allow me to elaborate a bit more.

Discovery learning became quite popular in American schooling and like all things in education (☺) there was suddenly a critique of it. Actually, I would like to share a reading with you on this. Anyhow, the critics' point is that **1) sometimes discovery learning activities take a lot of time and are thus not efficient, and 2) sometimes students come to wrong discoveries.** E.g., we look at the stars and we think that the sun revolves around us. So the critics said that discovery could be time consuming and lead to a lack of learning. So what then can teachers do? It's a long story to make concept based instruction clear but basically the idea is that **the teacher plays a crucial role in presenting the content in meaningful ways to students.** So in order to make meaning for themselves, students have to have a strong conceptual understanding. Through their activities in the classroom, they continue their sense-making processes, using the language and explaining their metacognition. **But it's quite focused. It's not discovery, but it is personal sense making through the use of conceptual tools**. Of course I could say that personal sense making through concepts is a kind of discovery if I used that word differently.

Nonetheless, I am saying this because looking back on my early years as a teacher, **I used a highly inductive approach that I thought was great at the time**. But I came to question it in terms of the quality of instruction it led to. In fact, **I had one powerfully bad experience with a student** that over time made me realize a lot of how I was doing my discovery learning. To be honest, I realized that I did not give myself credit for the role I should be playing as having knowledge in the classroom as the teacher. I didn't want to "give" my students knowledge but to let them "discover" it. I understand why I did what I did at the time and I'm not saying I was a bad teacher. I "think" I was good. But with new understandings and knowledge, I evaluate that teaching differently, somewhat negatively (and can say why). My philosophy of teaching now is quite detailed and explicit and I try to make my classrooms embody it though I know I have degrees of success. **Anyhow, perhaps this is more than you wanted to know ☺ But I am going to question you about what you mean by "discovery" because it's a loaded word. And I hope this is okay with you.**

In the first paragraph, the teacher educator signals that this is going to be a detailed, important commentary because she is writing *"in text rather than in margin"* as she typically does. Throughout her comments, the teacher educator uses a number of rhetorical strategies in order to push Arya's thinking while remaining sensitive to her level of confidence. The teacher educator lays the groundwork for *interthinking* about what discovery learning means by trying to clarify her understanding of what Arya means by 'discovery,' and then, so her commentary is less face threatening, positions herself as a beginning teacher similar to Arya: as a beginning teacher, *"I believed this* [discovery learning] *myself"* but then she had this idea *"challenged"* as she learned about Vygotskian sociocultural theory. The teacher educator is uncertain whether she and Arya have the same meaning in mind about 'discovery learning' as an *academic concept*, so wants to explain what she means when she uses this concept.

In the second paragraph, the teacher educator, so that Arya does not feel as though she is being attacked personally, prefaces her critique of discovery learning by noting with a smiley face how theories *"like all things in education"* are critiqued. She attunes Arya to her understanding of why discovery learning is problematic by summarizing Karpov's (2003) argument (*"sometimes discovery learning activities take a lot of time and are thus not efficient"* and *"sometimes students come to wrong discoveries"*). She provides an easy-to-understand example of the earth's revolution around the sun to show how discovery learning could go awry. The teacher educator knows that she cannot cursorily explain an alternative instructional approach grounded in sociocultural theory, concept based instruction: *"It's a long story to make concept based instruction clear"*—but highlights that *"teachers play a crucial role in presenting the content in meaningful ways to students."* She highlights the crucial role that teachers play in creating the *"focused"* conceptual understanding students need beforehand for *"using the language and explaining their metacognition."*

In the third paragraph, the teacher educator recalls *"one powerfully bad experience with a student"* that pushed her understanding of 'discovery learning' as she uses her expertise to mediate Arya's understanding. She normalizes Arya's understanding of 'discovery learning' by in essence saying "I thought like that too," but shares her own negative experience in order to push Arya's thinking. The teacher educator sets up what she (mis)understood at that time as the two alternatives in teaching conceptions—giving students knowledge versus students discovering knowledge. However, *"with new understandings and knowledge,"* the teacher educator now has a more complex conception, which she manifests in her own teaching and can justify, and hopes to continue to share ("*But I am going to question you about what you mean by 'discovery' because it's a loaded word. And I hope this is okay with you*"). By being attuned to Arya's lack of self-confidence, the teacher educator downplays the strength of her critique of 'discovery learning' ("*perhaps this is more than you wanted to know*") and inserts a smiley face emoticon[2] as another softener.

Through this series of written dialogic interactions an IDZ emerges and a more robust understanding of Arya's conception of teaching begins to take shape. This is accomplished as the teacher educator and Arya build this understanding by *thinking together*, simultaneously explaining and critiquing their understandings of discovery learning, and asking and answering questions about Arya's ideal conception of teaching and discovery learning; the teacher educator also shares her ineffective implementation of it. They engage in *responsive mediation* by staying attuned to Arya's fledgling self-confidence as the teacher educator retells her own experiences as a novice teacher practicing 'discovery learning' while also challenging Arya to deepen her conception of teaching by articulating the reasoning behind her instructional activities and asking a series of questions to help her to do so.

A growth point emerges

The teacher educator videotaped Arya teaching during her third week of teaching (the fourth week in the course, as she and Mark alternated teaching weeks). It is important to note that the earlier a teacher can be videotaped for a DVP interaction, the more time the teacher will have to try to implement new understandings into their teaching activity. The teacher educator and Arya conducted a DVP of a lesson in which Arya introduced the concept of intonation.

Arya began the lesson with a 10-minute mini-lecture on intonation in which she tried to elicit the meaning of intonation from students. Then, she distributed a transcript of a speech by President Obama that they would next watch. She told them to mark places on the transcript where the President seemed to be expressing emotion through intonation.[3] After watching the video, the class regrouped for a whole class discussion concerning what they marked as intonation. The pattern of teacher–student interaction repeatedly involved Arya asking for an example, a student giving an example, and Arya paraphrasing the student's answer, a common initiation-response-feedback (IRF) sequence. Arya recalled feeling "*uncomfortable*" at the time because she felt as though students always focused on her. Even when other students did participate, she expressed that "*rather than listening to their classmates they're just waiting for the classmate to be done so they can just have me go back over it all.*" Because the teacher educator has Arya's ideal conception of teaching in mind and because Arya stated that she did not want to be the one in the classroom doing the "*telling*" (DVP), the teacher educator works to construct an IDZ with Arya by encouraging her to articulate an alternative instructional response.

Excerpt 5

TE: **Could you change the activity so that not everything is (.) you leading the discussion?** (4.0)

Arya: I mean I **could have them in pairs discussing the questions** (6.0)

TE: and then y'know imagine if you had (.) and this is why I think transparencies are really great (.) if you have you have the um the uh (.) transcript on the transparency, and then (.) um (.) they could even highlight the things that they were talking about they **could literally stand in front of the classroom and highlight the things they were talking about** ((*interruption in hall*))

TE: y'know what I'm saying,

Arya: yeah I do

TE: I=

Arya: =I remember doing that in high school

TE: yeah. You did it in my class too with

Arya: oh wow. I forgot about that.

A *growth point* (McNeill, 2005) emerges as the teacher educator and Arya discuss the contradiction between Arya's ideal concept of teaching and the reality of what is transpiring in her classroom activity. The teacher educator asks her "*Could you change the activity so that not everything is (.) you leading the discussion*," allowing for a 'do over' in a 'safe zone.' Depending on how Arya answers this, the teacher educator will be able to gauge better how to enact *responsive mediation*. The teacher educator offers her a space to think by remaining silent after her question. And after a four-second pause, Arya presents a brief response, "*I could have them in pairs discussing the questions.*" The teacher educator again gives her the space to elaborate on her suggestion of pair activity by remaining silent. After six seconds of silence, the teacher educator builds on Arya's response by inviting her to "*imagine*" having students also look at a transcript on a transparency. Although we could imagine a less explicit form of mediation being offered, the teacher educator works to create joint mental activity through more explicit mediation by referencing what she thinks is a shared understanding of how she used transparencies to support student activity in her own class in which Arya had been a student. Using this shared understanding as a concrete model of what Arya could have done, the teacher educator makes clear how students could "*literally stand in front of the classroom and highlight the things they were talking about*" rather than the teacher eliciting and controlling the results of pair/small group work in a teacher-fronted way. Arya does confirm the value of students' working through their understandings with a transparency, but by recalling her experience doing this in high school. The teacher educator reminds Arya that they have a shared experience of using transparencies in this fashion from the teacher educator's class, to which Arya replies, "*oh wow. I forgot that.*" This is a useful reminder that what we, as teacher educators, assume to be shared knowledge may not be shared in ways we expect.

Arya later stops the video after another series of initiation-response-feedback (IRF) sequences prevalent in her instruction. She again expresses frustration about repeatedly creating teacher-fronted lessons in spite of her deliberate efforts to revise her lesson plans to make them less so, an example of emotional/cognitive dissonance. The teacher educator acknowledges Arya's efforts and frustration.

Excerpt 6

> TE: you think you're breaking out of it (0.5) I don't- **this is no: deficiency on your part, this is like speaks to how: POWERfully ingrained (1.0) that model is**
>
> Arya: yeah
>
> TE: even when you had (.5) examples trying to break away from that (.) they don't translate (.) it's not like (.) I said something to you and then it transfers to your way of thinking
>
> Arya: yeah
>
> TE: I think (.) I think what's happening now: is **an incredibly crucial step** (.) you see what your intention was and you see how it's playing out
>
> Arya: mm
>
> TE: and you're saying that this is still (2.0)
>
> Arya: uh so much to do (laughs)
>
> TE: so: instead of watching (1.0) let's talk about how this could've been different
>
> Arya: okay
>
> TE: and more (2.0) more what I think you want your class to be
>
> Arya: uh hm (2.0)

The teacher educator emphasizes "*how: POWERfully ingrained*" the teacher-fronted model of teaching is as a way to normalize Arya's struggle to make her activity of teaching align with her idealized conceptualization. This interaction highlights the *growth point* as the contradiction between Arya's thinking and doing of teaching comes squarely into focus. The teacher educator and Arya work to stay attuned to each other's changing states of knowledge, understanding, and emotion within an emerging IDZ about overcoming teacher-fronted instruction. The teacher educator notes that recognition of the contradiction and the difficulty of changing teaching "*is an incredibly crucial step*" in her development. The two-second pause after she notes that Arya is "*saying that this is still* [a problem]" suggests that the teacher educator is using that space to determine what *responsive mediation* might look like next. Arya attempts to save face through her inflated comment "*so much to do*" and laughter. The teacher educator makes a strategic choice to stop watching the video, especially given Arya's *perezhivanie* concerning her lack of self-confidence, in order to address this *growth point*. Rather than just asking what she could have done differently as she had done earlier, the teacher educator signals that they will participate in *interthinking* ("*let's talk about how this could've been different*") with an orientation to how she thinks Arya wants her class to be. As the DVP continues, the teacher educator tries to create joint mental activity with a more specific prompt.

Excerpt 7

TE: **how could you have the sa:me (1.0) resources (1.0) but changed (2.0) what was happening in this class (1.0) and from physically changing the class to activities changing the class**

Arya: well **I really like what you said about transparencies** (1.0) because there's an overhead projector in every UF classroom (1.0) which I used to think was ridiculous but now (1.0) I'm kind of (.) sensing (.) um I like the idea of (1.0) **maybe not the sa:me resources,**

TE: uh hmm

Arya: but having several things we watch with the transcripts printed ON (1.0) the transparencies,

TE: uh hm

Arya: and then having several STUdents go up and (2.0) y'know they don't have to provide all the information but kinda be the one-**like have a list of questions (.) to ask the class to find and circle words** but once again I don't want to do it within the framework of intonation cause (.) I don't know it

TE: right right right right right. But again again (.) y'know **think about how I use the transparencies** to work in a group,

Arya: uh hm

TE: you have specific things ya have to do (1.0) then you've gotta come back with your explanation (.) You gotta present your answer and justify it right? (.5) so if you think in terms of this, (1.0) y'know (1.0) so (2.0) what was (1.0) I don't know what your questions were (.), I can't remember what your questions were.

The teacher educator mediates responsively here by introducing "elements of the task's solution" (Vygotsky, 1987, p. 209) by orienting Arya to using "*the sa:me (1.0) resources*" while altering the physical arrangement of teacher and students ("*physically changing the class*") and what students were doing in class with the resources ("*activities changing the class*"). Arya takes up this mediation by appropriating the teacher educator's earlier suggestion to use transparencies ("*I really like what you said about transparencies*"), but expresses agency as she negatively appraises the resources she used ("*not the sa:me resources*"), suggesting she would like to come up with a better explanation of intonation and more appropriate texts. Arya continues to detail how she would change her instructional activity, "*have a list of questions to ask the class to find and circle words,*" but she would use a new "*framework*" to remedy her unclear explanation. The teacher educator emphatically approves of this idea (five "rights"), and then attempts to create *intersubjectivity* by referencing their shared knowledge, encouraging her to "*think about how I use transparencies.*" The teacher educator communicates her expert thinking by recapping her procedures for using transcripts, and reiterating that the teacher provides specific objectives for the students when doing the activity, and then has students present their answers and justify the reasoning behind the answers. In essence, the teacher educator is encouraging Arya to engage students in a similar kind of *interthinking* that was embodied in the instructional activities she enacted in the pedagogical grammar class and in her interactions with Arya in the DVP.

The *responsive mediation* that emerged in the *structured mediational space* of the DVP was predicated to some degree on the teacher educator's targeted understanding of Arya's *perezhivanie* and ideal conception of teaching as expressed in her teaching journals (and, of course, as discussed in their other interactions) as a *growth point* emerged. At the same time, *responsive mediation* was dynamic, contingent, and emergent in the real-time, moment-to-moment dialogic interaction in the DVP as the teacher educator tried to gauge where Arya was in her cognition, emotion, and activity concerning teaching. Though the teacher educator began with a more implicit approach by asking Arya what she could have done differently, the teacher educator engaged in joint mental activity by noticing silences and lack of detail, thereby providing explicit mediation when Arya needed assistance to change the activity of her teaching to align with her emerging conception of teaching. She offered a pedagogical strategy, using transparencies in pair or small group work, from their shared experiences in the teacher educator's class, as a way to engage students in the kind of sense making of language in context that Arya valued. Though Arya had not recognized the teacher educator's pedagogy in the pedagogical grammar class as a model for accomplishing the kind of student interaction that she desired, she could, once prompted, appropriate the model and reimagine what she could have done differently in the class she taught on intonation. As we will see in the next section, the consequences of this *responsive mediation* played out inconsistently when Arya tried to materialize her emerging conceptions of her teaching in the internship.

Arya's (inconsistent) aligning of her activity of teaching with her conception of teaching

In the week following the DVP, Arya and Mark were presenting a unit on politeness and directness in American English requests, responding to requests, and hedging. Arya attempted to implement her new conception of instruction when she introduced politeness in American English requests. She put students into pairs and gave each a transcript of a request dialogue between two native speakers of English. They were also given three questions about the transcript. The students were told that they had 15 minutes to analyze their dialogues and come up with answers for their questions. Once the 15 minutes were up, one member from each pair used the overhead to explain the group's ideas to the rest of the class. She evaluated this lesson in her teaching journal entry:

Excerpt 8

Arya	Teacher Educator
It **went great!** (I know **I'm supposed to say more than that,** but I want to say that, too!)	Actually, I am **quite relieved** to hear this. **Yah.**
I may have gone into the lesson nervous, but it went better than any other lesson so far. The **students were incredibly engaged in their groups, discussing what they thought was being accomplished and how.** During the presentation portion, there was an open conversation with the entire class. I never had to explain anything, **I just had to facilitate** the conversation by pointing out what I agreed with and what was really interesting and asking questions to further their thoughts about it.	**I can see you are explaining why here** ☺ I am **so excited** reading this. You are **describing everything** I have been trying to convey to you about this way of teaching. You have experienced it and **you "understand".** **Wow.**

Arya evaluates the lesson as going *"great"* but knows that the teacher educator expects an explanation for her evaluation (*"I know I'm supposed to say more"*). The teacher educator validates Arya with *"Yah."* Arya then provides evidence of why she believes the class went so well: *"students were incredibly engaged in their groups"* as they grappled with *"what they thought was being accomplished and how."* The students presented their ideas, the content that Arya wanted them to discover, and she *"just had to facilitate."* The teacher educator responds to Arya's earlier aside that she knows that the teacher educator will want her to explain by noting *"I can see you are explaining here,"* using the smiley face emoticon as evidence of their shared understanding. The teacher educator validates Arya's implementation of her emerging conceptualization in her instruction by expressing her excitement. She also signifies with 'understand' in quotes that Arya has enacted her new conceptualization into her material activity; from a Vygotskian sociocultural perspective, she has developed as a teacher. She expresses the significance of Arya's accomplishment with *"[W]ow."* However, given our understanding that teacher development occurs through sustained participation in the activities of teaching, it is hardly surprising that Arya does not experience the same success the next time she teaches.

Because of the success she experienced in this lesson on requests, Arya planned to do her next lesson on the different situational meanings of 'sorry' using a similar instructional activity. Classroom conditions changed as only three students showed up for class, and Arya expressed her disappointment with the lesson in her teaching journal. Once again we are reminded how a lesson plan is an idealized conception of teaching activity that will be influenced by various contextual factors emerging in the material activity of teaching.

Excerpt 9

Arya	**Teacher Educator**
Because of the lack of cultural variety (and the **lack of our normal, talkative, analytical students**) the lesson **did not go very well**. ~~My wait~~ time has never been so tested! I ended up having to completely change my question every time, essentially **walking them through each context** in order to reach the answer I was looking for.	**Did you have them analyze together or as individuals/pairs first?** It seems like the former or your wait time comment wouldn't have been such a concern. **I guess I'm just not to understanding** why this didn't work out if you had texts for analysis.
It was **incredibly frustrating** for me as the teacher, and I'm **sure uncomfortable for the students,** who **did not want to talk as much as they ended up having to.** Despite this, however, I feel as though the students got something out of the lesson. They were surprised by the number of different ways that sorry is used in American English. They also by the end had a grasp of how sorry can be used with sarcasm (they did not have a perfect understanding of sarcasm obviously, but they understood the possible relationship between I'm sorry and sarcasm).	**Are you sure about this? Did they NOT want to talk or did they not understand what you wanted from them? Did you give them an opportunity to prepare to talk?** Again, **I just don't understand what the problem was from what you describe. I would encourage you** to think more on this and what you did. **It may not be as you think**...

Arya attributes the lesson not going "*very well*" to the absence of the "*talkative, analytical students*" who normally participate. Students did not respond despite her varied questions and protracted wait time, so she took up a more teacher-centered role ("*walking them through each context*") to elicit appropriate answers. The teacher educator, assuming that Arya followed the similar pattern of interaction and activity as in the previous successful lesson on politeness in requests, expressed confusion by asking "*Did you have them analyze together or as individuals/pairs first?*" The teacher educator's expertise is evident in her response as she speculates that Arya changed the activity from pair analysis of text before returning for whole-class discussion to whole-class analysis of texts together with her ("*It seems like the former*"). The teacher educator, knowing from experience working with beginning teachers that they may initially blame students if a lesson goes awry as a kind of face-saving mechanism, speculates and then downplays her speculation ("*I guess I'm just not understanding*") as a way to encourage Arya to reflect and explain further.

Arya expresses negative emotions in the next paragraph as she describes what transpired in the class, describing it as *"frustrating"* for her and *"uncomfortable for the students."* She attributes her frustration and student discomfort to their unwillingness to participate (*"did not want to talk as much as they ended up having to"*). The teacher educator shifts to more direct questioning because if she is going to mediate Arya responsively, she needs to know more about what transpired. She directly asks Arya if she is *"sure about this* [her interpretation]," modeling questions she should ask herself about whether it was student unwillingness to participate, punctuated by 'not' in capital letters, or lack of an understanding of how to participate. She directly asks her if she enabled them to participate (*"Did you give them an opportunity to prepare to talk?"*) as a reminder of their shared understanding created through the DVP. The teacher educator uses a rhetorical strategy of modals as hedgers, hedging her inducement to reflect with a distancing modal (*"I would encourage you to think more on this and what you did"*) and then suggesting the possibility of another explanation through another modal (*"It may not be as you think"*).

To close this section, Arya's final week of teaching involved a number of review activities, so this lesson marked the end of her attempts to integrate her new conceptualization of students co-constructing their understandings of language through text analysis into her teaching activity with new subject matter. Arya's return to her teacher-centered style of teaching in the next lesson and her reflections in her teaching journal demonstrate the inconsistencies so prevalent in the learning-to-teach experience, representing what Vygotsky (1987) called the *twisting path* of development. Though Arya had some initial success addressing the contradiction of her *growth point*, she has not fully internalized her conceptualization of students co-constructing their understandings of language, that is, she is not fully self-regulating in her activity of teaching.

Re-storying what triggered Arya's return to teacher-fronted instruction

By including a *narrative inquiry* project at the end of the teaching internship, the teacher educator intended for the teachers to step back from their experience; revisit it through their journal entries, the audiotape of the DVP, videotapes of their teaching, and whatever other artifacts the teachers might have; narrate their experience; and, in the process, come to new understandings of their learning-to-teach experience. Arya's narrative reveals how she construed the teacher educator's and her *responsive mediation* as shaping her learning, as well as what she learned. In her narrative inquiry, Arya highlighted the importance of her interactions with the teacher educator during the DVP.

Excerpt 10

Being able to sit with [the teacher educator] and have my teaching analyzed in an interactive way, both of us being able to stop the video and talk about whatever came to our mind, **allowed me to see myself in a new way.** Watching myself teach and talking about it was incredibly helpful because **it took the abstract concepts that we had been discussing all semester and put them in a concrete framework.** Right in front of me was the evidence that my class, even though it was participatory, still remained teacher-centric. **Though I may be thinking about discovery learning or genre theory while creating my lessons, I was not applying them as well as I had thought.**

Arya describes how the experience of watching herself on video and discussing what she was doing and why with the teacher educator allowed her to *"see myself in a new way."* This was in part done by *"how abstract concepts that we had been discussing all semester"* were put *"in a concrete framework"*—Arya herself suggesting a Vygotskian notion of the dialectic between the abstract and concrete. What the DVP showed her was that even though her class was *"participatory"* (students were asking and answering questions), it was not the kind of participation she wanted because it was teacher-centered. A contradiction existed between her *"thinking about discovery learning or genre theory while creating my lessons"* and *"applying them"* in her actual teaching.

Arya also acknowledges in her narrative the impact of her journal writing and her and the teacher educator's *responsive mediation* of the entries as she re-stories her *"frustrating"* teaching experience with the lesson on 'sorry.'

Excerpt 11

I realized after the fact (**after a journal and a journal reaction from my professor**) that I could have handled the situation better…I allowed myself **to feel pressured** into changing the format of my lesson… **I was incredibly nervous** when I realized how few students had showed up, however. For some reason I did not think that this format would work. I think I was nervous about having all of the students work in one small group and how that would affect the atmosphere of the classroom.

Arya appears to have taken up the teacher educator's advice to reflect further on and reinterpret what happened by directly referencing the journal entries (*"I realized after the fact"*). Arya's narrative functions as *externalization* as she describes her emotions and thoughts when she was teaching that lesson. She describes feeling *"nervous"* first when she realizes that only three students were attending class that day and then when she thinks about them working together in one group. Consequently, she allowed herself *"to feel pressured"* and reverts to her teacher-centered pattern of interaction with students analyzing the varied situational meanings of 'sorry' one by one with her at the front of the class. Whereas previously in her journal entry Arya attributed her return to teacher-centered teaching to student unwillingness to participate, here she attributes it to her nervousness as she feels *"pressured"* to modify her plan. Arya explained that the students:

Excerpt 12

...felt pressured in the normal "classroom" environment to let the teacher be the one providing the information. Because of this dynamic, the class was **incredibly difficult to get through**. It felt like **it dragged**, taking a longer than usual amount of time because of how many long pauses there were following me asking a question and **no one having an answer to volunteer. In my nervousness I returned to my teacher-centric classroom model**, feeling more comfortable in the role of information-provider because I was unsure about how the students would participate in a less "standardized" classroom.

Students likewise felt *"pressured"* to revert to their previous norms of participation. Rather than forge ahead, albeit nervously, with the successful kinds of activity and interaction she established in the previous class, Arya resumes the comfort of being the information provider. Arya evaluates the resulting classroom interactions through negative emotional language (*"felt pressured," "incredibly difficult to get through," "it dragged"*). Because she has not given them the space to construct their understandings of the texts with a partner or group before whole-class discussion, she describes *"no one having an answer to volunteer."* Rather than trusting in her newly emerging cognitions, her conceptualization of teaching, she is regulated by her emotions (*"In my nervousness I returned to my teacher-centric classroom model"*). In describing her emotions and how they influenced her teaching activity, Arya, through her *narrative inquiry*, was able to reinterpret and re-story her experience. Arya's re-storying of this experience reveals what she learned.

Excerpt 13

I had prepared my lesson in a certain way that, in my mind, necessitated a larger group of students. In reality, however, any group of students could have completed my assignment. **I just needed to be sure to give them the information in an environment where they were primed to participate with answers they have had to time to figure out themselves** ...

The 3 students that I had come to class that day were all incredibly interested in sociocultural aspects of language. As we went through the lesson **it was apparent that they were understanding the points and were enjoying them**. They were not, however, primed to participate in the discussion. They did not have knowledge of the different usages of "sorry" and were not inclined to just speak up in class.

In order to make that class be much more successful, **I should have just stayed with my original plan**. Rather than allowing the low number of students to make me uncomfortable and change my mind for how to lead that day's class, **I should have trusted myself as the teacher** and carried forward with the lesson normally, allowing the students time to talk among themselves about the material before expecting them to be able to offer information in front of the class, however small it may have been that day.

Arya now believes that her lesson plan would have worked with any number of students. She reinterprets her students as being "*incredibly interested*," and re-stories what happened in class: "*it was apparent that they were understanding the points and were enjoying them*." Students were not unwilling to participate. They needed to be "*primed to participate*" and have time to construct their understandings of the language feature before they were expected to participate. She realizes she should have "*stayed with my original plan*" and "*trusted [her]self as the teacher*," an important reminder in light of her and the teacher educator's goal of her building her confidence through the learning-to-teach experience in the internship.

The teacher educator commented on Arya's narrative as she described her return to a more teacher-centered role.

Excerpt 14
This is so interesting because you showed that you had "learned" something important earlier. Yet when faced with quite a different context, what you had "learned" seemed not to be fully internalized. **This is not meant as a critique of you at all. I am trying to point out how "learning" is not linear. It is, as Vygotsky says, a twisting path.** It might be helpful for you to think about this in your own learning, but your students as well! **Their learning is not linear either.**

The teacher educator's response to Arya's resumption of her teacher-centered manner of teaching in the face of a changed context is "*not meant as a critique*" of her but as an acknowledgment of how learning to teach requires extended participation in the activity of teaching. The teacher educator revoices Vygotsky's (1987) image that development is a *twisting path* involving fits and starts, suggesting that Vygotsky's ideas were part of their dialogic interactions throughout the internship. In addition, the teacher educator connects Arya's learning experience to that of her students ("*Their learning is not linear either*"). Once again, the teacher educator tries to orient Arya to the impact of instruction on learning, but this time through Arya's learning.

Conclusion

The sequencing of *structured mediational spaces* that the internship provided—the teaching journal, DVP, and *narrative inquiry*—enabled the teacher educator and Arya to develop a shared understanding of her pre-understandings of her conception of teaching as students co-constructing their understanding of language as discourse through texts, her execution of this conception in her teaching, as well as her *perezhivanie*. As the teacher educator became attuned to Arya's conceptions of teaching and emotions expressed in her teaching journals, the teacher educator tried to mediate responsively in her written responses to push Arya at her 'ceiling' to articulate the justifications behind her conception of teaching. The contingent and dynamic mediation as they engaged in joint talk in the DVP assisted Arya's ability to identify and address the central reasons why she was not enacting her idealized conception of teaching and tangible pedagogical activities to do so, a *growth point*. Though Arya was successful in aligning her instructional activity with her idealized conception of teaching in her next class, she reverted back to her teacher-centered ways in the following class, a common experience for many beginning teachers. Through the reflection and externalization facilitated by the *narrative inquiry* she conducted, Arya was able to reinterpret both her and her students' activity, and re-story the experience to exhibit cognitive (knowing what she could have done) and emotional growth (trusting herself), exhibiting a more nuanced understanding of what participation means in the language classroom. Though she had some opportunities to materialize her emerging conceptualization of students co-constructing their understandings of language in meaning-based activity, Arya needs continued opportunities to enact her conceptualization in teaching activities in new and varied contexts if these written and spoken dialogic interactions with the teacher educator are to become psychological tools that regulate her teaching.

In this chapter we have highlighted how a teacher participating in an internship engaged in a sequence of *structured mediational spaces* that allowed for prolonged participation in the activities of language teaching. This sequence made *responsive mediation* possible, and the teacher experienced both gains and setbacks, with the opportunity to turn setbacks into gains in the learning-to-teach experience. In spite of having an ideal for teaching, the teacher struggled to enact that conceptualization, as is typical of many beginning teachers. The teacher thought that she was enacting her ideal, but realized otherwise when watching and talking about a video of her teaching with the teacher educator. Providing mediation that is responsive to the immediate needs of a teacher can be challenging when the teacher has to teach in next to no time, has limited resources to enact a conceptualization of teaching, and may feel insecure. We believe it was the teacher educator's sequencing of cultural activities with specific mediational intentions that allowed for an ongoing co-construction of an IDZ, which enabled a shared understanding of the teacher's cognitive and emotional needs to emerge through the journal entries before and during teaching, a *growth point* to emerge and be addressed through the DVP, and Arya's re-storying of an unsuccessful teaching experience to occur through the writing of the *narrative inquiry*. We also believe it was the teacher educator's balanced attention to pedagogy (such as using transparencies, providing guiding questions to work on in pair work before discussion) and the teacher's tenuous confidence that facilitated the teacher educator's *responsive mediation* as the teacher verbalized, materialized, and enacted her emerging conceptualization of teaching as students co-constructing their understanding of language as discourse through texts. Both her successful and unsuccessful experience with enacting her conceptualization, with supportive mediation, helped to foster the development of greater levels of teacher/teaching expertise. By tracing teacher development as it is in the process of formation in/ through the varied activities of the internship, we are able to see the interdependence between engaging teachers in different kinds of thinking about teaching and providing multiple opportunities to enact instruction, as well as the kinds of mediation that can emerge in these varied cultural practices of teacher education.

Notes

1 Mark undoubtedly mediated Arya's thinking and doing of teaching, but this interaction is beyond the scope of this chapter.
2 The teacher educator is not normally a user of emoticons, but finds them essential in softening critique and creating emotional solidarity with beginning teachers as they learn to teach.
3 Arya confused emotion as signaling intonation in her class. Although this was discussed in the DVP and no doubt contributed to her students' answers, it is beyond the scope of this chapter to address this issue.

References

Golombek, P. R., & Doran, M. (2014). Unifying cognition, emotion, and activity in language teacher professional development. *Teaching and Teacher Education, 39*, 102–111.

Karpov, Y. V. (2003). Vygotsky's doctrine of scientific concepts: Its role for contemporary education. In A. Kozulin, B. Gindis, V. S. Ageyev, & S. M. Miller (Eds.), *Vygotsky's educational theory in cultural context* (pp. 65–82). Cambridge: Cambridge University Press.

McNeill, D. (2005). *Gesture and thought*. Chicago: University of Chicago Press.

Mercer, N. (2004). Sociocultural discourse analysis: Analyzing classroom talk as a social mode of thinking. *Journal of Applied Linguistics, 1*(2), 137–168.

Vygotsky, L. S. (1987). Thinking and speech (N. Minick, Trans.). In R. W. Reiber (Ed.), *The collected works of L. S. Vygotsky, Vol. 3. Problems of the theory and history of Psychology* (pp. 37–285). New York: Plenum Press.

Vygotsky, L. S. (1988). The problem of age (M. Hall, Trans.). In R. W. Reiber (Ed.), *The collected works of L. S. Vygotsky, Vol. 5. Child psychology* (pp. 215–231). New York: Plenum Press.

PART IV

Mindful L2 Teacher Education

10

RESPONSIVE MEDIATION

The Nexus of Mindful L2 Teacher Education

In our earlier work, we argued that taking up a Vygotskian sociocultural *theory of mind* radically transforms how we understand L2 teacher learning, L2 teaching, and the entire enterprise of L2 teacher education (Johnson, 2009; Johnson & Golombek, 2011). In this project, by looking closely at our teachers as they are learning to teach and our activity in mediating their learning, we have become mindful of our role in cultivating their professional development. And this, according to Vygotsky, is the ultimate goal of formal education: "to point the road for development...to create conditions for certain cognitive processes to develop... for a child to transform an ability 'in itself' into an ability 'for himself'" (as cited in van der Veer & Valsiner, 1991, p. 331). As L2 teacher educators and applied linguistics researchers, writing this book has created the conditions for our own professional development, enabling us to become mindful of our pedagogy for L2 teacher education. By putting our pedagogy under a microscope, we have deliberately sought to unpack what we have fully internalized as L2 teacher educators, and, in true Vygotskian fashion, externalized our own expertise as we seek to cultivate L2 teachers' professional development. Doing so, we believe, has changed our expertise as well, cultivating a higher level of consciousness, a more nuanced understanding of our work, and a mindfulness of what, how, and why we do what we do and its consequences on and for our teachers. As we mentioned at the outset, we believe that the educational value of analyzing our practices with our teachers, in our programs, is in enabling others to scrutinize their practices, to hold themselves accountable to the teachers with whom they work, and to become mindful of their pedagogy for L2 teacher education.

Early on in this project, the notion of responsiveness captured our imagination. We could feel and see an intense level of responsiveness in how our interactions with teachers unfolded. Yet to articulate what we meant by *responsive mediation*, we needed to tease out its dynamic, emergent, and contingent qualities while also articulating a theoretically sound rationale for why we do what we do with the teachers with whom we work. We also needed to empirically document the consequences of our pedagogy on and for our teachers' professional development. The end result of this project, the writing of this book, has led us to conceptualize our pedagogy as *Mindful L2 Teacher Education*.

Framed as Vygotsky might, *Mindful L2 Teacher Education* is about creating the 'social conditions for the development' of L2 teacher/teaching expertise. It is about engaging in dialogic interactions that assist teachers as they transform knowledge, dispositions, skills, and abilities 'in itself, for themselves.' It is about exposing teachers to psychological tools that 'point the road toward' more theoretically and pedagogically sound instructional practices and greater levels of professional expertise. In practice, *Mindful L2 Teacher Education* requires that we recognize and intentionally direct what happens inside the practices of L2 teacher education. To do this, we need to be mindful of our motives, intentions, and goals when designing, sequencing, and enacting our pedagogy. We need to be mindful of who our teachers are, where they are in cognitive, affective, and experiential terms, how they are experiencing both being and becoming teachers, and what we collectively are attempting to accomplish throughout our time together. We need to maintain an intense level of responsiveness, one that permeates all of our interactions, whether moment-to-moment, asynchronous, or at-a-distance, in order to encourage collective responsiveness within our practices. We need to be mindful of the consequences of our pedagogy on how teachers come to understand both the scope and impact of their teaching. More now than at any point in our professional careers, we have become mindful of the tremendous level of reflexivity, sensitivity, and specialized expertise that is required of us if we are to cultivate L2 teachers' professional development.

Yet we are also well aware that in a time when there is growing public consensus that teachers matter, this has not been matched by a consensus that teacher education matters (Cochran-Smith, Feiman-Nemser, & McIntyre, 2008; Edwards, Gilroy, & Hartley, 2002). On the contrary, political challenges to the value of teacher education and alternative pathways into teaching through initiatives such as 'Teach for All' (http://teachforall.org/en) have reified the common sense notion that teaching is best learned on the job. Additionally, the neoliberal de-skilling of the teaching profession that is being propagated through teacher-proof, scripted curriculum (see Beatty, 2011) is purposefully designed to take the mindfulness out of teaching by telling teachers exactly what to think, say, and do irrespective of who the students are or where the educational setting is. These trends and their socially situated meanings both reflect and are reflective of contemporary societal, institutional, and political expectations that shape and are shaped by the sociocultural contexts in which teachers and teacher educators live, learn, and work. *Mindful L2 Teacher Education*, we believe, offers a counter-narrative to these discourses. *Mindful L2 Teacher Education* requires that we make visible the unique contributions that teacher educators as professionals and teacher education as professional preparation make toward the development of L2 teacher/teaching expertise and its deeply personal and moral consequences on and for L2 teachers.

We once again call attention to Vygotsky's idea that properly organized formal education is the exemplary activity to achieving a deeper understanding of the object of study, and thus argue that L2 teacher education can be that compelling force in teacher professional development. Vygotsky argued that children go through critical periods, not linked to age, but periods of upheavals, where new psychological tools (literacy, math, etc.) are introduced with the goal of reconstructing the child's mental structures. These critical periods are marred by contradictions between the child's current abilities and the dominant mental formations, what we described in Chapter 2 as *the social situation of development*. Overcoming these contradictions creates the potential for cognitive development. We thus envision *Mindful L2 Teacher Education* as a critical period in the learning of teaching, in which contradictions emerge between teachers' *apprenticeship of observation* (Lortie, 1975) and what they are experiencing and being exposed to in and through the practices of L2 teacher education. *Responsive mediation*, as the nexus of *Mindful L2 Teacher Education*, emerges during systematic instruction aimed at the ceilings of teachers' ZPDs and supports the emergence of new meanings, enabling teachers to gain increasing control over *true concepts* that regulate their teaching activity and burgeoning teaching expertise.

In Chapters 1–4 we offered the foundation of sociocultural theory and a collection of Vygotsky and Vygotskian-inspired theoretical concepts to situate and operationally define the concept of *responsive mediation*. In Chapters 5–9 we highlighted various iterations of *responsive mediation* that emerged in different material cultural activities that constitute our own L2 teacher education practices. In this chapter we shift our attention to a much more abstract level, one in which we consider the logic that is ignited when *responsive mediation* becomes a psychological tool for L2 teacher educators, teachers, and researchers to both examine and inform their own pedagogy. We propose *responsive mediation* as an *academic concept* that "develops dynamically through use, to be learned over time and formed through a process of synthesis and analysis while moving repeatedly between engagement in activity and abstract reasoning" (Johnson, 2009, p. 20).

Given our Vygotskian sociocultural stance on internalization as the ongoing process of transforming from the social-external to the personal-internal, we know that readers will not simply read about *responsive mediation* and use it to regulate their thinking and activities. Nor does *responsive mediation* include just any interaction. Through our description of *responsive mediation* as a psychological tool, we encourage readers to ascend to the concrete by externalizing and examining the conceptual and material features of their L2 teacher education practices (activity). We invite readers to document and analyze empirically the impact of *responsive mediation* on, for, and with the L2 teachers with whom they work.

Dialectics and responsive mediation

In proposing *responsive mediation* as a psychological tool for L2 teacher educators, we draw on the origins of Vygotsky's approach to investigating the development of higher-order mental functioning (i.e., human cognitive development). In his attempt to reformulate the dominant psychological theories of his time, Vygotsky sought to overcome the deficiencies of binary logic (i.e., mind versus body) by uncovering how dialectical principles functioned in the domain of human consciousness, specifically the uniquely human ability to use symbols to mediate the psyche (Mahn, 2009). Dialectical logic, based on the writings of Hegel (1965), is a method of reasoning that aims to understand the world concretely in all of its movement, change, and interconnections, unifying its opposite and contradictory sides. Put simply, to understand anything in our everyday experience, we must know something about how it arose and developed (processes) and how it fits into the larger context or system of which it is a part (relations). Vygotsky was attracted to how Marx had used dialectical principles in his political-economic analysis of capitalism, and thus he attempted to apply these same principles to the field of Psychology. Obviously much more can be said here, but for our purposes, it is Marx's dialectical methodology that we find fruitful in articulating the internal logic of *responsive mediation*. Briefly, Marxist methodology entails deconstructing the present to find its preconditions in the past (how did it come to be as it is), which allowed Marx to project its likely future (what it could be), in essence, seeking out the preconditions of the future in the present (what is happening now that allows us to imagine the future). Marx's 'dance of the dialect,' according to Ollman (2003), is never truly finished. Thus, while "change is always part of what things are, the central question becomes how, when, and into what they change and why they sometimes appear not to (ideology)" (Ollman, 2003, p. 66). For teacher educators, this means thinking dialectically and having a theorized idea of how, when, and into what we expect teachers to change their thinking and activity, all the while recognizing why they may not change, or choose not to change, in ways that we may have intended and/or imagined.

We find this dialectical methodology vital in defining the internal logic of *responsive mediation*. When we respond to our teachers' blog entries, when we discuss their videotaped instruction, or when we ask them to conduct narrative inquiry projects, we continually ask ourselves, "Given the activity we are currently asking our teachers to engage in (present), how have their ways of thinking, talking, and acting come to be as they are (past)?" Moreover, "How can we collaboratively co-construct an imagined future, one in which they come to embody theoretically and pedagogically sound ways of thinking, talking, and acting (future)?" Thus, while we are engaged in the present, we must collaboratively and cooperatively acknowledge the past and imagine the future, all the while recognizing what we are doing as happening in an evolving, ever-changing, and challenging system. And as a result, *responsive mediation* has come to represent the nexus of our pedagogy for L2 teacher education through which this process is accomplished. It is not simply about what we do, but how we think about what we do that matters. And how we think about what we do is grounded in an ideal/material dialect that (re)shapes *responsive mediation* continually.

Ideal/material dialect

In addition to being driven by dialectical logic, we also find *responsive mediation* as constituting an ideal/material dialectic. One opposition, the ideal (conceptual), represents our motives, intentions, and goals, which inform not only the design and sequencing of the mediational spaces, tools, and activities that we create, but also how we envision our teachers should begin to think, talk, and act. The other opposition, the material (activity), is what we actually say and do together, our moment-to-moment, asynchronous, and at-a-distance interactions, that are, of course, enacted with real people, with histories, needs, emotions, in real time and in real contexts. This dialectic is endemic to our work in that a new path forward, or a new way of thinking, must be put forth both ideally and materially for development to occur. And this is where *responsive mediation* comes into play. Teacher educators have an ideal of what they want to accomplish in an activity and an individualized sense of each teacher, but it is in the material, the *in situ* enactment of that activity, that teacher educators attempt to identify concretely the lower and upper thresholds of each teacher's ZPD as they seek to cultivate development. The *in situ* activity, on the social plane, may alter the teacher educator's ideal, as well as understanding of the teacher, while also, we hope, altering the teacher's ideal and activity. *Responsive mediation*, once again, functions as the mechanism through which to resolve the dialectical relationship between the ideal (conceptual) and the material (activity) that exists in the social conditions and interactional spaces, mediated through language, where *obuchenie* takes place. Not every interaction between a teacher educator and a teacher leads to development, so when enacting *responsive mediation*, the concept of *obuchenie* positions teacher educators squarely on the instructional side of expert/novice interactions, as the ultimate goal of *Mindful L2 Teacher Education* is to cultivate teachers' professional development.

The ideal/material dialectic does not only represent the teacher educator's mental processes and activity in L2 teacher education. Teachers likewise come into these interactions with an ideal (conceptual), though we expect that this ideal does not contain the specificity characteristic of the teacher educator's expertise. Teacher educators thus also need to have some understanding of the teacher's ideal if they are to mediate responsively. This is where intersubjectivity is particularly important as teacher educators try to create a shared understanding of the instructional situation that is the focus of their activity. This dialectic plays out in dialogic interactions with teachers, when teacher educators and teachers are highly responsive to one another, when they share some of the same motives and are working toward the same objective, and when their dialogic interactions are directed at the upper limits of teachers' current capabilities.

Junctures within mindful L2 teacher education

Given the complexity and dynamism of the dialectic we are describing, especially the ideal/material, readers may be struggling to understand how to place these abstract notions into concrete activity. We have found it helpful to consider the ideal/material dialectic emerging at three unique but continuously interacting junctures in our work as teacher educators—intentions, *in situ*, and consequences. The first encompasses our intentions. In whatever practice or sequence of practices that we are creating for and/or enacting with teachers, we begin with basic questions concerning what we hope teachers will accomplish, what we anticipate as being difficult for them, and what the consequences of activity may be on and for teachers. The second juncture is *in situ*, as it is happening, in moment-to-moment, asynchronous, or at-a-distance interactions. The dialogic nature is obvious in both moment-to-moment and asynchronous interactions, but it is also evident in the at-a-distance interactions. If we consider Bakhtin's (1986) notion of dialogism as *utterance* and *discourse*, chains of utterances and discourses not only anticipate a listener, but also anticipate a response, being "shaped and developed in continuous and constant interaction with others' individual utterances" (p. 89). As teacher educators, our mediational intentions at-a-distance serve to anticipate teachers' responses, and to maintain an ongoing dialogue. We again ask ourselves questions *in situ* concerning what we seem to be achieving and how it links with our and our teachers' intentions. The third juncture entails the end result, the consequences on and for professional development. As we enact our intentions in activity, we expect there will be significant consequences for teachers, for their students, and for ourselves, so we question what those consequences might be, both *in situ* and after the fact.

We emphasize both the recursive and interactive nature of these junctures. Even when one juncture is a focal point, the others are still present. When considering our intentions, we are concomitantly reflecting on what we anticipate, to some degree, will happen *in situ*, as well as the possible consequences. When interacting *in situ*, we are appraising whether and how our intentions are being carried out as well as their potential consequences. And when we experience and appraise the consequences, we are reflecting on their effect on our intentions and the *in situ*.

Responsive mediation

We emphasize that our concept of *responsive mediation* is theoretically informed and multifaceted and, thus, cannot be reduced to a bite-sized definition. Grounded in dialectical principles, *responsive mediation* starts with the teacher as a whole person, or as much of the person as teacher educators know or can come to know. It also requires establishing a sense of teachers' *perezhivanie*, both past and present, as well as recognizing teacher educators' own complex interplay of cognition and emotion, originating in and reshaped through their *perezhivanie*. Thus, *responsive mediation* recognizes how teachers have come to be who and where they are (processes) as well as how they and what they do fit into the larger sociocultural contexts in which they operate (relations). From here *responsive mediation* proceeds to the particulars: the challenges teachers are facing, the tensions they are experiencing, the excitement they are feeling. These particulars may represent potential *growth points* where *responsive mediation* may be most beneficial. For example, a teacher's idealized teaching persona (e.g., Kyla's persona as *fun and mellow*), or the partial understanding of an academic concept (e.g., Ryan's everyday notion of parallelism), or an externally imposed teacher identity (e.g., Patrick's identity as 'grammar inquisitor') all represent the particulars or preconditions that exist in the present that can help open up the past and imagine the future. As teacher educators work on and through these particulars, they must come to recognize the upper limits of teachers' potential, be strategic in the sort of assistance given, and remain highly responsive to teachers' immediate needs and emerging capacities. As we mentioned previously, we emphasize the multidirectional nature of these dialogic interactions and the fluidity with which *responsive mediation* evolves. Such responsiveness requires that teacher educators intentionally forge *intermental development zones* (IDZs)—multiple and sustained opportunities to *think together* about the problems, concerns, and/or issues at hand; offer assistance that is responsive to immediate needs and emerging capabilities; and design, sequence, and enact various mediational spaces, tools, and/or activities through which teachers can function successfully ahead of themselves. Yet, *responsive mediation* also entails moving back and forth between the particulars and the abstract, drawing on *academic concepts* to restructure *everyday concepts*, assisting teachers in naming or renaming new ways of reasoning about and enacting their teaching activity in various instructional situations, for different pedagogical purposes. As new generalizations take shape, *true concepts* begin to emerge and hopefully become the psychological tools that enable teachers to enact theoretically and pedagogically sound instructional practices in the settings and circumstances where they teach.

Responsive mediation also requires that teachers come to think dialectically too. We expect teachers to reflect on their experiences with us by recognizing the past in the present, and imagining the future, as predicated on the present. For example, in Chapter 6 Kyla's idealized teaching persona originated in her past and was challenged when she was unable to enact it in the present, but with the teacher educator's assistance and their dialogic blog exchanges, she became increasingly capable of materializing her idealized teaching persona. As a consequence, her idealized teaching persona had changed. Her *mellow and nice attitude* now had *a purpose* and *clear objectives* that regulated her thinking and activity. She was not only able to describe what she did, she was able to imagine what she could have done. Her newly imagined teaching persona emerged from the fluid social relations and dialogic interactions that she had with the teacher educator. These interactions were not and could not have been predicted ahead of time, but instead were negotiated and constituted *in situ* as teacher and teacher educator engaged in and with the blog during Kyla's practicum placement. We saw a similar tension unfold for Abra in Chapter 5. Her idealized conception of teaching originated in her *perezhivanie* about what it means to be a 'good' person in how she treated others. Even though she did not enact this conception materially in her instructional activities, at least to her way of thinking, engagement in the digital video protocol (DVP) with the teacher educator created a safe zone, a 'do over' of sorts, where she was able to express what she could have done differently to engineer student participation in the future. And in Chapter 9, we saw how Arya expressed her ideal conceptualization of teaching as students co-constructing their understanding of language as discourse through texts, and how she thought she was enacting it until she participated in the DVP. Even though the teacher educator's assistance through their emerging, moment-to-moment dialogic interactions in the DVP enabled Arya to design and enact material activity aligned with her ideal conceptualization in her next class, when faced with new classroom conditions, she resorted to her teacher-fronted approach. The self-inquiry and mediation provided through the process of writing a narrative inquiry enabled her to re-story this entire experience, transforming her understanding that she could implement her conceptualization in material activity with any number of students if they were '*primed to participate*' and she '*trusted [her]self as the teacher.*'

As we have argued throughout this book, L2 teacher education as a culturally embedded, socially constructed educational activity is designed and carried out to support the development of L2 teacher/teaching expertise. Yet, in many ways, and based on our analyses in Chapters 5–9, what we are really attempting to do in our pedagogy is to project an imagined future *on, with,* or sometimes *for* our teachers. For us, *Mindful L2 Teacher Education* is about how to enact *obuchenie*, focusing specifically on the central role of social interaction and meaning-making in building teaching repertoires for *how to be* and *how to mean* in the L2 teaching world. *Mindful L2 Teacher Education* entails attention to what teachers bring to their learning-to-teach experiences (*pre-understandings*), how teachers are experiencing what they are learning (*perezhivanie*), the emergent, contingent, and responsive nature of teacher/teacher educator mediation (*responsive mediation*), the development of new understandings (*concept development*) in situations where teachers' pre-understandings are inadequate, and the mediational means (*mediational spaces, tools, and activities*) through which teachers begin to reconceptualize how they think about and attempt to enact their instructional practices in the setting in which they teach. To enact *obuchenie* as Vygotsky intended, we argue, *responsive mediation* lies as the nexus of *Mindful L2 Teacher Education*.

An invitation for L2 teacher educators, teachers, and researchers

In the opening pages of van der Veer and Valsiner's (1991) book, *Understanding Vygotsky: A Quest for Synthesis*, they offer a quote from Vygotsky that captures the principles that have inspired us to write this book. In true dialectical thinking, Vygotsky states:

> Every inventor, even a genius, is always the outgrowth of his time and environment. His creativity stems from those needs that were created before him, and rest upon those possibilities that, again, exist outside of him. That is why we notice strict continuity in the historical development of technology and science. No invention or scientific discovery appears before the material and psychological conditions are created that are necessary for its emergence. Creativity is a historically continuous process in which every next form is determined by its preceding ones. (p. xi)

In this book we have opened up for closer scrutiny the material (practices) and psychological (conceptual) conditions of our work as 'inventors,' as teacher educators, and in doing so, unpacked what we know and do as L2 teacher educators and researchers. By turning our analytic gaze inward and grounding what we know and do in a sociocultural theoretical perspective, we have articulated our pedagogy for L2 teacher education by uncovering 'the material and psychological conditions' underlying it. It is our hope that by making our pedagogy accessible to others, we have created the theoretical and pedagogical conditions that will promote *Mindful L2 Teacher Education*. Our commitment to *Mindful L2 Teacher Education* and the concept of *responsive mediation* as the mechanism through which it is enacted would not have been possible if we had not empirically documented and analyzed the material and psychological conditions of our work as L2 teacher educators. Thus, to conclude, we invite readers to take up a mindful stance, one that we believe will enable them to enact *Mindful L2 Teacher Education* in the settings and circumstances in which they work and that offers a counter-narrative to dominant discourses that degrade teacher/teaching agency and the role of teacher education in the development of teaching/teacher expertise.

Cultivating development

Teachers do not enter L2 teacher education programs to mirror the experiences they have in the everyday world. Instead, they expect to engage in practices that will, by design, enable them to materialize and enact theoretically and pedagogically sound instructional practices that support productive language learning within the contexts in which they teach. In the introduction of our 2011 edited book, we argued that a Vygotskian sociocultural *theory of mind* offers tremendous explanatory power to both capture the elusive processes of teacher professional development and articulate sound ways to support and enhance teacher professional development within L2 teacher education programs (p. xi). While much of our earlier work focused on capturing the processes of teacher learning, our more recent work, and this book in particular, has focused on the deployment of specific Vygotskian-informed concepts and principles in order to intentionally promote the development of L2 teacher/teaching expertise. It is for these reasons that we have sought to examine not only how we attempt to cultivate teachers' professional development but also the consequences on and for the development of L2 teacher/teaching expertise. We see our work as very much in line with Lantolf and Poehner's (2014) recent attention to the *pedagogical imperative* in L2 education. They state that *the pedagogical imperative* reflects "Vygotsky's position that to be successful, psychology cannot be a science limited to observation of human psychological processes and their development, but it must become a science that takes seriously the obligation stated succinctly in Marx's Eleventh Thesis on Feuerbach: 'The philosophers have only *interpreted* the world in various ways; the point is to *change* it' (italics in original)" (Lantolf & Poehner, 2014, p. 7). This project and our conceptualization of *Mindful L2 Teacher Education* is a serious attempt to change L2 teachers, L2 teaching, and L2 teacher education.

Thinking dialectically

This is hard for most of us to do. Thinking dialectically about anything we do requires a sea change in how we understand the world. Aristotelian philosophy has long dominated Western thinking through its dualistic mind/body distinction, based on formal logic and characterized by a schism between the ideal (mind) world and the material (body) world. Thus, in L2 teacher education we are often stuck in dualisms such as theory/practice, novice/expert, or teaching/learning, positioned as if they represent fundamental distinctions that distort our understandings of the relationship between and consequences of teaching and learning, how and what we need to know to learn to teach, and what it means to be a teacher and a learner. Dialectic thinking, in contrast, is the logic of interconnectivity, of movement, of change, and accepts as fundamental that reality is constantly changing especially through the dialectic unity of opposing forces (Novack, 1971, pp. 77–78). To enact *Mindful L2 Teacher Education*, teacher educators and teachers must think dialectically. The present must be viewed as reflecting the preconditions of the past that made it possible and the future can only be imagined by reflecting on the preconditions in the present that make the future possible. We believe our characterization of *responsive mediation* does create the social conditions for dialectic thinking and, thus, makes development possible. But, as we mentioned above, we are also humbled by the reflexivity, sensitivity, and expertise that are needed to cultivate teachers' professional development.

Unpacking expertise

As we mentioned in Chapter 1, Ball and Forzani (2010) describe the activity of teaching as 'unnatural work' since it requires teachers to unpack something that they know so well, yet now must make accessible to and learnable by others. We argue that the same can be said for teacher educators. To enact *Mindful L2 Teacher Education*, teacher educators must unpack their own expertise, or what they have internalized; make it systematic, accessible to, and learnable by their teachers; and provide appropriate assistance as teachers attempt to first imitate, then play, and eventually internalize features of their expertise, moving from external (*interpsychological*) to internal (*intrapsychological*) and thus establishing the psychological basis of L2 teacher/teaching expertise. We have done this for our work in Chapters 5–9, and invite other teacher educators, teachers, and researchers to do the same. We believe for teacher educators and teachers, doing so will change the nature of their expertise, while for researchers, doing so will change the nature of their understanding of expertise. The materialization of teacher educator expertise, whether through self-study or study by others, reveals the complexity and socially situated nature of such expertise, *located L2 teacher education* (Johnson, 2006), and thus offers evidence against the de-skilling of teachers, discourses of teaching as 'learning on the job,' or teaching as scripted activity.

Forging true concepts

As we mentioned in Chapter 1, Vygotsky (1986) did not privilege *academic concepts* over *everyday concepts*, arguing that neither is sufficient for a child to become fully self-regulated. Instead, he argued that the goal of formal education is for *academic concepts* and *everyday concepts* to become united into *true concepts*; an *academic concept* "gradually comes down to concrete phenomena" and an *everyday concept* "goes from the phenomenon upward toward generalizations" (p. 148). We believe this same process of internalization is essential for the development of L2 teacher/teaching expertise. *Mindful L2 Teacher Education* that supports the internalization of *true concepts*, a concrete example of how we can think dialectically, assists teachers as they transform their tacit knowledge and beliefs acquired through their schooling histories, enabling them to rethink what they thought they knew about teachers, teaching, and student learning. *Mindful L2 Teacher Education* supports teachers as they begin to use *true concepts* as tools for thinking, enabling them to see themselves and classroom life and the activities of teaching/learning through new theoretical lenses. *Mindful L2 Teacher Education* assists teachers as they begin to *think in concepts* (Karpov, 2003), to reason about and enact their teaching effectively and appropriately in various instructional situations, for different pedagogical purposes, and to articulate theoretically sound reasons for doing so. Likewise, through unpacking expertise, we expect that teacher educators can, as they identify what they do in their pedagogy and why, engage in a similar process of thinking through concepts more intentionally and responsively—with the goal of cultivating teacher development.

Working responsively

In line with cultivating development, thinking dialectically, unpacking expertise, and forging true concepts, enacting *Mindful L2 Teacher Education* requires that teacher educators work responsively as the nexus. We invite readers to embrace *responsive mediation* as a continuous process of recognizing and then working at the upper limits of teachers' ZPD, mindful of their own and their teachers' *perezhivanie*, sociocultural history, idealized conceptions, motives, and goals, while continually responding to teachers' needs, motives, and goals as they unfold in moment-to-moment, asynchronous, and at-a-distance dialogic interactions while engaged in the practices of L2 teacher education. As we articulate our pedagogy, we are even more humbled by the reflexivity, sensitivity, and expertise that are needed to work responsively to, ultimately, cultivate L2 teachers' professional development.

Conclusion

In this book we offer *Mindful L2 Teacher Education* as a counter-narrative to the dominant political and educational discourses that teacher education doesn't matter. We believe it does. We see *Mindful L2 Teacher Education* as theoretical learning that is intentional, deliberate, and goal-directed by teacher educators who are skilled at moving teachers toward more theoretically and pedagogically sound instructional practices and greater levels of professional expertise. We have empirically documented how teacher learning and development are assisted by the dialogic interactions that emerge inside the practices of L2 teacher education. We propose *responsive mediation* as a psychological tool for examining the quality and character of the dialogic interactions that emerge inside the practices of L2 teacher education, as well as a mediational means for orienting to and enacting a mindful pedagogy that supports the development of L2 teacher/teaching expertise. We end by leaving our readers with the same 'quest for synthesis' that Vygotsky called for more than 85 years ago. Though this book may be completed, our quest for understanding, supporting, and enhancing L2 teacher professional development inside the practices of L2 teacher education continues to constitute the essence of our scholarly and professional work.

References

Bakhtin, M. M. (1986). *Speech genres and other late essays* (V. W. McGee, Trans.). Austin, TX: University of Texas Press.

Ball, D. L., & Forzani, F. M. (2010). The work of teaching and the challenge for teacher education. *Journal of Teacher Education, 60*, 497–511.

Beatty, B. (2011). The dilemma of scripted instruction: Comparing teacher autonomy, fidelity, and resistance in the Froebelian kindergarten, Montessori, direct instruction, and Success for All. *Teachers College Record, 11*(3), 395–430.

Cochran-Smith, M., Feiman-Nemser, S., & McIntyre, D. J. (Eds.) (2008). *Handbook of research on teacher education: Enduring questions in changing contexts.* New York: Routledge.

Edwards, A., Gilroy, P., & Hartley, D. (2002). *Rethinking teacher education: Collaborative responses to uncertainty.* London: Routledge.

Hegel, G. W. F. (1965). *The logic of Hegel* (W. Wallace, Trans.). Oxford: Oxford University Press.

Johnson, K. E. (2006). The sociocultural turn and its challenges for L2 teacher education. *TESOL Quarterly, 40*(1), 235–257.

Johnson, K. E. (2009). *Second language teacher education: A sociocultural perspective.* New York: Routledge.

Johnson, K. E., & Golombek, P. R. (Eds.) (2011). *Research on second language teacher education: A sociocultural perspective on professional development.* New York: Routledge.

Karpov, Y. V. (2003). Vygotsky's doctrine of scientific concepts: Its role for contemporary education. In A. Kozulin, B. Gindis, V. S. Ageyev, & S. M. Miller (Eds.), *Vygotsky's educational theory in cultural context* (pp. 65–82). Cambridge: Cambridge University Press.

Lantolf, J. P., & Poehner, M. E. (2014). *Sociocultural theory and the pedagogical imperative in L2 education.* New York: Routledge.

Lortie, D. (1975). *Schoolteacher: A sociological study.* Chicago: University of Chicago.

Mahn, H. (2009). Vygotsky's methodological approach. A blueprint for the future of psychology. In A. Toomela & J. Valsiner (Eds.), *Methodological thinking in psychology: 60 years gone astray?* (pp. 297–323). Charlotte, NC: Information Age Publisher.

Marx, K. (1978). Theses on Feuerbach. In R. C. Tucker (Ed.), *The Marx-Engels reader.* (2nd ed., pp. 143–145). New York: W. W. Norton.

Novack, G. (1971). *An introduction to the logic of Marxism.* New York: Pathfinder Press.

Ollman, B. (2003). *Dance of the dialect: Steps in Marx's method.* Urbana, IL: University of Illinois Press.

van der Veer, R., & Valsiner, J. (1991). *Understanding Vygotsky.* Oxford: Blackwell.

Vygotsky, L. S. (1986). *Thought and language* (A. Kozulin, Trans.). Cambridge, MA: MIT Press.

INDEX